PRAISE FOR
THE POWER OF EMERGENCE

"Brave, brilliant, and deeply human, *The Power of Emergence* tells a raw, often painful, but ultimately beautiful and uplifting story that demystifies gender identity. Ella Samson's courageous storytelling will move readers, deepen empathy, and help most people learn something new, creating many new allies for the transgender and gender-diverse community. Every executive who cares about workplaces and economies where everyone can contribute to their fullest potential should read this book."

—KEN JANSSENS (he, him), CEO, Open for Business

"My own lived experience has taught me that inclusion is not abstract—it is built when people are seen and valued in their full humanity. In *The Power of Emergence*, Ella Samson offers leaders a powerful and compassionate lens on gender identity that elevates belonging as a strategic and moral imperative for organizations."

—JUAN FERNANDO LOPERA (he, him, él), Chief Community and
Health Impact Officer, Beth Israel Lahey Health

"This memoir does something rare: it deepens understanding without simplifying complexity. Ella Samson invites leaders to move beyond policy and toward genuine recognition—the kind of understanding that makes belonging real rather than aspirational."

—**DALLAS DUCAR** (she/her), Executive Vice President of Donor Engagement and External Relations, Fenway Health

"Knowing Ella personally and reading her story are two different things—this memoir changed me. It deepened my understanding of gender identity and sharpened how I lead, pushing me to build cultures rooted in empathy, authenticity, and true belonging."

—**CURTISS BARNES** (he, him), CEO, 1EdTech

"An insightful memoir that not only shares a courageous personal journey but also equips business leaders with a deeper understanding of gender identity—empowering them to cultivate belonging and create workplaces rooted in empathy, openness, and inclusion."

—**JACK MITCHELL** (he, him), Executive Vice President in Financial Services

"A memoir that's persuasive in its clarity, restraint, and steady sense of dignity."

—*KIRKUS REVIEWS*

THE POWER OF EMERGENCE

A Memoir to Demystify Gender Identity
and Inspire Belonging in the Workplace

ELLA SAMSON

Published by River Grove Books
Austin, TX
www.rivergrovebooks.com

Distributed by River Grove Books

Design and composition by Greenleaf Book Group
Cover design by Greenleaf Book Group
Cover images used under license from ©Adobestock.com
Author photograph by Sandra Costello Photography

Publisher's Cataloging-in-Publication data is available.

Print ISBN: 979-8-90052-027-8

eBook ISBN: 979-8-90052-028-5

First Edition

This book is dedicated with love to Mama; Papa; Amalia; little Ella; you; the light of all past, present, and future gender-diverse and transgender souls; all who read this memoir with an open heart and mind; and all the energy in the universe.

CONTENTS

INTRODUCTION

Even though I didn't understand it in my early years, my spirit, mind, and soul were born female. My body presented as male, and thus, understandably and unfortunately, I was misgendered at birth. However, I was never a boy—and most certainly not a man who then became a woman. I did not "transition" from male to female. The inaccuracy of that language makes my stomach turn—a *transition* means that something fundamentally changed from one thing to another. I've always been female, so the word *transition* does not represent the most basic truth of my journey. A word that more accurately describes my experience is *emergence*. I *emerged* to fully become myself as a woman, and today, I walk the world as a whole woman—with gratitude and love—fully aligned with how I was born.

Although I didn't understand the concept of gender identity as separate from sex, what I knew with 100% certainty for the first several decades of my life was that my lower part was incorrect. The wrong thing was there—the thing that my parents had a rabbi circumcise when I was eight days old. In my mind's eye, it was always a vagina—a malformed vagina that I considered a birth defect. I was a transgender woman before I had my lower surgery, which treated the genital birth defect. Now, I am simply a woman, and the adjective *transgender* isn't necessary and feels both inaccurate and irrelevant. At this phase of my life, the *transgender* label is not aligned with who I am, but my transgender medical history remains an important and special part of my identity. It showcases my strength, and it has infused my worldview with more open-mindedness and compassion.

As a result of my experience, I have become humble. I recognize that things are not always as they appear and that it's folly to form opinions or perspectives on complex topics without firsthand experience or thorough research. In today's modern world, we all have easy access to information and to wide audiences, and it is tempting to claim an informed opinion or perspective. This happens regularly—we believe we understand something based on a quick internet search or a politician's statement, which might even contradict science or expert evaluations. There are examples of this across a wide swath of issues ranging from how we manage a pandemic to whether we believe in climate change and whether gender identity is real or different from sex.

I used to be such an offender. I held the common perspective that gender is obvious and a direct result of what's assigned at birth, which is based on what's between a person's legs. When I was young, I didn't understand gender and didn't know what it was. I was not able to comprehend or reconcile the true and deep knowledge that my part was wrong with the reality of my gender. It was a disconnection that I didn't fully recognize and didn't understand. However, on the very rare occasion when I looked inward at it, I recognized that being seen as a boy didn't feel right. In my forties, after I had done the inner work, I came to discern the truth. It was not a strong, overpowering feeling; rather, it was the soft, gentle, and absolute knowledge that I am female, which came from my mind, my brain.

There were moments from my early teens onward when my brain told me that my inner truth didn't match my outside, but I squashed any acknowledgment or consideration about it. I accepted my gender assignment as an absolute truth that could never and would never be fixed. I was told I was a boy, and my body had a part between my legs that boys have. I wasn't interested in roughhousing, tree climbing, or causing mischief like a lot of the boys I knew, but I was also not interested in girls' clothes or playing with dolls. I had no stereotypical personality traits that screamed there was an issue, so my dissonance was easy to ignore. I had a boy part, and I was treated like boys are typically treated, so it must have been true. I didn't dwell on it. I didn't know the language of gender assignment at the time. I ignored the truth of what I would come to think of as the "disconnect" inside me with hope that I was wrong, or that it would go away, or that I would simply learn to live with it.

I grew up to be an arguably handsome boy—or so I was told by more than just my grandmothers. In reality, on my exterior, I was the ugliest girl in the world. I was not seen or treated or understood for who I was. From about the time we immigrated to the US, when I was nine, I often went to bed in anguish, wishing to a greater power that things could be different. I wanted the disconnect and its related discomfort to go away. However, I had neither the desire nor the ability to dig deeper to understand, let alone possibly do something about it.

When I got older, hair grew on my chest, my back, my arms, and my legs, and my voice deepened. It's what I expected and accepted as part of getting older and maturing. On the one hand, I was happy to grow up and experience the associated milestones, like shaving. My maturity was exciting because it meant I could have more freedom and do adult things, like drive and make my own decisions. On the other hand, I had a deep-rooted fear about growing up. I couldn't see myself in an intimate emotional and physical relationship with anyone given what I was physically becoming. It didn't feel right; it scared me, and the thought made me feel physically ill. I didn't want that part of growing up.

As I was going through puberty, I couldn't comprehend it at all. I didn't know what I was, didn't have words to apply to it, didn't think anything could be done about it, and was really excellent at burying and ignoring the feelings and thoughts. From today's perspective, I can see the cognitive dissonance between being fine with hair growth and general maturation and the disconnect between my actual gender and what was happening with my body. Now in my fifties, I have a much different perspective from the one I had as a child and as a younger adult. Although I once believed that sex equated to gender, my lived experiences have taught me otherwise and have reminded me of the importance and power of curiosity, education, and growth.

Why did I wait so long?

I was in my forties when I emerged, and I've been asked why I didn't do it sooner. There were many reasons for it. My lack of action was driven by denial, fear, overwhelm, and gratitude:

- **Denial** that I was transgender. I didn't know what it was and didn't have examples in my life or in the media to understand it. For multiple reasons, I didn't think I fit the definition of transgender. The few examples I had seen were absolutely not reflective of me. I didn't identify with the little I knew about transgender people. There was simply a lack of knowledge, clarity, and understanding.

- **Fear** of not being able to live the life I wanted and deserved. And fear of what others, including my family, would think.

- **Overwhelm** at the impact across the entirety of my life if I were to do something about it. Overwhelm at the sheer amount of work, strength, and stress that would be required to tackle it. Overwhelm at the thought of having to do it alone.

- And **gratitude** for everything that I did have, including my health, my career, my financial security, my friends, and my family, all of which I thought should have been more than enough to provide me with a happy and fulfilling life. Gratitude that I didn't have to live in hiding to survive like my grandparents and gratitude for everything my parents provided, from our nice house and the great vacations to the exquisite food and the opportunities we found after immigrating. I believed that my life was pretty privileged and it would need to be good enough.

Beneath my gratitude, however, I didn't have what I needed. I felt constricted and constrained. I was unable to really be myself and unable to live in the moment. The truth of my malformed vagina and gender disconnect slowly built up and manifested as an underlying anger, sadness, and hopelessness. Those emotions compounded over time until it became clear that my truth would never allow me to have a truly authentic, connecting, and vulnerable romantic love. I was mostly able to suppress my emotional pain by diverting energy into my career, health, and friends. However, I was quickly triggered into outward anger over minor inconveniences and the sorts of misunderstandings that often arose in my family. My pain also created a shell around me that took the form of a healthy dose of sarcasm, and my sadness caused me to have an air of moodiness; it would appear to my family that I was moping and generally grumpy.

I didn't dare talk about my struggle with anyone—until I took steps to tackle it in my early forties—because I was scared, embarrassed, and thought the whole thing was crazy. How could I make someone else understand if it felt incomprehensible even to the one experiencing it? But as time went by, the hopelessness and emotional pain eventually became too much to bear, and all those reasons to keep silent about it became less important. I couldn't ignore it any longer.

Privilege, euphoria, and opportunity

I emerged as myself in 2015, when I was forty-four, and subsequent to the initial bang, I have mostly enjoyed the privilege of not needing to talk about it again. Because of my genetic privilege, my medical history rarely comes up. My physical proportions are well aligned with the traditional Western standards of beauty for White women: I am 5'7" and around 130 pounds. I have warm blonde hair, which is long and naturally wavy. I'm fairly narrow shouldered, leggy with a short upper body, and blessed with my mother's looks.

Having presented as an overweight boy in my childhood, my father made me run to lose weight. That unwelcome (at the time) push and my upbringing led to lifestyle choices and habits that have shaped how I live my life and how I physically present today. I started working out at around age thirteen and have never stopped. I stay fit by speed-walking my dog two miles every morning, and four times a week, I lift weights and partake in cardio. Exercise is not only a passion; it provides me with emotional and mental balance, allows me to indulge my passion for cuisine, and keeps me physically fit and young. Additionally, I value my seven to eight hours of sleep, don't smoke, have generally kept away from party drugs, eat a well-balanced, healthy diet, drink lots of water, and have since the age of twenty-three—per the urging of an older boyfriend—religiously applied sunscreen daily. My healthy lifestyle choices are an important factor in how I present; however, my genetic privilege is a gift for which I'm grateful every day.

Right after my emergence, I had opportunities to share my story publicly, but for years, I chose not to do so. Beyond deepening romantic connections and new friendships, I have not talked about it, whether within the workplace, on social media, or with neighbors, friends, or casual acquaintances. I haven't talked about it because doing so feels like I'm shooting myself in the foot. By talking about it, I know that there will be some people who will see me for something other than a woman. That thought is terrifying. After forty painful years of inaccurately presenting as a man and existing in an impenetrable cloud of sadness, why would I risk talking about something that would take away the very thing that I have worked so hard for? I'm a woman who is finally recognized every day, all day, and in various ways for who I am, and there are many reasons for me not to undermine all that.

Some in the LGBTQIA+ community might say that my privileges give me the ability to *pass*, meaning that others see me correctly as a woman. I dislike the word *pass* for three reasons and will not use it beyond this paragraph. First, it implies that those who don't pass are not real women. Second, it perpetuates unrealistic and narrow standards of femininity and beauty. There are plenty of cisgender women (i.e., women whose gender identity aligns with that assigned at birth) who are masculine leaning in appearance and dress and are perceived to possibly be transgender. For what are they not passing? They are still women; they are each their own unique and special flavor of woman. All women and men come in different physical sizes and variations. Third, passing implies that all transgender people should have a goal of passing in order to be fully recognized for who they are. Such beliefs are inaccurate, unhealthy, and dangerous, especially because passing is unattainable for many who have to deal with the same experience of questioning gender identity and discovering the harsh reality of an incorrect gender assignment. These men and women are just as much men and women as those who pass. I recognize that it is a privilege for me to reject the word in large part because I am seen for exactly who I am and have not had to navigate hatred. I have struggled with feelings of guilt for my genetic privilege, and through a journey of investigation and self-reflection, I have come to a place of supreme gratitude for the gift and what it provides me. It is one of the reasons I've chosen to write this memoir.

I think it's relevant and important to share my euphoria with how others perceive me today so I can better illustrate my life before my emergence and the emergence journey itself. Even ten years after having emerged as myself, I experience regular innocuous interactions that—although they're no different from or more special than those experienced by others—have an outsize impact on me. I'm referring to the kind of interactions that I may have when a barista hands me my tea and says, "Here you go, ma'am," or when entering a clothing store with some girlfriends, the clerk greets us with, "Hi, ladies!" On an average day by eight a.m., I may have already had a few gender-affirming interactions. These might include flirting from the middle-aged neighbor or inquiries directed at my insanely cute dog from passersby wondering if *Mommy* is taking good care of him and giving him enough treats. In the workplace, I feel affirmed when my colleagues refer to me correctly by my name and pronouns. A server in a restaurant at dinner might induce joy when he turns to me to ask, "What would the lady like to eat tonight?" Or at some point that same evening, when I inevitably need to use the bathroom and someone points me to exactly where I need to be.

I love these affirmations. I'm grateful for them, and I allow myself to feel and experience each one of them. They make me smile inwardly with gratitude for being seen for who I am. Each incident brings me joy.

My feelings of euphoria can be further amplified at the gym. In those moments when I'm already on the natural high of workout endorphins, I'm filled with amazement and limitless gratitude about how I'm now seen for who I am. Given my starting point and the journey I've traveled, I feel powerful gratitude as I'm rocking my skin-hugging, gender-aligned workout clothes and finding myself on the receiving end of friendly smiles from women in the locker room and sometimes the shy (or not-so-shy) flirtations of men. During those moments at the gym, the intensity of the gender euphoria can be so strong and joyous that it provides me with a strong natural high to support productive workouts. Those moments have the capacity to make my heart swell with appreciation; bring a smile to my face; deliver rising feelings of fuzzy gratitude to my abdomen; fill my body with happiness and joy; provide my brain with hope, peace, and present-moment awareness; and allow me to see beauty, love, and freedom.

It hasn't always been this way. When I first started to hear these affirming compliments and receive warm looks, I was suspicious. I didn't believe it. In the years just after my emergence, I sometimes doubted their sincerity. Sometimes, I wondered whether the comments or looks were the result of discomfort. Other times, I'd catch myself holding my breath in the presence of children, who often ask blunt, piercing questions. I was terrified of being on the receiving end of an innocent child's observations about me, my journey, or how I presented outwardly. Was this the time someone would look me up and down and deliver a comment or question about my appearance or clothes? Would this child see that I'd emerged and ask a question of their parent or me? I don't think I fully accepted the reality of my physical changes until one day, about three years after I emerged, when I was in a line behind a mom and a young boy, who was perhaps five or six years old. He shyly looked me over and then said to his mom, "She's so pretty." I don't think the smile could have been blasted off my face for the rest of the day.

Others' opinions shouldn't impact how we feel about ourselves, but at the same time, they do make a difference. I'll venture so far as to say that everyone has a desire to be seen for exactly who they are and that a sincere affirming compliment lifts one up and has the potential to make someone's day.

The opposite of gender euphoria is gender dysphoria. Gender dysphoria is experienced when one is *not* seen for who they are, such as when there is a mismatch between one's biological sex and their gender identity or a mismatch between their assigned sex and the way they express their gender. Those struggling with gender dysphoria feel varying intensities of sadness and pain due to this lack of alignment. Gender dysphoria can be so intensely strong that—when combined with a lack of acceptance by family, friends, or society—it can lead to suicide. My gender dysphoria was not clear to me while I was experiencing it for the first forty years of my life. This memoir will dive deep into my experience with gender dysphoria, which I became a master of ignoring and suppressing and only fully understood once I was able to experience the intensity of its opposite.

Although my medical history is something that most don't see about me, I can still struggle on those infrequent occasions when someone has a hunch about it. My reaction is rooted in my historical transphobia and my feelings of how transphobia impacts what others might think about me and whether they see me for who I am as a woman. I've had to recognize and work to let go of my own transphobia as it relates to others with transgender medical history, and I'm still working at managing my beliefs about how transphobia might impact others in their assessments of me. I'm relieved and grateful when the hunch comes with acceptance and the understanding that I am a woman—a woman who has had a journey to fight and stand in the world as herself. But I still struggle with disappointment, frustration, and hurt when that hunch comes with the inability or the refusal to see me for who I am.

Why now?

People with transgender medical history, as well as those who are gender diverse, are gravely misunderstood by most. These experiences are nearly inconceivable, understandably, for those who have never struggled with gender identity. As a result of this misunderstanding, there are unnecessary barriers, poor enterprise and public policy, a lack of compassion and support, and disproportionate occurrences of deadly violence and suicides. Here are some statistics that illustrate some of the challenges this population faces:

- 28% of transgender women are victims of violent hate crimes, in comparison to 9% of cisgender women.[1]

- Trans people "earn 32% less" than their peers.[2]

- 50% of transgender and nonbinary employees reported experiencing verbal harassment at work compared to 28% of cisgender LGBQ employees.[3]

- "30% of transgender employees have been fired, denied a promotion, or experienced another form of workplace mistreatment due to their gender identity or expression (Human Rights Campaign, 2018)."[4]

- Eight in ten Americans acknowledge that there is discrimination against transgender individuals.[5]

- More than 500 anti-LGBTQ+ bills were proposed—and more than seventy-five of those bills were passed—in 2023 alone; most of the bills specifically targeted transgender communities.[6]

- 66% of gender-diverse employees won't even apply for a job in a company "where they perceive the culture to be noninclusive."[7]

- "62% of all victims of fatal violence against transgender and gender-nonconforming people" are Black transgender women.[8]

- 81% of transgender individuals contemplated suicide in their lifetime, in comparison with 30% of their cisgender peers.[9]

- "42% of transgender individuals reported attempting suicide to cope with transgender-related discrimination."[10]

- 2% of the global population identifies as transgender, although this number could be higher because some countries do not have proper reporting mechanisms in place for gender identity and expression on their surveys.*[11]

- 28% of Gen Z adults identify as LGBTQ according to a 2023 PRRI study, and according to a 2023 Trevor Project study, 59% of LGBTQ+ Gen Z identify as transgender, nonbinary, or questioning.[12]

With a lack of understanding comes fear, which leads to violence against people who have emerged and drives harmful legislation that restricts the rights of people who have emerged or still need to emerge. I hope that compassion can spring from understanding gender identity and that, as a society, we will begin to do better.

I've been much more fortunate than many. In addition to the

---

* These numbers are underreported because of fear of identification and do not include those who are nonbinary, gender nonconforming, gender fluid, agender, etc.

benefits that my Whiteness and general genetic privilege have granted me, I am also grateful for the financial privilege that supported my emergence, my access to top-notch medical care, the support of a quality progressive employer, and the love and companionship of family and friends who stayed by my side. I wouldn't have a story to tell if it weren't for all these privileges. My aim is to make a positive difference by sharing my story with the objective to help others understand gender identity. Furthermore, it's my specific goal to use my story, my career experience, and my platforms—including my professional reach, education network, and community service—to inspire leaders of large enterprises, including my network of former Wharton classmates, to increase demonstration of enterprise allyship and improve a sense of belonging for their gender-diverse and transgender workforces.

For fourteen years, I had the privilege of making an impact in various leadership roles at Deloitte Consulting LLP, which provided me with a deeper appreciation about the inner workings of large firms and consulting. As a member of the board of directors for the Massachusetts LGBT Chamber of Commerce, I learned from and support businesses and entrepreneurs all across the Commonwealth. Harnessing those experiences with a thirty-year career rooted in driving internal change at large enterprises through improved processes, policies, and systems, I combined my functional expertise with my personal life journey and launched Emerge Collaborations, a workforce gender-equity consulting firm that helps organizations understand gender identity and addresses structural inequities that impact gender diverse and transgender employees.

Why a memoir?

I take pride in how I navigated my emergence privately, with a conservative pace and a deliberate approach. Now, at the time of writing this memoir, and as I begin talking more openly about my story, I am taking a similarly deliberate approach. I'm intentionally leading with my memoir, which includes my complete story and which I hope will have the greatest impact while reducing the likelihood that my words will be taken out of context or misinterpreted. My story is unique and will likely be considered controversial by some in terms of how I speak about my truth. I'm okay with that. It's my truth, and it does not need any defending. This is my story and my story only. I don't represent an entire community. I don't speak for other people who share a transgender experience. I did my best to be brutally honest—inclusive of both the sexiness and the warts—and tell my truth as I remember it. I'm sure I don't remember everything exactly as it happened, and my perceptions are only one side of the story.

I have written my story for those who have never had to think about their gender identities. I lived with gender dysphoria for more than forty years, and during that time, I didn't know what I was. I didn't understand my gender identity and certainly didn't accept that I might be someone other than what I appeared to be. Given my personal experience, I fully appreciate how difficult it might be to understand that gender identity is its own thing and could be incongruent with sex. This lack of understanding is the primary reason why many who emerge as themselves face serious challenges, including violence. I hope this book will contribute to changing that.

Additionally, I'm passionately motivated to tell my story to connect with enterprise leaders to help them improve their understanding of gender identity. I hope that by sharing my own personal experiences, I will make gender identity more relatable and thereby increase compassion and empathy in the workplace. Most leaders strive to ensure they create working environments that affirm and respect a variety of human experiences and enable their workforces to bring their authentic selves to work. Among the general population, at least 2% identify as transgender, which can mean thousands of individuals in the workforces of large organizations. Keeping in mind that this number excludes the majority of other genders under the gender-diverse umbrella (e.g., agender, pangender, gender nonconforming, nonbinary, gender fluid, etc.) and that gender-diverse populations are often underreported due to stigma, lack of inclusive options in surveys, and differences in definitions, this number is likely significantly higher. With increased awareness and visibility, we're seeing higher numbers reflected in the younger generations. For Generation Z, which now makes up the youngest demographic in the workforce, the numbers of those identifying as transgender, nonbinary, or questioning is higher than ever. The aforementioned studies suggest that among this cohort, 15%–17% identify as such, and for those in the workforce, 10%–11% don't feel a sense of belonging in their workplace because of their gender identities. This creates a meaningful opportunity for leaders to improve workforce satisfaction within their enterprises. That can only start with a better understanding of gender identity and the transgender experience. In this memoir, I focus on just telling my story—before, during, and after my emergence. I have resisted the urge to include details and information about what enterprises can do to improve allyship as that will dilute my primary goal of humanizing this struggle. It is my hope that after turning the last page, enterprise leaders will better understand gender identity and feel inspired to learn how their enterprises can do better to support those who are grappling with it.

I am adding my story to the mix of other unique, inspiring stories to support a better understanding of our journeys. While the primary reason for this memoir is improving workforce inequities, it's also my hope that the depth in these pages will inspire a family to better understand and support their child. I hope to help a manager provide a more easeful experience for someone who emerges, and I hope to open the eyes of a straight man who has met an amazing woman and help him understand that his interest does not impact his sexuality or change his straightness. I hope to reduce incidents of random verbal abuse from strangers on the street directed at unsuspecting people going about their day. I hope to improve the health-care experience by changing how practitioners engage, and I hope to shift the thinking of legislators.

I do not include photographs of myself before my emergence. The photo at the back of this memoir and those on my business website show the reader how I walk the world today as my vibrant self. They reflect who I am and are there to support my descriptions of my life today. They show the wholeness that is me now that I have fully emerged as myself. You will not find the typical before-and-after pictures dramatically displayed side by side in this memoir. That is intentional. I have always believed that those juxtapositions, although striking, are a red herring that distract from the real story and from the opportunity for a real discussion about what happens on the inside. The purpose of my story is to share what was happening inside me before, during, and after my emergence. That is the real story, one that is not often told. That's the story I hope to tell without the distraction of the exterior. By sharing, I'm hopeful I can help those who never had to think about gender identity begin to understand. In this way, I hope to make a positive impact.

1

MY ROOTS

I stood at the kitchen counter in my Boston apartment on a quiet Sunday morning in early 2015. Winter had just turned to spring, but a cold front was arriving in New England, and the rising sun had been unable to stop the plummeting temperatures. This time tomorrow morning, I'd already be at my home-office desk, working in my middle-management role for Deloitte Consulting. Today, my only real plans were to go the gym, and I was already in my workout clothes. Bosco, my wirehaired dachshund, was in the other room, resting after his breakfast. He'd need a walk in a little bit. I wasn't thinking about any of that, however; my mind was entirely focused on the contents of my cupped hand.

Three small tablets rested in my palm. Two of them were oblong, a shade of mint green. The third was white and round. Together, they would fix my blood chemistry, increasing my estrogen and decreasing my testosterone so the ratio would come to match what scientists define as a woman's biology. Those changes would lead to a cascade of other changes that would collectively, finally, after forty-four years, rectify a birth defect and enable others to recognize my actual gen-der. They would grant me what the majority of the population takes for granted: the consonance of mind, body, and soul. For as long as I could remember, there had been a disconnect within me, an under-lying sadness that permeated every stage of my life, from my early childhood through my teen years and my twenties and thirties, per-sisting through my various attempts to create identity. Only within the last few years had I figured out what it was and why it had lodged in me so deeply. These little pills would bring that chapter to a close and open up another very different one.

There was zero hesitation in me; my every fiber was ready for this. I'd been extremely deliberate about my journey, taking one small step after another for years now and allowing each step and its effects to fully sink in and settle before considering another. I'd made much progress, and there was much more yet to come, but this step was special. This was far more than appearance, or expression, or presentation—this was about true alignment. In my weightless cupped hand, I could feel the sheer magnitude of the decision and the momentum of my journey to this point. At the same time, how-ever, it also struck me how commonplace it felt to simply be standing at my counter, alone, with a few pills of medicine and a glass of water. It was an act I'd performed countless times before with ibuprofen or vitamins, as mundane as brushing my teeth in the morning. It felt appropriate that I would be standing here in solitude, in a moment of quiet contemplation. My emergence to that point had been very much internal—in my personal life, only my immediate family and my closest friends Ryan and Michelle knew who I really was and understood my trajectory. So it was fitting that I would cross this threshold without fanfare or hoopla. It was, after all, my body, my mind, my soul.

I didn't know exactly what would happen. The response to hormones varied widely and was affected by age and genetics. I would see breast growth, but when, and how much? My sister and Mama were both well-endowed in that department, but there was no other data for me to consider. My body would start distributing fat differently, but where, and how much? This redistribution is also what underlies facial feminization. I was hoping to avoid surgery—would the hormones' effects alone be enough?

Though I was eager for these changes to be underway, I was terrified they might unfold *too* quickly. I had an extensive professional network not only locally in Boston but also nationally, and many of us met in person at team meetings in Atlanta every month. Although Georgia lacked comprehensive protections for transgender individuals, Atlanta had local ordinances ensuring access to health care, so I felt grateful that my leadership had chosen a city where I wouldn't need to worry about such issues in case of an emergency. I had very specific plans for how I would handle my emergence among my colleagues, but only when I was completely ready. It was very important to me that I control my own story; the last thing I needed was for someone to notice something that might make me the target of the rumor mill. It wasn't just that I was anxious to avoid unwanted attention. Losing control of my narrative could have a major impact on my career, my very livelihood. When the time was right, I'd craft a careful announcement. But when would that be?

I didn't have the answers to any of these questions, but I was prepared to wait and let them reveal themselves. In the meantime, I had plenty else to occupy my mind and my time. Given the pact I'd made with myself to take only one small step at a time, this milestone meant I could start planning for what was to come next—and my excitement over that vastly outweighed my uncertainties.

Gratitude came over me—for this trio of pills, for the handful of people who had supported me to get to this point, and also for the privilege I enjoyed, which had helped me to acquire the resources I needed to undertake this journey safely, with support for both my physical and mental health. I reached for my water glass.

———

About forty years earlier, I had been standing over another sink in Emmen, Netherlands, in the northeast corner of the country, just ten miles west of the German border. Our neighborhood, Borgerbrink, was a brand-new grassy suburb of brick and wood homes, tidy and inviting yet unpretentious in their northern European simplicity. The modern brick streets formed a zigzag pattern, evoking a Bauhaus-inspired puzzle design.

The bathroom had plain medium-tone walls, bright lights, and a pedestal sink. As a five-year-old, I was still a few years away from being able to reach it on my own, so I was perched on a step stool, washing my hands with my mom's help. As I looked down at myself, the frustration built in my body until it became too large for the task. I pushed myself away from the sink and jumped down from my step stool, my eyes brimming with tears, my throat tight. With my wet fists balled, I shouted at Mama, "Het is verkeerd!" *It's wrong.*

"Wat?" she asked, completely perplexed. "Wat bedoel je?"

"Mijn ding is verkeerd!" I screamed again, through great sobs, pointing down at that thing that people called a penis. *My thing is wrong.* I knew the word for it, of course, but I didn't want to name it. I did not want to have that label attached to a part of *my* body. I had every belief that I was a boy. I had the body of one, everybody treated me as one, and at that time and for many subsequent years, I showed no other outward signs of femininity. I was still decades away from the realization that assigned gender was something I could question or even fix. And while I felt fine with much of my body, I knew with certainty that that thing was wrong, and there was nothing I could do about it. That sense of unfairness swelled in me until it became a white-hot anger, and it was there at the sink that day when it erupted.

I was blubbering loudly now, a mixed-up mess of tears and snot and fury. I screamed out again, and my mom winced, perhaps fearful that my outburst would awaken my little sister, Amalia, who was napping in the other room. But no matter how many times or how loudly I yelled it, I couldn't make my mom understand. The confusion stayed there, fixed on her face, as the frustration flooded my every cell and blurred my vision. Not knowing what else to do, she directed me to finish washing my hands, and we attempted to go on about the day.

That specific memory disappeared soon after that, occluded by the schoolwork, friendships, and family life that fill a child's days, and it would only resurface decades later, when I was deep in the process of uncovering my gender identity. And in fact, I harbor some doubt that it really happened—it might have been a dream I had. Either way, the frustration and anger were real, and that was the first time I can remember that disconnection erupting into my consciousness with such violence. And though the memory might have been submerged, that anger did not vanish. Instead, it transformed into a layer of sadness, which would lie beneath everything until I finally figured out what it was, why it was there, and what I could do about it.

Even with that undercurrent of sadness, much of my childhood felt idyllic. I remember in the early years, we had a warm and loving home. One of my strongest, most cherished memories of that time comes from a morning when I was about four years old. For some reason, I recall it was a Tuesday. I emerged from the hallway into the living room, where Mama was walking around, likely working on something. The sun was shining brightly into the living room, and dust motes were floating through the air. There were vivid shades of green from the plants, and orange tones, probably from the fabric of the furniture. I remember feeling the warmth of the sun and smelling the comfortable and clean smells of home. I recall a powerful sense of pure love. I *was* love, I received love, and I poured loving energy from my being, sending it out to everything around me, including and especially Mama. I was fully immersed in that happy moment, uninhibited, aware and appreciative of who I was, feeling and sharing the love that was my spirit and inner light.

Our home life revolved around my parents' business. My dad was a trained butcher who handled sales and operations, and my mom handled all other functions, from billing and accounting to human resources, marketing, and technology. She was also the homemaker and an excellent cook, so there was always heavenly, hearty food on the table, usually vegetables and boiled potatoes alongside perfectly cooked generous portions of meat. I still salivate at the thought of my mom's veal chops, which she often served with an onion curry dish. Their business did well and provided us with a great many privileges. Amalia and I had new clothes to begin each school year, and we took exciting family vacations to destinations like France, Sicily, Israel, and the US.

Papa solved most mechanical problems with a meat cleaver and duct tape. He wasn't exactly handy—a fact he would readily admit— but he had confidence in his abilities to work minor miracles. Once, on a family vacation from the Netherlands to the coast of France, we found ourselves towing a camper behind our Mercedes through the tree-lined narrow streets of old Paris neighborhoods. Most families planned these trips well in advance, reserving a campground six months earlier, but ours were usually last-minute. With the unpredictability of their free time, my parents weren't able to be so prepared. We found places to stay, and it always worked out.

I think the original plan was to go *around* the city, but Papa is disastrous with directions, and so we found ourselves driving through the heart of the city. The farther we drove, the more curious I became about the old architecture and the people we passed by. Then there was a scraping noise, and our car stopped moving altogether. The camper had met a low-hanging branch it couldn't drive under. Papa tried to coax the car along, his foot growing increasingly heavier on the gas pedal, the engine revving and whining, but all of his effort was in vain.

Amalia and I looked at each other, wide-eyed and smiling. It wasn't clear what was going to happen, but we were both very invested in the adventure of it all. A gaggle of pedestrians were looking at us, pointing, gesturing, talking among themselves. Amalia leaned over me to look out the window at the crowd.

"Papa?" I asked. "What are you going to do?"

He looked at us in the rearview mirror, gave a smile, and said, "Hang on, and don't look back."

He pushed the pedal to the floor. The car moved an inch and then another, and then finally, with a great screeching noise, it broke free, and we were off. The assembled Parisians who had gathered on the sidewalk laughed, waving as we drove away. *Bon voyage!*

Amalia and I giggled and cheered.

"Shouldn't we pull over?" Mama asked.

And he did, a little farther down the road. We all got out of the Mercedes to inspect what had happened. The branch had opened the camper's metal roof like it was a soup can, peeling back a corner and exposing a hole that was at least three feet wide. There weren't any clouds overhead, but there was rain in the forecast. We were far from home with a damaged camper, our vacation only a few days old. Where were we going to get it repaired in a foreign country? How long would it take? Would we get wet tonight? Would they cut our vacation short?

"Well," Papa said. "I've got this. Get back in the car." First, he grabbed his cleaver from the pocket on the driver's side door. Then he went to the trunk, where he kept a carefully arranged collection of items, and retrieved two garbage bags and a roll of duct tape. Using the cleaver as a hammer, he did his best to pound and push the metal back into place. It was like trying to make a sardine can whole again. Then he laid the bags over the hole and secured them with duct tape. An imperfect solution, but it was the best he could do, and he seemed to have confidence it would hold.

I loved our trips—it was so exciting to pack our bags and head off somewhere, bound for adventure. The change of routine, our family unity, and the laughter when things started to go awry are among my favorite memories of my childhood. The spirit of playful improvisation permeated our home life, too. It snowed so heavily in the winter of 1978 that my mom often took a sled with her to the grocery store to make it easier to haul the food back. Amalia and I would watch as my mom tugged on the rope during her approach to the house. I had the idea that when she was done with the sled, Amalia and I could wrap the rope around the chest of Boris, our Rottweiler, and he could pull us down the hill—a slight incline, really, since the Netherlands is so flat. It hinted at a hill, though, so for our purposes, it would have to suffice. I suggested it to Amalia, and she needed no nudging. The only thing left to do was convince Mama. As soon as she came through the door, my sister and I started shouting over each other about this *great* idea we'd come up with. Surprisingly, Mama went along with it. Amalia and I bundled up in our hats and scarves and mittens and boots. The way we saw it unfolding was that Boris would see a cat—where or why it was out in the snow weren't important details to us—and then he would shoot out like a bolt of lightning, and we'd have to hang on for dear life. The only thing that gave me pause, at seven years old, was that we might get going fast and out of control and that Boris could head toward an oncoming train. The tracks were only a couple hundred yards away from our house.

To our surprise and delight, Boris *did* see a cat, and Boris *did* take off like a bolt of lightning, and when he did, Amalia and I and the sled got thrown almost immediately. We watched as Boris ran down the slope and disappeared into the trees. Amalia and I couldn't stop laughing. We wanted to try again, but Boris was gone, and Mama was left worrying about how to get him back.

When I was about six, my parents enrolled me in swimming lessons. The local swimming facility had an Olympic-size pool with a roof that opened on nice days. I liked learning how to swim, and Mama and Papa regularly took Amalia and me. As the years passed, I came to dislike the smelly, dirty locker rooms but found another reason to enjoy going: I began to notice men. I knew then that my curiosity about men, rather than women, was different. But I didn't know what any of it meant. Some confusion set in, but I knew not to bring it up with anyone. Like my unhappiness with my wrong part, I did my best to set it aside and to enjoy our prosperity and the rhythms of our home.

There were other unsettling currents that ran through our family life, many of which I did not recognize until later. Perhaps the most significant of these was my relationship with Papa, which was and remains complex and challenging for me. It's hard for me to remember just when I became aware of this discord, but one early memory stands out. I was perhaps seven at the time, and it was a school morning. Our school was about a mile away, and I often walked there and back with

Amalia, who was two grades behind me in school. Or perhaps I should say I was supposed to walk there and back with her; most days, I tried to avoid it. On this particular morning, the walk in would be a trudge because snow had been coming down all night, so I got an early start, peacefully alone. I began making my way carefully along the edge of the plowed road, walking past drifts that were taller than I was. The warmth of our cozy home wore off, and the cold set in, along with the discomfort of having to walk in too many layers of clothes. I still had a long way to go when a familiar car drove past—my dad's Mercedes. In the rear window was my sister's face, wearing a look of glee and triumph. Papa didn't stop.

I was confused, hurt, and angry. That night, I went to my mom and asked her why he hadn't stopped to pick me up. It made me feel like he didn't like me. Although I can't recall any earlier occurrences, I remember with certainty that this was neither the first time he'd made me feel that way nor the first time I'd sought help—unsuccessfully— from my mom.

"He probably just didn't see you," she said, with annoyance. "Stop complaining about it."

Not wanting to accept that he would just blow past me on purpose, I tried to believe that. I tried other explanations, too. My sister and I fought regularly, as siblings close in age often do, about everything and nothing. One of our recurring fights was about territory in the car's backseat, so maybe my dad had opted for a peaceful ride to school instead of giving me a lift. Whatever his reasoning was that day, it would prove not to be an isolated event. He'd make me feel that way many more times to come.

In other realms, Papa does have a wealth of admirable personality traits and strengths. He possesses an innate ability to connect with people and always has a captivating story filled with laughs at the ready. He has a strong sense of humor, which he inherited from my grandmother, Oma Resi. This gift served him well in his butcher shop and subsequent wholesale businesses—he ran thriving operations for more than fifty years and served long-standing loyal clients in the finest restaurants and hotels across Europe and North America. He prided himself on his creativity with specialty products, the high-caliber quality of his meats, and his gold-standard customer service, all of which set him apart from any real competition.

My favorite of his recipes was a dried beef sausage with a proprietary spice blend he made from scratch. The entire family loved it. He didn't make it often—perhaps only once a year if we were lucky. Whenever he'd make it, he'd give Amalia and me a few to dry in our respective bedrooms and to eat as we pleased. We'd protect them like gold, carefully pinching off a few bites every day to make it last as long as possible. Those sausages are among my favorite childhood memories. The American palate wasn't too interested in them, however, and after we moved to the US, he made it less and less.

Beyond his professional life, he was also known for his generosity; he was quick to spend to support the family, and he freely gave his time to others. His friends called him when they didn't know where else to turn, and he'd unfailingly help them solve their problems. This generosity of time rarely extended to his kids, however, and definitely not to me. His focus was entirely on his role as the provider, and most everything that happened in the home was Mama's job. His expectations of my sister and me were that we do well in school, complete the chores around the house, and keep our opinions and thoughts to ourselves, especially at dinnertime, which was generally time for my parents to discuss unresolved business matters of the day. The business was at the forefront of everything they did, and as I grew older, I came to recognize the cost. During those dinnertime meetings, Amalia and I sat quietly, eating, forbidden to bring forth our problems and questions.

Mama was the embodiment of love. I felt this in all the little ways growing up. In addition to supporting Papa's business and running the household, she raised my sister and me. She made our meals and got us to our activities and taught us how to do things for ourselves as soon as we were able. She was organized and pragmatic, supporting our needs while giving us lots of love. But there wasn't much she could do to mitigate the strain in my relationship with Papa. Sometimes when I asked her about him and why he treated us the way he did, she would tell me to remember where he'd come from.

We are Jewish, and most of my extended family was murdered during World War II. Three of my grandparents were born and raised in Germany, and when the Nazis took over, they fled into the Netherlands, saying goodbye to parents, siblings, aunts, and uncles, most of whom would eventually be gassed. When Hitler invaded the Netherlands, one side of the family survived years by hiding in a peat hut, and the other side survived by hiding in the farm attic of a sympathetic family. There were days and weeks when their hideouts were compromised or unavailable and they needed to spend extended periods hiding in chicken coops, stables, and open rye fields.

After the war ended, they found their businesses intentionally demolished and other families living in their homes. They'd lost everything and chose to remain in the Netherlands to slowly rebuild their lives. My parents were both born within a few years of the end of the war into families suffering from unthinkable trauma, in an era when these things were poorly understood and little discussed. When my dad was thirteen, his father died. My Opa Benni, my namesake, was a well-loved figure in the community and a cantor in the local congregation, and his loss must have been devastating to Oma Resi and her three sons. I've asked what caused his death, and the answer I've gotten was that it was due to numerous health complications stemming from the war. It's not a medical explanation, but I have no doubts about its truth. The stress and exposure, the cold and malnutrition, or any of a thousand other terrors could have led to long-term impacts. He had not escaped the Nazis, after all.

My dad was the oldest of three, just barely a teenager when my grandfather died. My dad's uncle informed him that he had become man of the house. Soon after that, my dad apprenticed with butchers, made his way through butchery school, and launched the career that would support our family for decades.

Although Oma Resi raised her sons with resolve and exuberant humor, my dad learned a deep mistrust of everyone around him as a result of the specter of his parents' trials and his upbringing. This was not just something I observed; it was explicit. And given what had happened to my family, I understood it. In general, he didn't trust people, and he certainly had no trust of white-collar, professional-service providers and institutions like insurance companies, banks, and the stock market. He much preferred to keep gold over trusting banks with his money. He taught Amalia and me not to trust anyone, either, a lesson that would hinder me from getting close to anyone until well into my thirties, when I realized I had to make a conscious effort to overcome this legacy. And he worked relentlessly, perhaps mindful of how everything could be taken away at any time.

In Mama he found another descendent of a hard-working line of entrepreneurs and someone who also knew well the horrors of the Holocaust, including the murder of family, destruction of businesses, and loss of home. Like the rest of my great-grandparents, my great-grandmother was also gassed, and I was told that her son, my Opa Herbert, never recovered from the atrocity. How could he, though? When we'd go visit him and my Oma Linie, I found their home to be a solemn and somber place. Perhaps it was the persistent weight of grief.

Mama shared Papa's work ethic and worked hard alongside him throughout the entirety of their marriage. My first days were spent in a baby carriage in the back room of their butcher shop because she had gone back to work immediately after being discharged from the hospital. They tell me I didn't mind this and that I exuded joy to be in the world. In their stories of those months, I was a sweet, happy baby, calm and quiet, who smiled a lot. They called me their sweet little duck. Although I was to go through long periods of turbulence, some of it a direct result of my family's dynamics, I feel that at my core, that calm, joyful essence has remained intact. It's one of the many things for which I'm extremely grateful.

In the stories I've heard of that era, the shop was a lively place—a bustling business, full of conversation and laughter, not to mention cigarette smoke and the occasional nips from the flask. Knowing the lineage of humor in my dad's family line, I imagine there were lots of harmless pranks and practical jokes. But underneath the camaraderie, there was a subtle undercurrent, dark and persistent. We were the only Jewish family in the area, and not only did everybody know it, but they were also quick to point it out. At school, when I met someone new, I was without fail introduced as "the Jewish kid," even by teachers. At the time, it didn't bother me much; I was proud of my lineage and comfortable owning my Jewish identity. I didn't feel ostracized or excluded. In fact, the teachers picked me to play the coveted lead role in our student production of *The Emperor's New Clothes*. There's a significant dose of irony in me playing the lead in a story about trusting oneself and being honest, but I was a long way off from recognizing that.

It was only later, after we moved to America, where my classmates didn't refer to me as "the Jewish kid," that I realized how completely my family and I had been othered. When I returned to the Netherlands as an adult to visit my grandparents, the differing perspectives on Judaism became even clearer. On one trip, a stranger at a bar reacted with aversion when I told him I'd moved to America. When I asked him why, he said, "There are just too many goddamn Jews there." On another trip, in a small town in the north, where my grandmother lived, I discovered a large swastika spray-painted on the side of a phone booth. This happens all over the world, but in the States, it was my sense that it'd be removed fairly expediently. This one stayed up for the entirety of my five-day visit. I wonder how often my grandparents were subjected to such hateful reminders.

My parents had always wanted to immigrate to the US, for a number of reasons. First, they felt the US would provide more opportunities for their kids. Second, they valued the entrepreneurial culture in the US as well as the business-friendly tax laws. Lastly—though they didn't talk about this with us at the time—they wanted to distance themselves from the memory of what had happened to our family on that continent and from the ongoing anti-Semitism.

When I was nine, just before the end of third grade, their five-year application process finally wrapped up, and we received our green cards. My parents had already sold our house in anticipation, and now my dad quickly shut his business down, passing his clients over to one of his brothers. We packed up our furniture and household items, loaded them on a container ship bound for Oakland, and after a big farewell party, we were on our way: my parents, my sister and I, and

Boris. I loved my grandparents, and I would miss them, but the move felt like a grand adventure, and I was excited for all that awaited us. Our destination was California. My parents wanted snow-free winters and had made a couple of scouting expeditions to numerous cities, finally narrowing their choices down to Atlanta and the San Francisco Bay Area.

Papa had a German expression he was fond of using: *ruck zuck*. Most of the times he said it, he did so with a big smile on his face. It was frequently voiced in the context of describing the objective of a new project he had for Amalia and me, indicating that the project was to be completed quickly and orderly, all things with straight angles. Tidy. On the day we left for America, he'd managed to downsize everything we would take with us into ten suitcases, all of them facing the same direction, perfectly aligned, ordered by size from small to large, and each with their name tags properly positioned in the same spot. *Ruck zuck.*

As we took our seats on the plane and I watched the men loading luggage into the cargo hold, the reality of the move and where we were going filled me with both a sense of sadness at saying goodbye to what I'd always known and the hope of what could be somewhere else. I clicked my lap belt and closed my eyes, feeling the deep rumble of the double-decker 747 course through my body as the plane sped down the runway.

2

THE GREEN DREAM

Our first stop was a motel along Highway 101, just north of San Francisco, where we lived for six months while our parents investigated the area for a permanent home and explored work opportunities. In that time, Amalia and I attended school in a one-room private schoolhouse, doing our best to absorb the new language. The school headmistress was an imposing figure. She had unnaturally tall red hair that must have required an obscene amount of hairspray in order for it to comply with its lot in life. She was as militant with us as she was with her hair. One day, I proudly used my new English to ask her if I could go to the bathroom. She said no and told me I needed to ask correctly. I didn't know what she wanted from me; I was certain I'd said the right thing. Many years later, I shot up in the middle of the night with the realization that she'd wanted me to ask her "may I" rather than "can I." Pedantic subtleties aside, Mama's English was already pretty good, and Amalia and I learned quickly. Papa did, too, although his English was colored with a thick accent that would never go away, and in the early years, there were a number of cultural and language-related incidents and misunderstandings, many of them quite funny.

Once, Mama and Papa were at a business dinner in a white-tablecloth restaurant with potential clients. Papa was discussing the business of rabbit-raising, but he didn't know the word for *breeding* in English, so he substituted the Dutch word *fokken*. Their dining companions were perplexed, and Papa, frustrated that they didn't seem to understand his point, iterated numerous times that he thought it'd be great to "fok" rabbits, with no clue how it sounded. Papa mastered English in time, but my parents would always speak to each other in Dutch. That rabbit story persisted. Once Papa discovered the reason behind the confusion, he found it uproariously funny and told it over and over, for years.

Near the end of that first summer in the States, we moved to a new home in the hills in Santa Rosa, a wine-country town about an hour north of San Francisco. The house, which would be our family home for more than thirty years, was a two-story, dark-brown shingled home surrounded by oak trees, with a view of the hills.

After months of talking with chefs and studying the market, Papa started a new meat business, which he initially ran out of our home, and the rhythms of our life returned to the familiar patterns we'd grown up with. He created a series of new products and had the local chefs clamoring for them. He introduced them to tomahawk steaks decades before they became so trendy. With his innovation, work ethic, sales, and service skills, he rapidly developed a loyal clientele. Before long, he had accounts all over California, as well as in Las Vegas and Hawaii. Eventually, he would open a plant in Petaluma, a town twenty minutes south.

We had a strict regimen of chores. Papa insisted on hospital-style cleanliness and perfection—definitely a carryover from our German roots. If it wasn't up to his standards, he'd be quick to bark at us, and we'd need to do it again—and again if it wasn't just so, until it was. If he had any appreciation for our contributions, he didn't show it. In fact, he reminded us that our work was expected. And if we were caught being idle or doing something personal, we'd most certainly be recruited for something else, so Amalia and I learned to navigate around it. It became a running joke between us that we had mastered the art of looking busy—or simply being scarce. It became second nature for me to look over my shoulder, and I resented him for that.

At dinners, he vented about work while Mama listened and, when requested, offered up an opinion while my sister and I ate quietly and quickly. Our parents insisted we speak Dutch at home because they wanted us to maintain the language to be able to communicate with the family we'd left behind in the Netherlands. I understood their reasoning, but it became increasingly difficult, since most of the things Amalia and I wanted to speak about had occurred in the context of English. My thinking was shifting from Dutch to English, too. Sometimes I chose to stay silent rather than expend the dual efforts of finding an acceptable time to share my thoughts and translate them to Dutch. Amalia and I often slipped into a mix of both languages, but as long as we were under that roof, our parents spoke only Dutch to us. Only much later, once we'd both reached adulthood, did they begin to mix their Dutch with English with us.

In the fall, I began fourth grade and Amalia began second grade at our local elementary school. At school, I was self-conscious of my accent and strived to sound like a California native, but the other kids were fascinated with it, and they took to asking me to speak Dutch to them. After I was put on the spot a few times, I selected a go-to line: *De koe sprong over de maan en landde op de kerktorens,* which meant, "The cow jumped over the moon and landed on the church towers."

Once I had that at the ready, I came to enjoy the attention. One of the kids I came across in those first months was a lanky boy named Robert. He loved riding his ATV, learning how to fix engines, playing video games, fishing, and climbing trees. I didn't much care for most of those things, but he got a kick out of my clumsiness, and he appreciated my confidence. I appreciated his relaxed vibe and had fun hanging out with him. We shared a goofy sense of humor, made each other laugh, and connected in spirit. His friendship helped me to feel at home in California, and we've been connected ever since.

Despite my relatively recent introduction to English, I excelled in school, and when the time came, my parents enrolled me in a private middle school. Robert was a student there, too, which cemented our friendship. We had a couple of other friends in our little friend group, and we supported each other through our classes and through the changing social dynamics of adolescence.

Amalia and I excelled at pushing each other's buttons, anywhere and anytime. One Friday after dinner, the evening took a turn to the comical. I loved Friday evenings—Mama put extra effort into the meals, which almost always started with homemade soup and ended with dessert. A family favorite was chocolate pudding with homemade whipped cream, which waited in the fridge until after dinner, when Mama would ceremoniously add a large dollop onto each bowl of pudding. Boris got to lick the near-empty whipped cream bowl, which we all watched with delight.

On this particular evening, it was Amalia's turn to wash the dishes, which meant that it was my role to dry, standing next to her with a dish towel at the ready. Inevitably, I'd return a pot or a piece of cutlery that still had some food on it for a rewash, which always caused conflict. This time, our bickering quickly escalated into a food fight. Feeling goofy, I took it a step further and put a half-finished bowl of pudding on my head, which caused us both to howl with laughter. Because we'd been fighting, Papa mistook the commotion for a prolonged fight. Exasperated, he flew up from his spot on the couch, where he'd settled after dinner to get his dose of the nightly news, and came into the kitchen.

He grabbed two large butcher knives, holding them high as he approached us. "Here! Finish each other off and be done with it so I can get some peace." Incredibly, he didn't seem to notice the pudding sliding down my face, which only served to exacerbate our stifled laughter.

Amalia and I shared happy times, and we bonded over the challenges of living under Papa's roof and finding our way in a new country, in new schools. We had our moments of rivalry, but I was also protective of her. In these ways, our relationship was not unlike many other siblings', but my birth defect gave ours an extra layer of psychological complexity for me. Our dad referred to her as *meisje*, which is the Dutch equivalent of "little girl." He referred to me as *mejonge* (*mijn jongen*), which translates to "my boy." They are affectionate terms—but I wasn't actually a boy. I was many years away from a thorough grasp of the pain of misgendering, but I could feel something was off. His name for me just didn't land right. Now I understand that Amalia was being seen and named for who she was, and I wasn't, and that difference created some subconscious jealousy, which fed into my growing resentment. She was his little girl and was treated as such.

Papa gave her hugs, and he gave me handshakes. We shook hands when one of us was leaving or arriving or congratulations were in order, but he almost always made a game out of it to see who was stronger. His years of butchery made his hands very strong, and he'd crush my knuckles until I cried uncle, which he'd generally follow with a show of disgust. I hated it. I hated being measured for something I didn't care about, something I'd never be better at. To be fair, most of our interactions were neutral, but there were enough that left me feeling demeaned that I found myself wanting to avoid him as much as I could.

Amalia wasn't the only target of my subconscious envy. In elementary school, the boys and girls had all played together at recess as one big group. But as my classmates and I hit our teen years and middle school, that began to shift. The girls began developing, receiving attention from the boys and experiencing many firsts—hand-holding, stolen kisses—as themselves. They were also banding together more, experimenting and supporting one another through all those lessons of adolescent girlhood: gossip, periods, flirting, dating, makeup, and hair. The boys my age were doing their own versions of these. I didn't fit in either group. Instead, I was learning how to keep my eyes down.

It was at about this time that I was first visited by a recurring nightmare I would come to think of as the "Green Dream." It was short and to the point—just one scene. It began in a dark, dingy apartment where everything was some shade of a hazy pea green. There was a living room, a tiny galley kitchen, and a small bathroom, all of it dirty. Next to the front door, a sheer white curtain covered the apartment's only window. A woman lived there. She was alone and miserable, and somehow, I knew that she subsisted on sex work and that she was transgender. She wore a nightgown, and her face was ashen from smoking. There would be a knock at the door, and she'd open it reluctantly. The white curtain would flutter a little. A man in a long beige raincoat and a beige fedora, who had been there before, many times, stood at the door. Wordlessly, she'd step to the side, and the man would walk in, also without a word. When she closed the door, I'd always wake up with a knot in my stomach, a dry mouth, and a deep sense of sadness and fear.

I didn't feel that I was the woman in the dream; there was no connection that direct or clear. At the time, I didn't believe that transgender was a real thing. I also didn't believe this woman was actually a woman. I didn't understand that gender identity was something separate from sex or separate from assigned gender and that assigned gender could be incorrect. I didn't see how it could have anything to do with me. I had no interest in cross-dressing, and as best I knew, the two went hand in hand. What little I knew about transgender people I had picked up from the media or from popular culture, in which they were often portrayed in a negative light, whether as murderers, sociopaths, sex workers, or sexual predators.

But there was some connection there that made me feel afraid. Regardless of my muddled, poorly formed understanding of transgender people, one thing was certain about the dream: it was a painful, powerful reminder of the disconnect I felt inside and the wrongness of my lower part. Although I didn't consciously identify the woman in the Green Dream as a part of me, the nightmare did seem to be a sort of warning. It amplified many of my fears, such as physical danger, poverty, and the loss of friends, family, and the possibility for romance. That first occurrence marked a resurgence of the acute frustration and sadness I'd first tried to give voice to when I'd howled at my mom as a five-year-old. But just as I had then, I pushed it all to the side and tried to forget about it so I could get back to the safety of what was expected of me.

When I was about thirteen, we took a trip to San Francisco that underlined the role I was supposed to play. We had relatives in town from the Netherlands, and everyone squeezed into the wood-paneled station wagon, with me sitting right behind Papa, who was driving. As part of the day, he wanted to take our guests sightseeing on Polk Street, which at the time was the hub of San Francisco's gay community. For him, the excitement was in mocking the cross-dressers and laughing at whomever didn't meet his definition of manhood. As we drove up and down the street, his eyes would flick up to the rearview mirror to gauge my reaction. I can still feel the heat of his gaze. I didn't know which way to turn; I wanted to dissolve into the cracks of the seats and disappear. All I could do was stare out the window, keeping my face impassive so as to give away nothing to him.

The message was clear: no son of his should be anything like these "soft eggs," a name he had coined for men who fell short of his strong, masculine ideal. Worse than a soft egg was a woman who fell short of his feminine ideals, like outspoken, assertive women, especially those who challenged him. He referred to them as "dirty women," and he'd utter those words under his breath in Dutch whenever faced with one. Even at the time, I found his perspective perplexing and annoying. But subconsciously, his beliefs were building layers of homophobia and transphobia in me, teaching me that my acceptance depended on me presenting myself as a particular kind of man.

Yet I wasn't even a boy, let alone a man. I was still a long way from recognizing my truth as female, but I had known for many years that women were not for me. I was attracted to men—and men only. I had discovered Papa's secret hiding spot for issues of *Playboy*, and I snuck off with them when I knew I could get away with it for a time. But I'd flip quickly past the naked women, looking for the occasional photograph of a man. On that car ride, though, I did everything I could not to betray my truth.

I was supremely grateful for all we had, an awareness I can trace back to the Holocaust and to my grandparents' experience with it. They had lost most everything and endured hardships that left me with a powerful appreciation for our home, our family, and my parents' livelihood. Knowing how things could be taken away, I took nothing for granted. I recall nights in bed thinking about what my grandparents had been through and what my parents had been through as kids and feeling enormous gratitude for my comparably cushy life situation. I carry awe in my heart for their tenacity to survive, rebuild, and shine with so much love. I recognized appreciation for what I had and the importance of effort and vigilance to keep it. Much of it was the result of their work ethic. Their examples taught me that hard work and dedication were the only way to counter life's uncertainties, so that's where I put my attention.

Much later, I'd come to understand that there was another dimension to this gratitude—one that didn't serve me. My appreciation for our prosperity and all that was right in my life made it difficult for me to engage with the things that *weren't* right. I had some signs, going all the way back to early childhood, that my gender identity was different from the sex I'd been assigned at birth. I had unrecognized feelings of frustration, which I would later recognize as pangs of jealousy, for Amalia and for the girls I knew at school, but I could not explore them with everything I had that was good in my life. And every once in a great while, in the quiet moments of the night before sleep, my disconnect would surface into my consciousness, just a bit. I'd pray to the universe that it would go away, and by morning, I'd busy myself with other things and forget about it. Someone with a different family legacy might have started to investigate that deep sense of disconnection earlier, but that didn't feel like an option for me. I had no safe way of following my own natural curiosity, and it would be many years before I could.

Middle school gave way to high school. I was a chunky kid with contraptions in my mouth. I had retainers multiple times, braces twice, and also the dreaded headgear. The headgear, thankfully, only needed to be worn at night. Between my weight, the braces, and my accent, I was an easy target for some kids and on the receiving end of some occasional light bullying. It was frustrating, but I didn't let it take over my life. Papa attempted to help me out by teaching me unconventional self-defense moves. School was easy, but those years were not fun. I didn't go to most of the big weekend parties where the real fun and connection happened. I didn't like them, and it didn't register why I didn't like them at the time. Although I wasn't widely popular, I generally blended in and got along with a majority of the kids at school. Robert and I remained close friends, and I hung out with him and our small friend group often, and it was all I needed.

When I turned sixteen, I got my driver's license and the hand-me-down of the family Chevrolet station wagon, which gave me more freedom to be outside the house, away from my parents and the routines of the business. It was the mid-eighties, and the preppy style was on the rise. Its clean-cut smartness appealed to me, and its colorful accents reflected the brightness deep inside me. The true, full expression of my complete self was heavily constrained, but this seemed like a pretty safe way for me to experiment with some different looks and see how I felt.

One fall afternoon, I was preparing to head out to meet some friends. It was still too warm for a sweater, but in the evenings in Santa Rosa, the fog could roll in and with it sudden temperature drops. I'd seen both boys and girls wearing sweaters on their backs with the sleeves draped over their shoulders and knotted at the neck, and I wanted to give it a try. I spent some time at the mirror, experimenting with knots until I had it just right. I liked how it looked and felt. And I knew I was taking a big risk.

There was a good chance that Papa would interpret the look as feminine and make fun of me for it—or worse. I hoped I'd be able to slip out of the house and get to my car without attracting his attention. Of course, I could have waited until I'd left the house before getting the sweater arranged, but I wanted to do it in front of the mirror to get the knot just so, and there was a small part of me that wanted to see how he'd react. A couple of years earlier, my parents had agreed to my request to repaint my room a different color. After extensive comparison of swatches and test patches on my walls, I decided on peach and expected blowback at least from Papa for choosing a "girl's color." Neither of them balked, though, and I loved the walls of my room now. How would this sweater land? Were his feelings about masculinity so ridiculously rigid that he'd lose it over this?

I made my way down the stairs, trying to hear where he was in the house. All was quiet. I turned on the landing, and when I was just a few steps from the bottom, he suddenly appeared in front of me, and all my questions were instantly answered.

"What are you wearing!?" he roared, all the blood rushing into his face.

I froze on the step, my stomach tight, my heart hammering. "It's the style," I said. "It's preppy." But in the face of his sudden wrath, my voice was weak and thin.

"Why are you wearing it like that?" he yelled. He was so angry, spittle was flying out of his mouth now.

"This is what people do," I said. "Why can't I wear it like this?"

"Go upstairs and change right now, and don't ever do that again!" he yelled at me before continuing to wherever he'd been going.

I turned around and went back upstairs, my fear turning instantly to boiling anger and blistering frustration. It was the same feeling that had gripped me as a child when I was searching for words to explain that my lower part was wrong. I stayed in my room for a time, shaking with rage, and when I left, I was still filled with anger over his reaction. My experiment had been a failure. I had stuck out a toe, and my whole foot had been ripped off. My desire to express a small part of my internal truth retreated and went into hiding. As absurd as it might sound, given how innocuous my experiment had been in the first place, I never tried anything like it again. Papa's disapproval was just too overwhelming a force.

As if to make sure this remained the case, Papa brought this incident up regularly for years to come. To him, it was a funny story that showed how ridiculous I could be, and he'd have a good laugh at my expense. Amalia and Mama went along with the laughter, never really realizing how much it had hurt me or why, and I resented both of them for it.

Mama's larger role in all this was hard for me to pin down. She generally steered clear of these flash points between Papa and me, leaving me to fend for myself. Those closest to Papa knew him to be an obstinate person who was quick to anger. He wouldn't let anyone, not even Mama, tell him what to do, what not to do, what to say, and what not to say. I know she sometimes came to my defense in private—to her own peril, I would speculate—but I wished that she could have stood up to him and stopped him on the occasions when things turned ugly. She did listen to my pleas with sympathy, and she would sometimes remind me of his love for me and remind me that he would lay down his life for me if needed. I knew both to be true. But even with her sympathy, she didn't think any of it was a very big deal. She'd often tell me to lighten up, go along with it, and be more easygoing. She couldn't see how his treatment of me was a threat to my very essence.

As a family, we never discussed the cyclical challenges in the relationship I shared with Papa. From today's perch, the reasons for our conflict seem very obvious to me. I believe the flareups were rooted in Papa's disappointment and exasperation at my lack of interest in meeting his expectations. That led to his unsuccessful attempts to try to change me, which caused me anger and sadness while I continued to ache for the rare signs of his acceptance and love. I learned to tiptoe around him. I relied on inner strength, calmness, and pragmatism. I didn't rebel or turn to escapism through drugs or other means. I knew which way my bread was buttered and did what I needed to do to get through it. I learned to live with the dynamic and focused on my studies, being a good friend, taking care of all my obligations at home, and suppressing my true self.

The high school years ticked by. Puberty and my running regimen had helped me shed the extra weight, and though I was not very athletic, I joined the junior varsity cross-country team. I left the orthodontia behind. I was feeling a little better about how the other kids perceived me, but deep inside, my disconnect was only growing more acute, and I was continuing to accumulate unhappiness, jealousy, and resentment. I was quick to anger, as I did one afternoon following a fight with Amalia just before I was to leave for college. The fight started inside and carried out to the street, where our cars were parked in tandem. I'd saved up enough to proudly buy myself a new entry-level Volkswagen Golf, which meant the Chevrolet became hers. I don't remember why the fight started, but I remember climbing into my car, trying to get away while she threw punches at me through the open window. While trying to crank the window up, I intentionally hit the back of her car a number of times. I was moving slowly and was protective of my own car, so I didn't cause any real damage, but looking back, I see my actions that day as an expression of the deep, pent-up frustration that had been building through my entire childhood.

3

ACCEPTING MY REALITY

In the fall, I headed to the University of California at Davis, a town in California's Central Valley, about a ninety-minute drive east from Santa Rosa. I landed in a brand-new Spanish-style dorm complex, in a four-bedroom suite I shared with seven other students, two of whom became friends. I was interested in studying business, but UC Davis didn't offer that as a major, and economics seemed a little dry to me, so I settled on international relations. With my classes lined up, I was ready for this next step in my education. I was grateful that my parents were footing the bill for my tuition, room, and board, but I would have to buy my own clothes, pay for my evenings out, and cover my car expenses, so I took a job in the university's cavernous book warehouse, tracking inventory.

My roommates and I had just begun the work of getting to know one another and learning how to live together when something happened that kicked that process into high gear. It was a Tuesday evening in October. I'd caught a cold and was in my room fighting the effects of my cold medicine while trying to focus on my French homework.

My roommates were in the living room, sitting around the television, getting ready to watch the World Series. Our two local teams, the Giants and the A's, were about to square off in game three (details I learned only when writing this memoir). The effects of the cold medicine seemed to suddenly worsen. A dizzy wooziness came over me, and everything around me went into motion. I tried to clear my head but then heard that my roommates were also reacting.

The Loma Prieta earthquake lasted several seconds, cracked the top corner of the brand-new building, and quickly united us in our alarm and vulnerability. We were lucky, though. Closer to the epicenter and in the cities where freeways were collapsing, there were dozens of deaths and thousands of injuries.

Natural disasters notwithstanding, it was a lot of fun being away from home and exploring my newfound freedom, but I missed my mom, my sister, and my Rottweiler, Junior, so on most Friday afternoons, I'd drive home to stay until Sunday night. My relationship with Amalia made an instantaneous turnaround once I moved out. Now that we lived in different places, our rivalries evaporated, and we were able to stop fighting and be together in a way that reflected the love we'd shared all along. I'd hang out with her and our friends, including Robert, who was attending Santa Rosa Junior College. My relationship with my dad remained neutral. There were occasional moments of tension, but we were getting along well enough, and I liked being back at home. I was always a little sad when I had to climb into my VW and head back to Davis.

With thousands of newly independent eighteen-year-olds from all over the state thrown together, a part of those first months at school was overhearing stories of my fellow freshmen exploring dating, casual sex, or even, in some cases, the beginnings of serious relationships. I had always been a late bloomer and didn't have overwhelming sexual needs, so I kept my focus on my studies and my friends and looked forward to my weekends at home with my family. Or at least that's the story I told myself at the time. There was far more happening beneath the surface.

I'd always felt some jealousy in high school when I saw my peers pairing off—almost exclusively boyfriend–girlfriend relationships, since it was very rare at the time for anyone to be out as publicly gay in high school. In college, now that we were spending much more of our lives with one another, I saw a great deal more of others' relationships, and this served as an ongoing reminder that I was on the outside, looking in. But more than ever, I was frightened about my sexuality. I'd known with complete certainty that women were not for me. From what I understood, the only other alternative was that I was a gay man. But this didn't feel right either, and the possibility of it brought up additional fears.

There was a tiny part of me that questioned whether this fear was a result of my own internalized homophobia, which manifested in numerous ways, such as in the fear I had of being seen as feminine. Some of that I could trace to my dad, although there were plenty of other places where that message was loudly broadcasted. Another fear came from the HIV/AIDS epidemic, which had just grabbed a hold of the gay community a couple of years earlier. Diagnoses and deaths were both on a steep uphill climb, and I was terrified of it.

Of course, my reluctance to think of myself as a gay man went far deeper than either of those reasons. There were moments even before the bathroom incident with my mom when I knew that my part was wrong. In my mind's eye, I'd always had and seen a vagina, but when I had to face the anatomical reality of it, I could only think of it as malformed. That was my disconnect. Back then, I never dwelled on it more than moments at a time, and I didn't stop to consider the impact on my emotional and mental health of never being able to make love in the way my mind and soul were intended to. I didn't know what this meant for my identity or sexuality.

It did not occur to me that I could be a woman. How could it have? To start, I simply didn't believe that someone could be transgender. I didn't believe it was real. The few representations that appeared in the media were uniformly negative and marginalizing—the sorts of mentions that my brain had used to construct the Green Dream, which I was continuing to have once or twice a year, its fearsome power undiminished. I was devoted to my studies and enjoying many aspects of my new independence, but the undercurrent of frustration and sadness I'd always felt was getting stronger.

This was obvious to my family, most notably my mom. Now that I was out of the house, we chatted on the phone several times a week, and she could hear the pain in my voice. She often asked me what was wrong. Not only was I filled with fear, but I also had no understanding of—and no ability to articulate—what was happening inside me. So I'd always respond with a grunt and say that I was fine. She'd sigh, and we'd move onto something more mundane.

Looking back, I can see that part of the reason I liked going home on those weekends was because it gave me an escape—at least a partial one—from all this torment. I didn't have to see couples hanging out all weekend, blissfully oblivious to how straightforward love and romance were for them. I could meld right back into the comfort of my earlier life, with my parents and Amalia and Junior and Robert and our safe Santa Rosa hangouts.

———

With those supports, and with my dedication to my studies and the distraction of my job, I made it through my freshman year without upheaval. That summer, I worked with Amalia at Papa's plant in Petaluma, which was a good experience. Not only was I making good money, but it was easier to relate to my dad in that context. I was a diligent, conscientious employee, and I knew he recognized it and appreciated it, though he might not have said it out loud. He trusted me and my attention to detail when it came to things like preparing his proprietary recipes, and Amalia and I strove to be model employees, ensuring that the other workers couldn't accuse us of using our relationship with Papa to collect easy paychecks. Inevitably, however, he'd do or say something to demean me, and I'd complain to my mom about it, with no more effect than in the past.

When I returned to Davis for my sophomore year, I moved into an off-campus home with two of my former dorm roommates. I settled back into my studies, and most of the year went by without significant developments. But then, toward the end of my sophomore year, I was hired by a house-painting company called Student Works Painting, which franchises operations out to students to paint homes in assigned territories. The job got me out of that dim, dusty book warehouse, away from my MS-DOS workstation, and into the California suburbs.

By that time, my desire for human touch and my curiosity about sex had grown to the point where I could no longer brush them to the side or distract myself with schoolwork or trips home. Despite my disconnect, which felt ever present when I dared glance at it, my growing sexual needs were becoming stronger. Even though I felt I had limited options, I was determined to take the step.

On my drive to one of my painting jobs, I began to take notice of one of the neighbors, who was always out in his beautiful front yard, tending to his flowers or his lawn. That was a common enough sight in Davis's neighborhoods, but this guy was tall and muscular, almost always shirtless . . . and he wore leather pants *every time* I saw him.

He was about twice my age, and it seemed absurd that someone would be doing yard work in the Central Valley heat in leather pants. But absurdity aside, it signaled to me that he likely was gay.

So I changed my routine and began to park a few blocks away from his home so I could conveniently, albeit nervously, walk past his house on the way to my jobsite. Within days, after a few nodded greetings, we moved on to brief friendly exchanges, and then one day, with my heart beating out of my chest, I took the leap and made a point of holding eye contact a little longer than normal. Sure enough, he invited me in for a drink.

It was a mixed experience. I'd finally experienced the touch I'd been craving. And it was awful, because it felt entirely wrong. I felt *molecularly* wrong. From appearances, there had been two men in that bed, but that was not accurate. Although I didn't understand it, I was a woman and—understandably—I was neither appreciated nor seen as one. He hadn't been able to see me, talk with me, or touch me for who I was. And of course, I hadn't been able to use my vagina. While he and I were wrapped in a postcoital cuddle, the force of my disconnection erupted through my whole being. I became lightheaded and nauseous and began to heave. It felt like I was falling down a bottomless well.

This would never change; it was hopeless. It was an unfixable truth of my life, and I would go to my deathbed like this. I was forever broken. I didn't know what I was and certainly didn't know I was living a transgender experience. The disconnect I'd always felt with that part of my body shoved its way to the center of my mind. My vagina would always be malformed, never aligning with its intention, never able to receive my guy—or any guy. I'd been sentenced to a lifetime of punishment, and that day, in that moment, the clarity of the inescapable truth made me physically sick. I jumped out of bed and threw up right there on the floor.

That encounter felt deeply wrong, but it did nothing to diminish my desire for the intimacy of a caring romantic partner. To be touched, held, kissed. I wanted someone I could experience life with, travel with, and take home and introduce to my family. The only option I had was to resign myself to the prison of my disconnect. Knowing it would come with me to my grave, I made a conscious decision to overlook it and focus on living the best life I could. I would never be seen and treated for who I was, and my vagina was never going to be whole, but I could still find love and companionship.

I couldn't fully embrace an identity as a gay man, but it seemed less wrong than being in a relationship with a woman, so I pushed myself in that direction. I'd noticed advertisements for a coming-out group on campus, and shortly after the Christmas break of my junior year, I decided to attend. Meetings took place in a community room on campus. On my first day, I walked in nervously, but the respectful, welcoming vibe quickly put me at ease. There were about a dozen attendees, and we sat in a circle on the floor and shared stories. Some of the attendees were anxious, others excited, and others timid, but we were all grateful for the community and the support.

I was immediately drawn to a guy named Ryan, a scruffy guy with brown hair who looked a little younger than I was. I found him to be kind, smart, and sweet, and we began spending more and more time together. We had an easy connection, and we often met to listen to music, get sushi, or go to parties. With our caring, genuine connection, we decided to date. Strictly speaking, this was against the policies of the group, but we went for it anyway, since the group would be winding down at the end of the school year, in just a few weeks. Not wanting to spark a coming-out-group scandal, though, we kept our activities to ourselves. It was a little closer to the sort of relationship I'd always hoped for.

———

On a Friday night in May at the end of my junior year, I turned 21. I'd never cared for being drunk, but I did enjoy a nice drink or two on occasion, and I stayed out late that night, celebrating with friends. I finally got to bed about two in the morning, about four hours after I typically went to sleep. I've always been an early bird, so it wasn't surprising when I woke up at my usual time, feeling groggy from the alcohol and lack of sleep. That wouldn't have been a problem if I'd had nothing on my schedule, but my family had planned a family dinner at a fancy San Francisco steakhouse for me that evening. Mouthwatering food and quality time with my family—I was looking forward to both. By the time I left for the ninety-minute drive, my night of celebrations was catching up with me, and I was exhausted.

When I was about halfway there, I found myself in danger of falling asleep at the wheel. I tried rolling the windows down, blaring the music, and even slapping myself in the face, but none of it worked. I could see I would have no choice but to pull over to attempt a quick twenty-minute nap. This was not an easy realization—I'm always on time. Actually, I'm almost always early. It's genetically coded. But this was before cell phones, and I had no way to reach my family to let them know I'd be a little late.

When I showed up to the restaurant, only ten minutes late, I found Mama and Amalia at the table. Amalia was stoic; Mama's eyes were red, and she was clearly upset. I asked where Papa was and learned he'd left in a huff five minutes earlier, taking the car and abandoning them at the restaurant, an hour from home. We ate in silence, and then I drove them home. During our drive, I found out that he'd declared I would be late just to spite him. Beneath my disappointment and anger, I wanted to understand why he'd left, so when we arrived, I searched him out.

"Papa, can we talk and work out what's going on?"

"No. I don't want to talk with you. I do want to give you your birthday present, though. Follow me."

He headed for the garage, and I followed. "I don't need a birthday present," I said. "I just want to talk."

In the garage, he pointed to a battered suitcase in the corner. "There's your present. My old suitcase. I would never give you a new one. Take your dog, and get the hell out of my house. I never want to see you again."

"Why are you doing this?" I asked him. Beneath my feet, the floor felt uneven; colors were blurring. "What have I done?"

But he was done talking to me. He walked out, leaving me alone in the garage with a cast-off suitcase, grappling with the meaning of all this. How would I visit Mama and Amalia? Did this mean he was cutting me off financially, too? How would I pay for my final year of college?

I tried to find Mama, but I couldn't. Amalia, who was now a freshman at Davis, said she'd join me in solidarity and return with me. I was grateful for her show of support. I collected Junior, left the suitcase in the garage, and drove away, wondering what was happening to our tight-knit family.

In the subsequent week, I tried to call Papa a few times to see whether he'd talk and let me in on what had transpired. He didn't return my calls. I wondered whether he'd overheard one of the 1-900 calls I'd made over the previous years to gay chat lines. Maybe the reality of my sexuality had triggered him to kick me out. I couldn't think of any other possible reasons, so I decided it was time to come out to Mama. That week when we spoke, I told her that I was attracted to men and was sure that was why Papa had kicked me out. True to form with her pragmatism, she didn't react to my news with any drama or fanfare. She told me she hadn't known about my sexuality, and to my relief, she also told me that she loved me and accepted me. She went on to share her fear of HIV, and she asked me to tell Papa so that he could hear it from me and not her. She didn't know why he had kicked me out but didn't think that had been the reason.

I made a number of additional attempts to reach him via phone, and eventually, he picked up. I told him that I didn't understand why he had kicked me out, that I loved him, and that I just wanted to talk. He agreed, and we set a time the next weekend to meet back in Sonoma County. They had begun a big remodeling project and were staying in a local hotel called The Flamingo, a famous Santa Rosa landmark. I'd meet him there, and we'd attempt to clear the air.

The exchange made me feel like I was the adult, placating an upset child who had acted out, but I very much wanted to fix things, so I was committed to taking the high road. If I had done something wrong, I wanted to know what it was. Maybe there was something I needed to apologize for or rectify.

That next weekend, my sister and I drove back to Sonoma County, my heart beating at a rapid clip, my body tense. Mama and Amalia went off, and Papa and I settled into chairs at a small round table that sat just under a large window that let the spring light into their hotel room.

"Why did you kick me out?" I asked him.

"I'm sorry," he began, which floored me. I couldn't remember him ever apologizing to me before. It seemed completely sincere. "You're my child, and I never should have done that. I want you to be in my life. It was a mistake, and I hope you'll forgive me."

I told him that made me happy to hear and that I loved him, and I asked him again what had angered him so much. He explained to me that he'd overheard conversations in which I'd been complaining about him to my mom. This was certainly a possibility. Many such conversations had taken place over the years. I think it also hurt him that Mama was my confidante. He knew she kept things from him, things I felt comfortable enough to share with her. But also, I still had to wonder whether he'd overheard some of those 1-900 calls. I didn't ask.

I forgave him, and he asked that we strive to share things with each other, which I agreed to. After a brief pause, I decided it was time to come out to him, and my nervousness surged back up.

"In the spirit of not keeping things from you, I told Mama this a few days ago, and I want you to know, too," I began. "I'm attracted to men." I was so scared that it felt like my heart and soul were about to leave my body, but something new was happening, too. His unprecedented display of vulnerability had empowered me and connected the two of us in a new way.

"I didn't know that," he said. I wasn't entirely convinced of this, but in the moment, that wasn't relevant. "But I love you no matter what," he continued. "Thank you for telling me. You're my son, and I don't care who you're attracted to. Let's not have secrets from each other, okay? Does Amalia know?"

"No, not yet," I said.

He nodded. "How about we go find her and you let her know, and then let's all get some dinner and drinks." We're not a hugging family, but we stood, and he folded me into his arms, and then we walked out together.

The very next day, my parents burned up the phone lines to the Netherlands. It seemed a little insane that they would go to the effort to announce it to everyone: all the grandparents, each of my dad's two brothers, my mom's sister, and even their close friends received calls, informing them of my interest in men. Oma on Papa's side responded with warmth and love, telling me she had a close gay friend in her knitting group and inquiring whether there were any nice Jewish boys in my school. My other grandmother's response was cooler, which was in line with her personality. She was accepting but wanted to make sure I wouldn't be marching in those "flamboyant" parades. With the Bay Area as a major center for gay culture, I had every intention of exploring the fun and participating to the degree I'd find comfortable, but I wasn't ready to engage in a conversation about visibility and equal rights, so I didn't let myself get snared by her discomfort. That was her problem, not mine.

It had been a little shocking to find myself at the center of a family-wide, intercontinental closet outing, but ultimately, I was relieved to get it over with in one fell swoop. And just like that, I was right back in the fold of my family and entirely out of the closet. Or so it might have seemed.

Back at school, we broke for summer, and Ryan and I continued to see each other, making a trip to San Francisco together to attend the Pride Parade in June. When classes began, we reunited with our cohort from the coming-out group, now as a friend group. No longer constrained by the group's policies and with me fully out of the closet, Ryan and I were now free to go public with our relationship, which felt great. But within weeks, we came to the mutual realization that our connection lacked romantic excitement, and we realized we were better off as friends. We had a gentle, loving breakup, and Ryan shifted from being my boyfriend to being my best friend, a position he would occupy well into my forties. Like Robert—my childhood best friend—and a few others I originally met in that coming-out group, Ryan remains a dear friend today.

I loved Ryan's companionship and the intimate connection of a monogamous partnership, but in the course of that relationship, I learned that gay partners would want things from me that I was unable to give. They were, understandably, interested in my malformed vagina, but I didn't want it to get any attention. Any focus on it made my brain immediately malfunction. Sex was bearable at best but almost always sparked the disconnect which made it a painful experience, both emotionally and mentally. When he really wanted to touch my malformed vagina, I'd tense up and look the other way. I hated receiving oral sex. On the rare occasion when I allowed him to perform it, I held my breath, bit the inside of my cheek, and looked at the wall, fully tense. It was always a strong "no!" when I was asked to penetrate. There was no part of me that wanted to do that. Thankfully, Ryan was versatile, and his preference was to "top" me, which is why we worked for a while. Given the limited choices, I relegated myself to being a "bottom," even though it never felt aligned. I didn't like anal sex. I didn't like the prep and was always mildly revolted by the act. And worse, even though I tried not to think about it too much, anal sex just reminded me of my limitations. Ultimately, I felt both resentment and gratitude for it. I was grateful that at least I was able to receive but resented that I needed to settle for something that felt so far out of alignment with who I really was, even though I was still many years from learning the true magnitude of what that meant.

———

After graduating, I moved to San Francisco and set about looking for work. I'd grown up around the business of food and had developed some experience in supply-chain management from my work at the bookstore, so I put my resume together and soon landed a job with a food products company, Burns, Philp & Company, working on inventory management and forecasting. It was fairly boring. Supply chain tended to have a strong old-boys' network, and I didn't feel like I belonged, so I kept my personal life to myself. It paid the bills, though, and I was enjoying living in San Francisco, so I kept my head down, did my best, and learned what I could.

The following summer, a group of friends invited me to come on a trip with them for a long weekend in Manhattan, on the occasion of the twenty-fifth anniversary of the Stonewall uprising. In 1969, police raided the Stonewall Inn, a gay bar in Greenwich Village. They roughed up patrons and made arrests based on the state's gender-appropriate clothing statutes. Rather than dispersing, the large crowd of evicted patrons, which included a significant number of transgender people, particularly transgender women of color, fought back. Protests and clashes with the police continued in the neighborhood for several days. The events were a turning point for the LGBT rights movement, which led to the birth of numerous LGBT rights organizations and demonstrated the importance of visibility. I didn't fully understand the impact of that uprising when I attended the twenty-fifth anniversary. I was just looking to have fun with my friends and widen my experiences in the world of gay culture—and I did.

I met a handsome Australian lawyer on that trip. He was most definitely my type: strong masculine energy, sharp, and fit. We hung out a bit, and that led to him inviting me back to his hotel room. After a lot of sexy, fun making out, he asked that I top him. I didn't know whether to laugh with surprise or cry with disappointment. You never know whether someone will be a top, bottom, or versatile, but I hadn't learned this lesson yet, and I'd assumed he was a top based on his appearance and energy.

I told him I didn't want to top, had never done so, and would rather he take that role. He argued that I couldn't possibly know I didn't like something if I'd never tried it before, and though my gut said no, I found myself swayed by his logic. He must have been a good lawyer. So with condom in hand, I made a conscious decision to give it a try.

Even if it turned out to be a disaster, I'd learn something, and at least I could say I tried.

It was, in fact, a disaster. Within the first moment, my body and mind revolted. I was instantly nauseous and mentally disconnected, and I felt the free fall down the well again. An overwhelming sadness and anger swelled up in me. I stopped and told him that I needed to go, which he accepted without much of a reaction. I got dressed and left, vowing never to do that again, wondering anew whether I would ever be able to feel comfortable and fully present in bed with someone.

I returned to San Francisco, and a few months later, I met David. He was thirteen years my senior, but I was attracted to his amiability, his sense of humor, and his outgoing, confident, and decisive personality. He was also into me, and we began dating. We had fun together, but ultimately, the gap in our ages proved to be an incompatible difference, and we split up amicably. David remains a dear friend to this day as well.

I continued to date, but nothing developed into anything meaningful. I was, by all appearances, a gay man in one of the most exciting and vibrant places to be a gay man in the world, but I still felt a disconnection from the culture and community. My romantic liaisons weren't satisfying—gay men just weren't for me somehow. They expected, rightfully, that I would show up with the energy and appetites they expected of men, but I just didn't connect with that energy, sexual or otherwise. Actually, the men I'd had the most meaningful, intimate relationships with had all had previous relationships with women. These men each made me feel more seen and had an indescribable masculine energy I was drawn to. But without yet knowing how to name that or seek it out, I was stuck in the world of gay dating, and even then, only when I became desperate for touch and intimacy— about once or twice per year. With little emotional connection, those trysts did little but amplify my feelings of disconnection, both with gay men and with my own part.

That wasn't the only realm where things were feeling stagnant and unsatisfying. By my fourth year in supply-chain management, it felt unfulfilling. I found it to be an uninteresting niche in the business world, and I wanted a career that was more creative and dynamic, with innovative colleagues who would inspire me. I applied to MBA programs, seeing the degree as a good means to widen my opportunities. I was ecstatic to be accepted into the highly regarded Wharton School of the University of Pennsylvania. Living on the East Coast was a huge change for me. I'd never been more than a couple of hours away from my family, and now I'd be moving across the country, where I didn't know anybody. I felt ready for that.

With just a few months before I was to move, I met Joe. He was about my age and funny, and I loved his relaxed vibe. Even though I still hadn't shaken that underlying layer of unnamed dysphoria, he kept me intrigued. We had an easy connection, and I had hopes that our young relationship might survive my cross-country move. He was supportive and even came with me to help me settle into my new place in Philadelphia. With our relationship only a few months old, however, we didn't have the sort of bond that would carry us through a long-distance stretch. He broke up with me within months, which stung. But I had my coursework and a new life to build, which helped ease the hurt.

———

Business school was a wonderful educational experience, in large part because of my wildly unique, brilliant, kind, genuine, and driven peers. I made lifelong friends, had the opportunity to participate in a multiweek summer group trip to visit businesses in Europe, and learned across disciplines from excellent professors. And at the same time, I passed up untold opportunities to make deep connections with these extraordinary people, which remains one of my few regrets in life. There were a number of reasons for this.

Cancer had taken Junior, and now I had a new Rottweiler puppy whom I named Baxter. As a militantly responsible dog owner, I took his care and well-being seriously. This meant a lot of time for regular exercise and timely feedings. I also made it a point to study at home in my apartment rather than studying with my friends at the library. My body's natural rhythms continued to put me in bed by nine or ten o'clock, which caused me to miss a lot of evening activities.

I think I would have found more motivation to go out in the evening if it weren't for the deeper issue of my gender identity and how I was seen. I was unable to let go and simply have fun. Without understanding why, I was often on guard, uncomfortable, and sad. I had little hope or excitement of anything magical blooming from any new connections; they could only go so far because I was not at peace. I wasn't whole. My jealousy of other women was also intensifying at the time. It never impacted my behavior, but it was there, just under the surface. I was also getting angrier about my inability to be seen and connect with people, straight men in particular. They couldn't see me for who I was. Nobody could. And I couldn't connect with them because I was so disconnected from myself. I couldn't talk about myself beyond superficial facts. My confusion, my phobias and misconceptions, and my hopelessness persisted, leaving me where I'd always been—with no other option but to try to live as well as I could, with no hope that anything could ever change.

To make matters worse, I was feeling more and more disconnected from the gay community. I received plenty of invitations to gatherings and had ample opportunities for sexual escapades, but I wasn't interested in the parties or the casual sex. It was hard for me to even create or maintain friendships. I'd found that around gay men, a lot of the conversations revolved around sex: tops, bottoms, escapades, etc. Hearing all this just heightened my acute disconnect and made me even more forlorn about my situation.

———

As I'd done all my life, I sought refuge in the realm I knew and where I excelled: work. Toward the end of business school, I had the opportunity to join two other students, Bob and JP, in a business-plan competition. The business—related to managing excess inventory—was aligned with my work experience. We didn't win, but we were excited to be finalists, so after graduating, the three of us chose to forego job offers, and instead, we focused on making our idea into a reality. I was thrilled; I admired both Bob's and JP's thoughtfulness and smarts.

We started in the basement of Bob's brownstone, where he lived with his wife in the center of Philadelphia near the Italian Market. It was a tight space but comfortable, and there was a lot of laughter and hard work as we geared up for our launch. I took responsibility for operations and marketing, and Bob navigated his role as president with care and wit. JP astonished me with his passionate work ethic while balancing dad duties. In addition to taking on the strategy role, he agreed to also take charge of finance, as I was adamant that the numbers role shouldn't default to the Jew. Baxter and Bob's dog, Emma, were also part of the team. Baxter would provide comic relief with expressing his anal glands, and Bob, not to be outdone, passed his share of gas. We received funding from friends and family as well as an investor, and we grew our business enough to hire a small team. Eventually, we moved into a larger loft in an artists' community building, in a part of town where the rent was cheaper.

We ran the business for four years, but after a series of obstacles— unfortunate strategic decisions, poor timing, 9/11, the misleading and disingenuous intent of a strategic investor who was also a customer—we saw we had to wind it down. We transferred our intellectual property to a new entity to try to recoup some value for our investors and said goodbye to the loft. Entrepreneurship had been a rewarding challenge. I enjoyed running a company. I embraced the decision-making, the strategizing, the flexibility, and the freedom from heavy office politics, and I was also proud of being a cofounder. More than those benefits, though, I'm so grateful for the dear friendships I developed with Bob and JP. Before we formed our team, I hadn't had much opportunity to connect with straight men. Their camaraderie meant a great deal to me, and they unknowingly helped me to develop my comfort and confidence.

After we shut our business down, I decided to move to Boston. Ryan had moved there a decade earlier, and through a series of visits, I had fallen in love with New England. The directness of the New Englander—which felt natural to me as a Dutch person—was refreshing. I also loved Boston's cleanliness and its elegantly integrated juxtapositions of old and new architecture. I had also come to love Cape Cod, the mountains of New Hampshire, the Maine coast, the proximity to the rest of the Eastern Seaboard, and the ease of getting to Europe. Most people migrate from Boston to sunny California, but I proudly went the other way.

On a crisp spring weekend morning, I was walking to the gym, moving fast to warm up, still feeling high on the novelty of my new city. I saw him from a distance as I was approaching from behind: a tall, muscular man in gray sweatpants—cliché, but he wore them well—walking slowly with a corgi on either side of him. All three butts were swaying side to side, including his strong one.

The words fell out of my mouth as I passed. "Three nice asses," I said, and gave him a smile. Dating hadn't provided much satisfaction in quite some time, but I hadn't lost my confidence or my optimism, and I was feeling particularly good that morning. He gave me a quick up-and-down and smirked.

"Have a great day," I said, still smiling, and continued on my way without slowing down.

It turned out that he was also a member at my new gym. Later that week, I saw him on the StairMaster, where, upon recognizing me, he spoke rapidly in a foreign language and with much laughter to a friend who was on the adjacent StairMaster. I walked over, introduced myself, and met him and his friend. His name was Johan, and he was also an immigrant who'd come to America by way of Sweden, and he looked as good as I'd remembered. We had a brief chat, and then I went back to my workout.

A few weeks later, a friend of mine, who was trying to help me meet new people, set up a coffee date for me to meet another of his local friends—nothing intentionally romantic, but someone he figured I'd enjoy getting to know. I walked into the café at the appointed hour and found myself again face-to-face with Johan, who would shape the next decade of my life.

4

THE DEEP LOW

Johan and I soon became an item. Since we were both seeking new jobs and had plenty of time on our hands, we spent a lot of it together and got to know each other quickly. I loved his sense of humor, his heart, and his easygoing masculine vibe. He balanced my more serious type-A personality well. Our dogs got along well, too, which gave us plenty of opportunities to be outside together.

About six months after we met, our respective leases expired, which triggered talk about moving in together. I wasn't looking for work outside of Boston, but an offer came up through my network back in San Francisco, with a midsize high-growth coffee roaster and retailer, Peet's Coffee & Tea. They wanted me to come help improve the efficiency of their internal operations. It was a great opportunity in a city I knew well, so in the new year of 2003, Johan and I decided to make the move together.

We rented a bright, sunny apartment in West Portal and settled into a comfortable life: taking care of our dogs, cooking and exploring restaurants, and curling up on the couch at the end of the day to watch

TV. Johan secured a great job with an international charitable organization whose mission was to deliver medicine to communities in need around the world. I joined him on one of his trips to Nairobi, Kenya, to deliver a shipment. We both loved traveling, and we had adventures in destinations like Hawaii, Mexico, and Paris. The most memorable trip was one Mama and Papa took us on. My Oma Resi was nearing the end of her life, and my parents treated Johan and me as well as Amalia and her new husband to a trip back to the Netherlands to visit to say our goodbyes. Although the reason for the trip was somewhat somber, it was connecting to be with everyone and to show Johan my birth country.

I loved our relationship. I loved the intimacy and companionship, the stability, the touch, and the deepening of our knowledge of each other. I loved the shared experiences and the intermingling of our families. I was also thrilled with my decision to accept the Peet's offer. I worked in various roles, reporting directly to senior leadership, doing work that had a meaningful impact. I also felt right at home in the company's culture, which was progressive, culturally diverse, and collaborative, its people immensely competent. I vaguely remember how supportive the company culture was of those who were gender diverse or gender nonconforming. It seemed to be a nonissue, which contributed to a feeling of cultural belonging for everyone, which in turn encouraged open communication and invited a diverse range of ideas when it came to problem-solving. The open, accepting approach espoused by the leadership at Peet's gave the company a reputation as a great place to work and attracted the best talent. I harbored my own personal discomforts when I came across instances of gender diversity, as I always had, but I recognized how important the company's policies and culture were in fostering inclusivity and overall effectiveness.

It all felt like our version of the American dream. We had meaningful work, our own place in a thriving city, our dog family, and each other. But as with many couples, we had deeper, hidden issues, and after a few years, we both began to notice the strains.

There were some critical things missing from our relationship: vulnerability and healthy communication. I don't think either of us was good at expressing our needs and desires. Although my command of the English language was strong, I didn't know how to feel my body and tap into my needs, let alone express them. We loved each other, but meaningful intimacy was lacking because we didn't truly know each other. I don't think I received it from him, and I know with certainty he didn't receive it from me. I wasn't honest about who I truly was, which became harder as the years went by. He treated me like a man, which was understandable, but it left me feeling unseen and lacking the tenderness I needed from him. He didn't look at me or touch me in the way that I needed and deserved. He couldn't hold me emotionally or sexually satisfy me mentally, emotionally, or physically. He certainly takes no blame for any of that. He couldn't be expected to see me for who I was if I hadn't told him. I hadn't even sorted it out for myself. Our agreement, as officially recognized by the State of California, was that he was in a domestic partnership with a person who presented as a man.

About five years after we moved to San Francisco, Johan discovered a home for sale in the Ingleside neighborhood of San Francisco, near the city's southern edge. Interest rates were low, and with pooled money, we had a down payment. He really wanted to purchase a home with me. I had misgivings, mostly because of our rocky relationship, but I went along with it, and our offer was accepted. We moved our furniture and our dogs, hoping that the new neighborhood and our shared home ownership would create new bonds for us.

In the following year, we unexpectedly lost Baxter, as we had lost Junior, to cancer. He was only nine and in what seemed to be great health when he suddenly started having problems with incontinence and vomiting. Our local vet discovered a massive tumor on his spleen and advised us that it'd be best for Baxter if we were to help him over the doggy rainbow bridge. In shock, we drove to Santa Rosa for a second opinion. Baxter had been my steady companion since before graduate school, traveling with me from San Francisco to Philadelphia to Boston and back to San Francisco. He was a major part of our family, and I'd assumed he'd still have a few good years with us. The vet in Santa Rosa echoed the original diagnosis. Going through the motions in a daze and with a pit in my stomach, we took him out for a burger and then brought him back to the clinic for a sobbing goodbye. I held him while he received his shot.

Not long after that, a senior executive at Peet's left the company to become the CEO of a small beverage business and asked whether I would join him there in a finance capacity. I was ready for a change and agreed. My responsibilities were varied and the hours demanding, so it distracted me from everything else that was going wrong. At least for a few months it did—this was 2008, just a few months before the Great Recession hit hard, and I soon lost my brand-new job.

At the same time, Johan and I were in the last gasps of our relationship. Therapy wasn't turning it around, and after much reflection and discussion, we made the decision to end it. I'd lost a lot in a short period of time: a stable income, my sweet good boy Baxter, and the most significant relationship I'd had. I was out of work during a major recession, and I had the responsibility for half of an expensive mortgage. Worse, I didn't have a private space to grieve and rebuild. Johan and I were still living under the same roof, and within weeks, he had a new romantic interest, which turned serious very quickly. I was glad to be free of our ties, but it didn't help to have his new love in my face every day. And beneath it all, my own familiar demons were still there, taunting me, reminding me that I would never be truly happy or truly connected with anyone.

One day, I was sitting at our dining table, searching through the limited job openings in the area, when Johan returned from a date. I watched him walk by, found myself thinking, "Wow, this really fucking sucks right now," and felt what little energy I had just drain away. I needed to protect my sanity, and one of the few things I had immediate control over was my living situation. I needed to get out of there.

Unfortunately, Johan didn't want to sell. His suggestion was that we stop paying our mortgage and allow a foreclosure process to run its course. Not only did I want to protect my credit, but that felt wrong to me, so I proposed a different plan, which he agreed to. I found a cheap room for rent in the home of an elderly gentleman and moved in. Johan's new love moved into our home and paid me rent, and I continued to cover my half of the mortgage. It didn't feel fair, but it was a price I was willing to pay to protect my credit and my energy and give myself a new start. It was the start of a turnaround that ignited a chain of positive events.

I'd had no success in finding employment, so I launched my own operations and strategy consultancy. Through some heavy networking and luck, I found some traction and won work with a few start-ups as well as a significant multimonth consulting gig with a large global medical device company. That big project led to more projects and provided me the income I needed to get my own one-bedroom apartment. I was grateful for the work, but the pressure of running a one-person business was stressful. It felt hard to focus on exemplary consulting deliverables while also doing the billing, operations, marketing, and sales. I didn't like all that weight, and without the security of a steady paycheck, it didn't feel worth it, particularly on top of my neglected underlying sadness and the feelings of my disconnect.

When I stepped away from work, in the evenings or perhaps to have a drink by myself on the weekends, my unexplained sadness would bubble into inexplicable slow-flowing tears that sometimes evolved to sobs. I tried dating on occasion, soldiering on with my habit of infrequent encounters, but they continued to leave me feeling unsatisfied. I still hadn't shared my sadness with anyone, so I continued to shoulder the struggle by myself. Mama and I were still in the habit of our regular phone calls. It was a ritual now: her telling me I didn't sound right and asking me what was wrong, and me replying with, "Nothing, I'm fine" and a grunt. Every once in a while, I'd add, "I can't talk about it."

For the last several years, I'd occupied myself with engaging life activities: grad school, my relationship with Johan, staying fit, and building businesses. But alone in my apartment, without even a dog, I couldn't hide from it anymore. I had to make a change. My immediate challenge was providing for myself, so in the summer of 2010, after running my own business for about a year and a half, I reached out to my Wharton network, applied to two consulting firms, and crossed my fingers. A predictable income would alleviate my financial insecurity, and there could also be another benefit to such a position—it would afford me the time and space to begin therapy, which I thought I should get underway if I had any hope of shaking off this sadness that had plagued my life.

I was ecstatic to receive offers from both of the companies to which I'd applied. I chose the lower-entry position at Deloitte Consulting LLP because I was drawn to its collaborative and human-centered culture. I felt both relief and trepidation. Consulting, which was a popular route for many of my business school peers, hadn't drawn me previously, and I would soon find out whether it was a fit. It required heavy travel, and I had valued work–life balance, which is why I'd opted for the startup with Bob and JP. Ironically, life had steered me toward consulting after all. I hoped I could handle the traveling. I put a note on my calendar exactly two years from my start date that said, *If you're not happy, leave.*

Just as I had at Peet's, I found Deloitte to be full of intelligent, productive, and caring people, and I was grateful for the financial security. The learning curve was intense and engrossing, and for a time, the intellectual challenge made it easy to push the other stresses out of my mind. But as the weeks and months wore on, the novelty dissipated, and there, beneath everything, were the same long-standing frustrations. I was now traveling constantly, spending the majority of every week away from home, and in those quiet moments, in unfamiliar hotels and in airport terminals, my sadness was free to come surging back to the surface. Would I ever be seen and known for who I truly was? Would I be able to find deeply connecting romantic love? My life felt dim, and I felt dim. And what about this certainty that I'd been born with the wrong part? What was I to make of that? I still could not bring myself to believe that sex and gender were two different things. Transgender people seemed to be a bit crazy, to have something psychologically wrong with them, to be attention seeking, or perhaps some combination of those, I felt. But how could I reconcile that with my own experiences and feelings about myself? Was I crazy, too?

I really didn't think I was. Nor was I attention seeking, as the spotlight made me squirm. Also, there was my disinterest in cross-dressing—and as best I knew, all transgender women cross-dressed from an early age. Sure, there are men who enjoy cross-dressing as a kink or simply for fun, but that doesn't mean they're transgender. A man can cross-dress, identify as a male, live a happy and fulfilling life as such, and not be transgender. However, a cross-dresser certainly *could* be transgender because they are dressing to support being seen for the feminine beings who they truly are. As far as I knew, transgender women almost always cross-dressed. My lack of interest in women's clothes played a major role in my confusion about who I was.

My confusion wore on me, and before long, my new road-warrior lifestyle did too. The late dinners, late nights, and different hotel beds made sleep a challenge. My fitness suffered—it's hard to find healthy food on the road, and even though I was partaking of the hotel weight rooms, I missed a good gym and truly satisfying workouts. I also missed my friends, and even though my dating life was generally dismal, it became nonexistent on the road. I couldn't even think about getting a dog because I was away from home constantly. Additionally, I've always valued building long-term working relationships, as I had with Bob and JP. But this was a very different working style, with a new client, a new team, and a new city every eight weeks, on average. Piled on top of all that, flying takes a physical toll on my body, and I often need a full day to recover.

Just before my 40th birthday, when I'd been with Deloitte for six months, there was a flash point where the unhappiness of my job, the deep frustrations of my disconnect, and my exhaustion all collided. I was running between flights at Chicago's O'Hare International Airport, hurrying through the famous tunnel that connects Concourses B and C in Terminal 1. The underground tunnel is several hundred feet long, with brightly colored walls, mirrored ceilings, and thousands of feet of neon tubing running its entire length, with music playing throughout. There's a beauty to the installation, but the energy is frenetic, and it combined with my physical and emotional exhaustion to push me over the edge. As I was hurrying along the moving walkway, I broke down into tears. I had to get off the road. My physical and mental health depended on it. And I'd put therapy off for long enough. It was time to start the process if I wanted even a chance at happiness.

It was a daunting prospect, and I knew I needed a little push to provide the momentum. I also knew where I could get that push. While still on the moving walkway, traveling through that chaos of color and sound, I took out my phone and called Papa.

He had always given it straight; I'd seen him help countless others through hard situations. I knew he could be a reassuring, calm, and present voice of reason, a voice that erred on the side of taking risks, especially when it meant doing the right thing or standing up for oneself, even if that meant going against the proverbial herd. As hard and unpredictable as he'd always been with me, I also knew he wanted me to be okay.

To my relief, he picked up. Through my crying, I said, "Papa, I'm miserable, and I need to get off the road and figure some things out."

"What about Deloitte?" he asked. "Would you be able to get something else there?"

"I don't know," I said. "Maybe." I had seen others at Deloitte move into roles that didn't require as much travel, but I didn't know whether I could make the switch. I hoped I could. If not, I'd have to find something else.

"What does your gut say?" he asked.

"That I need to try," I said. "I can't do this anymore."

He listened, staying calm the whole time, and when he'd heard me out, he told me that he believed in me and supported me, that giving up on a great job in favor of happiness made sense, and that I should follow my gut. His counsel was exactly what I'd hoped for, and it gave me the push I needed to seek change. I shifted my focus to figuring out how to approach Deloitte's leadership. It was risky—I'd only been on the job for six months, and I didn't know how my request would be received. Would it impede my career or restrict the types of projects they'd trust me with, if I could even make a shift within the organization? Would they see me as a quitter? Would I have to actually quit to get off the road? In the end, Deloitte and its leadership were amazing. They were receptive to my request, and I was placed in a temporary internal analytics role, with the possibility of future opportunities, without travel. I was off the road, with none of the negative consequences I'd feared.

Following that shift, I made another big decision in support of my health and happiness. The offer from Peet's all those years ago had been too good to pass up, but at the time, I'd only just begun to get acquainted with Boston and New England. My new role at Deloitte was largely remote and allowed me to be anywhere, so I took the opportunity to return. I found a quiet 700-square-foot garden-level, two-bedroom apartment in Boston's South End and signed a lease that would go into effect in another month. Once I got there and got established, I'd start looking for a therapist who could help with the deeper problems, but for now, I dedicated myself to enjoying my remaining time—and the closing weeks of my thirties—with my family and my friends.

I love birthdays and was not the least bit upset to turn 40. I craved a meaningful celebration for this milestone, and my wish was to have my closest friends and family together to meet and get acquainted with one another. Most of my friends, beyond Ryan, had never met my family. My gay friends and my straight friends had inhabited separate realms, and I was excited to bring everyone together and mix it all up. Amalia, my parents, and about ten friends converged in Palm

Springs, California, a central location for most, where the weather would be great in early May. My vision was for a relaxing do-what-you-want weekend, during which the only official scheduled activity was my Saturday-night birthday dinner outside on the patio of a nice restaurant, where I was looking forward to treating everyone to a spectacular meal. I had planned a special menu with the chef that would end with an over-the-top dessert spread—I have a dessert fetish, and you can never have too many dessert options. I was especially looking forward to treating Papa since he's always the first to pay for a group dinner, and I wanted to show my appreciation for him. Beyond that, I'd planned a few other informal get-togethers, like coffee and a hike, but kept it casual because I didn't want anyone to feel pressured or overscheduled during the quick weekend getaway.

Most everyone arrived Friday evening, and we met for a low-key Mexican dinner. This was the first intersection of family and friends, and it made my heart swell with love. Papa was in fine form, entertaining the group with stories of the past and plenty of his innuendo-filled jokes.

"Do you know why my wife married me?" he asked the group, looking for anybody to answer. They were all leaning forward, clearly enthralled with whatever he was going to say next. "She married me for my meat!" I'd heard him tell that same joke dozens of times growing up. He has great comedic timing, and without fail, the audience would erupt in laughter with him. My friends were no different.

As the meal was winding down, we discussed meeting for coffee in the morning. It was an informal plan, and we agreed we'd figure out the location and timing in the morning and coordinate over group text.

At the time, Papa hadn't quite figured out texting yet. And Mama could receive them but hadn't mastered returning texts. So the next morning, I followed up the group text with a quick call to them. Mama was in the shower, so Papa picked up, and I told him that if they were interested, the details of the coffee plan were in the text chain, and I was looking forward to seeing them if they wanted to come. I didn't think anything of it.

That evening, I drove to pick up my family for dinner. As planned, Mama and Amalia were waiting for me, but Papa was missing. Surprised and inwardly groaning, I inquired where he was and whether he was coming. Mama informed me that he would not be joining us. I asked why, and she said she didn't know. It felt like a redo of my 21st birthday: this was the second time he'd abandoned me on a milestone birthday.

By this time, I had internalized that Papa could be a difficult man. I wasn't the only victim of his poor, unpredictable treatment. He'd had many feuds and rifts with people close to him, including his mom, both of his brothers, a cousin, and a number of his friends. Several times, I'd witnessed his silent treatments toward others, which could last for years. He was quick to feel offense about seemingly inconsequential, unintended actions or unmet expectations he'd never communicated in the first place.

In that moment, I made a conscious decision to shake it off and not allow him to ruin my evening. This wasn't personal. I wasn't the issue. It was all in his head, and I was determined to rise above his selfish and unpredictable behavior. I'd focus on enjoying those who did attend. And I did. We had a wonderful meal in a magnificent setting, with genial conversation all around the table as the people who were dearest to me got to know one another.

Late in the meal, while we were relishing the expansive dessert spread, I felt time slowing down, like when you slow a movie to catch nuances. I surveyed the faces of my loving friends and family and felt the understanding that the next ten years had the potential to bring dramatic change. The following month, I'd be in Boston. Soon after,

I'd begin therapy and possibly begin to understand the disconnect that had plagued my sense of my gender, my lower part, and my very sense of self.

What would my 50th birthday party look like? Who, from this table, would be there to celebrate with me? I hoped it would be all of them. My curiosity felt new to me—a sudden light amid the muddy confusion that had plagued me since I'd been a young child. In the coming decade, I might finally come to be seen. That thought triggered a surprising, ever-so-small, very warm inward smile. I scanned the beautiful faces surrounding me again. If only they knew what might be coming.

A few weeks later, I moved into my new apartment in Boston. It was a fresh decade and an empty slate, and I was back in the city where I wanted to be, in a job I liked, working for a company I felt great about. I had the income and the flexibility to take the next big step. It was time.

5

LOOKING IN THE MIRROR

Once I adapted to my new routine, I prepared myself for my journey into therapy. I continued to doubt that transgender people were authentic or even sane. I trusted that most were sincere, but I still didn't see how one could be a different gender from their sex. I could see that my happiness might depend on having an open enough mind to question my beliefs. I had no idea where that would take me, but it was time to start the process of finding out.

I needed to be as deliberate and conscientious about this as I'd always been about everything—perhaps even more so. Most important to me was that I bring my dear friends and family along with me, wherever I might be going. I had lived with this disconnect for forty years, and if *I* didn't understand it, then I figured it would be even harder for others to understand it. I knew it would take patience, time, and some strategy to bring the right people along. But at the same time, I needed them for support and understanding as I began to explore. There had been no significant secrets between me and my mom or my sister, or between me and my close friends, and I didn't want that to start now.

The desire for support conflicted with other needs. I was heading into unknown territory and knew it would be important to minimize the noise of outside influences and other peoples' agendas if I was to make pure, honest decisions. I was also anxious to avoid being the target of gossip, especially when I was already struggling with my own phobias, misconceptions, and questions. Furthermore, my job and my financial security were on the line. Many people lose their jobs simply for being transgender, and I was deathly afraid of others at work learning of anything before I figured things out myself. It would require a careful balancing act to line up the right kind of support but also to maintain my privacy and autonomy. I opted to talk first with Amalia and Ryan. Other than Mama, they were the two people closest to me in the world. I'd start with Amalia. She was hosting Thanksgiving for our family that year, minus Papa, at her home on the Oregon coast.

Papa had opted out since I would be there. Since my 40th birthday, I'd made numerous attempts to reach out to him. He wouldn't pick up the phone when I called, and Mama told me, sadly, that he didn't want to see me. The only explanation I'd ever been offered had come from her: she said that he'd been upset because he felt that I hadn't wanted him at the coffee gathering in Palm Springs. I never fully believed that explanation but didn't dwell on it. Whatever his reasons were, his behavior felt childish, and I grew tired of trying to communicate with him, so I gave up on our relationship and moved on.

His actions made it harder for me to maintain my relationship with Mama. I couldn't see her as often as I would have liked, and our telephone conversations were stilted. He'd brood and direct anger her way when he discovered her chatting with me on the phone, so she'd only talk with me when he wasn't nearby, and she'd abruptly hang up when he approached. The situation broke my heart, but I put it behind me. It felt sad but at the same time more peaceful to not have him in my life.

I was looking forward to visiting Mama that Thanksgiving but was nervous for a whole week leading up to my planned talk with Amalia. Once I arrived in Oregon, it was hard to find alone time with her, so I suggested we work out together at the local gym. I was hoping for a good moment to present itself and seized the opportunity when we took adjacent StairMasters—as if my heart wasn't already beating fast enough. I don't remember exactly what I told her, but I know it was filled with uncertainty and disclaimers. It was terrifying to give some voice to something that I had bottled inside myself for forty years—and about which I was utterly confused. I shared that I had been struggling with a deep, underlying sadness for a long time and thought that perhaps it had to do with gender. I told her that I didn't know what the issue was. I also told her I'd be starting therapy, that I didn't know where it would take me, and I asked her not to tell Mama.

She was so surprised, she almost fell off the StairMaster, but she took it all in stride and received me with open-mindedness and sweetness. She agreed to keep it to herself and said that she, too, was curious where it would take me. Her one request was that the next time I had such big news to share, to please wait until she was sitting. We laugh about that today. It was a huge relief to have her in my confidence and to know I had her support and love.

I had a conversation with Ryan a few weeks later at a bistro in Boston's South End. We were seated for dinner at the bar, and again, I was shakingly nervous. I told him the same things I'd told Amalia and asked him not to tell any of our mutual friends. He was surprised and showed concern and wanted to dig deeper, which I wasn't ready for. It was hard for him to digest since I hadn't shared the extent of my struggles with him and he hadn't noticed any outward signs. He felt it might be a leap for me to assume that my unhappiness could be related to my gender, and given that I was barely able to articulate the nature of my disconnect, he was concerned that my explorations might unfold too quickly. But ultimately, he was encouraging, and most importantly, he articulated his love for me, his desire for me to be happy, and his support. Our conversation ended with him saying, "Knowing you, whatever decision you make, I know you will be happy."

With my closest allies in the know, I felt better about beginning my exploration. Decades earlier, when I had come out to my family as being attracted to men, I had done so with the offer to explore therapy, knowing full well it wouldn't change a thing. At the time, I thought it might soften the impact. That led to three visits with a therapist before I bowed out. More recently, Johan and I had gone to a couples' counselor for about six months, which I found to be helpful both as we tried to make things work and as we explored graceful decoupling. Although I hadn't had a lot of therapy experience, I had done enough to trust it could be helpful and felt ready to embark on this exploration with an open mind and with a very deliberate, gradual approach. I would take small steps, focusing only on the current step without committing to its duration or any subsequent steps and without attachment to outcomes. This would give me the time and space to proceed slowly and to fully process each lesson or insight that might arise.

My intention for the initial therapy was to focus on everything *but* gender. I wanted to explore all the other areas of my life, including my relationship with Papa, before I pulled on the gender thread. I needed to know that the root of my sadness was indeed gender related because that exploration had the potential to lead to tremendous emotional and mental work and to major upheavals that would impact every aspect of my life. I was still a long way from any solid, conscious conclusions, but I was beginning to accept the possibility that I could indeed be transgender. I had little knowledge about such experiences and still harbored severe fears and phobias, but I knew enough to have a general idea about the emergence process for others who identified as such. There could be any number of steps that they might take: hair removal, shifts in presentation and clothing, voice fixes, name and pronoun alignment, and hormone and surgical treatments. And all that was to say nothing of the social and psychological impacts. Sharing the emergence with family, friends, and colleagues would invite a wide range of reactions.

There was—and still is—a dearth of understanding and acceptance for transgender people and their experiences, which contributed to my desire to write this book. Transgender people are disproportionately the targets of ridicule, hatred, and violence. By the time I was ready to conduct my own explorations, I had also heard stories of people who had emerged, only to discover they were wrong about their identity and needed to reverse their emergence—a prospect that added more terror to the process.

In all, the possibilities seemed overwhelmingly difficult and beyond frightening. If this was a path I needed to travel, I wanted to be able to focus on it with absolute certainty and with as much confidence as I could muster, and that meant first identifying and addressing all other potential issues first and clearing them out of the way. A large part of me hoped that I'd find issues in other areas and that working through those could alleviate my sadness enough to negate the need to explore gender.

I first signed on with a licensed independent clinical social worker who had expertise in gender. I told her that I required a slow and conservative approach and that I wanted to begin with a focus in other areas, but she kept bringing the conversation back to gender before I felt ready. At what turned out to be our last session, she made the grossly premature suggestion that I grow out my hair, which completely freaked me out. It quickly became apparent that it had been a mistake to start with her, and after three months, I ended the relationship.

I took a step back to reconsider what type of therapist I needed for that early stage of my journey. There was a possibility I needed to work through emotional and mental baggage related to family dynamics or that I had an undiagnosed mental illness, so I decided on a psychiatrist, who would be able to not only make any required diagnoses but also prescribe medicine if I needed it. With a little more experience and knowledge, I went back to searching.

At about that time, a big piece of the puzzle was falling into place elsewhere. I had performed well in the temporary internal role I'd been assigned at Deloitte, and in mid-2012, I landed in a more stable entrepreneurial role, which didn't require travel, in a brand-new strategic area of the firm. It was perfect for me. Soon afterward, I ran across the two-year milestone note on my calendar: *if you're not happy, leave.* I smiled, recognizing the perspective I'd gained. I had experienced so much variety in my career, ranging from startups and midsize high-growth companies to large companies, and I had learned that no job is ever perfect. I had found a role in which I was able to make a difference while also working for and with intelligent, compassionate people, and that was all I could ask for. Deloitte provided a balance of entrepreneurialism and stability, and with my career on solid footing, I could better focus on my therapeutic process.

I lucked out with the next therapist, a well-respected psychiatrist whom Ryan recommended. I worked with him weekly for about six months, and during that time, I sorted through all the other areas of my life without touching on gender. We worked through dating, career, and my upbringing and family. I gained a lot of clarity about my relationship with Papa and all the related family dynamics. I asked my therapist whether he thought I was depressed and whether he thought antidepressants might help me. He surprised me with his directness when he quickly answered no to both questions. I asked him whether he would prescribe them anyway, if just for a short time, so that I could be sure. He consented, and I took them for about three months but experienced no positive impact.

In the course of those intensive six months, we eliminated all the other possibilities, and it became clear that there was nothing, outside of the possibility of my gender disconnect, that could explain my consistent sadness. I was ready to shift over to someone with deep expertise in supporting clients through gender exploration and therapy.

I found a therapist with a doctorate in psychology and twenty years of experience in her field who was widely recognized for her specialization in gender topics. We began weekly sessions in January, and it soon became clear that it was a perfect fit. She asked questions, and I did a lot of talking while she listened and provided perspective, sometimes gently challenging me. She also steered me to helpful outside resources.

We began our examination of gender and working toward an understanding of what it meant to be transgender. I still didn't understand how I—or how anyone assigned male at birth—could be a woman. I continued to carry a lot of transphobia due to my fear of the unknown. My phobia never manifested as feelings of malice or jokes but showed up instead as discomfort. I just didn't understand, and therefore, it felt scary.

At first, I wasn't sure where my discomfort came from, but after much reflection, I identified the reasons. One was that I held the misguided belief that a transgender woman was simply a man trying to be a woman by wearing a dress—a dress that wasn't fooling anyone. It seemed farcical and clownish to me, and I felt bad for them. I didn't believe that a transgender woman could be a real woman and that—for those who wore traditional women's clothes—the act of putting on female clothes or makeup didn't take away from the fact that he was still a man. He was just a man in a dress. Clothes didn't change gender, and I thought it absurd that someone might think they could. Eventually, I came to realize that my beliefs were the result of how I'd been raised and from a lack of education about transgender people and topics.

My own demons, specifically my disconnect, were another more powerful source of my discomfort. Discussing transgender topics and being around transgender women—as I had been on occasion while out in public or while at LGBTQ+ fundraisers—brought them forth and amplified them, making it impossible for me to ignore them. Even when I did muster the courage, in those early stages, to look at my disconnect directly, I was still confounded by my own experiences. I'd never been interested in cross-dressing, never felt I'd been born into the "wrong" body, and never leaned toward stereotypical adolescent female behaviors, clothes, or interests, which were all phenomena I associated with transgender people.

As such, the first part of my work with this therapist focused on exploring the female gender and womanhood. I needed an answer to the basic question, "What defines a woman?" I knew that neither gender roles nor gender presentation would provide the answer, so I conducted an analysis with support from my therapist.

Here I should note that this approach was something that I, a non-expert, created at the time to try to attain some clarity. It's not exhaustive and likely wouldn't pass the scrutiny of the latest societal and scientific thinking. Today, there are a lot of experts who are doing excellent gender work that is more comprehensive, includes the latest thinking, and encompasses more layers, including the lens of nonbinary and the concept of the gender spectrum. I would advise any readers who are grappling with similar questions to seek advice and support from contemporary experts. My idea at the time was to make a pie chart of all the elements that I believed could inform gender—and womanhood in particular. So here it is, my crude, elementary, and novice analysis:

Features: My first instincts were to include height, body shape, facial structure, facial hair, breasts and breast size, voice, and skeletal structure. When I thought about this more, I saw that none of these were defining. There are plenty of tall women. There are plenty of women with small breasts, and there are women who need to have their breasts removed for various reasons. They, of course, are still women. There are women with deep voices and men who would be mistaken for women on the phone. There are men who have facial features that would traditionally be considered "feminine" and women who have "masculine" features. There are men with wide hips and narrow shoulders, and there are women with narrow hips and wide shoulders. There are women with varying degrees of hair, including those who have hirsutism, a condition that causes excess facial or body hair. Women with this symptom may choose to remove their hair; however, that's not always the case. Some celebrate it. There is no question whether these women are still women; they are. Physical features signal a *likely* gender, but they do not define it.

Gender presentation: This might include the types and colors of clothing and shoes, the use and type of makeup, the types of jewelry, and the length and style of one's hair. Generations ago, men wore dresses, and it's still commonplace for men in Scotland to wear kilts. Men have worn heels throughout history, from cavalrymen in tenth-century Persia to aristocrats in seventeenth-century Europe. Haircuts have also evolved over the generations, and the shorter cuts that many women sport today might have been perceived as cuts that only men would have had seventy years ago. There are plenty of men who have long hair today. And men do wear pink and can look damn hot doing so. Men have also worn makeup in various cultures throughout history. Many women dress in clothes typically associated with men, and vice versa. In this category, too, I concluded that gender presentation has little to do with actual gender. As a social construct, it can help to signal perceived gender, but it doesn't say much about actual gender.

Gender roles: Modern Western society seems to have evolved enough that most people understand that roles don't define gender. We've come a long way since the stereotypical roles of the 1950s, when women were expected to be homemakers, teachers, nurses, or secretaries and little else. In today's households, men often share—or might even take primary responsibility for—the work of raising kids or homemaking. These antiquated concepts had nothing to do with gender, either.

Sexual orientation: I included this in my analysis because of some people's ideas about sexual orientation and gender, but I knew full well that sexual orientation does not define who you are, nor does your gender. It only defines whom you find sexually attractive. During the course of my work, I read something that struck me as an elegant way to understand the difference between one's gender and sexual orientation: Sexual orientation defines who you go to bed *with*, and gender defines who you go to bed *as*. A woman who is attracted to men is straight, and her gender is female. A woman who is attracted to other women is gay, and her gender is also female.

Indirect signals: This one fascinates me. There are many indirect things we all do that send signals about our gender to those around us. They range from our bodily affect, like how we walk and hold up our bodies, to how we eat and the way we move our hands. For example, women often walk with more hip movement, and regardless of height differences, they generally have a lighter tread with shorter strides. Men often walk with a faster pace and more determination. Women tend to eat more delicately than men and would be more likely to cut a burger in half. Many younger women will often cover their mouths—even when eating with their mouths closed—as if to hide their eating. There are also differences in how men and women talk and engage with other people. Women tend to be more apologetic and deferential, and their voices tend to be more singsong, with more inflection than many men's voices.

These are rough generalizations, of course, and many of these examples vary by age and by geography. Much of my list is specific to the US; in some cultures outside of the US, there are altogether different variations. Indirect gender signals are societal, cultural, generational, and geographic constructs that are learned and (often) indirectly taught. There are no strict rules, but these signals all contribute to perceived gender—and only to perceptions. They don't define gender, either.

Sex organs or reproductive organs: The primary sex organs for men are the testes and for women, the ovaries. The external sex organs are the penis and scrotum for men and the vulva for women. The internal reproductive system for women includes the ovaries, fallopian tubes, uterus, cervix, and vagina. Most of the reproductive system for men is external, but the internal reproductive system for men includes the vas deferens, prostate, and urethra.

But it's not that clear cut. Some women are born without a uterus or with an underdeveloped uterus. This is called Mayer-Rokitansky-Küster-Hauser syndrome, and it occurs in one of every 4,500 births, according to the National Institutes of Health. Some women have a medical need for hysterectomies, in which the uterus and cervix are removed. A subset of these women also have their fallopian tubes and ovaries removed. These women are all still undeniably women. Some men have their prostates removed, and they are, of course, still men. Both men and women have urethras. That leaves as remaining plausible differences between a man and a woman the penis, vas deferens, scrotum, vulva, and vagina.

Hormones and chromosomes: Men and women each produce sex hormones, including testosterone, androgens, progesterone, and estrogen. Testosterone comes primarily from the testes in men and estrogen from the ovaries for women. Men and women do have different levels of these hormones: men have higher levels of androgens, including testosterone, and women have higher levels of estrogen. These hormones determine the secondary sex characteristics, which develop during puberty. For men, these include deepening of the voice, increased body hair, and muscle development. Women experience breast development, rounding of the figure, and the start of the menstrual cycle. The determination of the proportion of hormones—which leads to the development of secondary sex characteristics—is driven by a gene that comes from our chromosomes.

Humans have twenty-three pairs of chromosomes, and one of them determines biological sex. The chromosomal pair for females is XX, and for males, it is XY. The egg always delivers an X chromosome, and the sperm either will deliver an X or Y. When the sperm delivers a Y chromosome, it carries within it a gene called the sex-determining region Y, or SRY, gene. At about the sixth week after fertilization, the SRY gene causes testes to develop in an embryo. The testes then produce androgens, which lead to further development of the fetus with typical male characteristics, including the penis, vas deferens, and scrotum.

The testes begin to develop at the six-week mark. Prior to that, the fetuses of both males and females are virtually indistinguishable—and develop as females. In both cases, breasts and nipples begin to develop, as does a genital bud. The beginnings of a vagina also appear. If there is a second X chromosome present, the breast tissue continues to develop, and at the time of puberty—under the stimulation of estrogen and progesterone—they'll develop into mature female breasts with the potential for milk production. The genital bud becomes a clitoris, and the vagina continues to develop, along with the ovaries. While the development of undifferentiated reproductive organs into either a male or female embryo comprises a coordinated and sequential series of biological and genetic processes, simply put, if instead of an X chromosome, the sperm delivers a Y chromosome, along with its accompanying SRY gene, then at the six-week mark, testes develop, and the genital bud becomes the glans penis. The vagina closes and fuses—the evidence of this is the raphe line, the seam on the scrotum. The nipples, obviously, remain in place, as lasting evidence that our "default" sex is female.

———

My analysis taught me a lot about everything that *doesn't* define gender, and that alleviated a good deal of my confusion. My feelings about cross-dressing, for example, did not matter, so I could eliminate them from consideration. The work led me down the path of reflection and helped me understand that I could, indeed, be transgender. As my confusion dissipated, two deep truths surfaced: I was absolutely certain that my lower parts were wrong, and there was a stark disconnection between who I was and how the world saw me.

I began to realize that the root cause of my disconnect was the development that followed the path of the SRY gene. That's where things had gone wrong. Had the gene not been present, my vagina would not have developed into a penis, and my androgen production would not have led to all the wrong secondary sex characteristics, like increased body hair and a deeper voice. It's the SRY gene that caused the disconnection between my physical manifestation and my innate gender identity.

In the years since I conducted those preliminary explorations, I have come to understand it's possible that I might not have XY chromosomes. I don't know, as I have not been genetically tested. According to my superstar vagina surgeon—based on what she saw inside me—it's possible that I'm intersex. *Intersex* is a general term used for a variety of conditions in which a person is born with a reproductive or sexual anatomy that doesn't fit the typical definitions of female or male. Intersex people could have XX, XY, or one of many other chromosome configurations, including no sex chromosomes, an extra chromosome (XXY, XXX), or just an X chromosome. Studies yield various percentages, but even the lowest estimates indicate that millions of people have inconsistencies between their reproductive or sexual anatomy and the standard expectations for males and females. In those instances in which there are ambiguous genitalia, doctors in the US since at least the 1950s have performed surgeries on babies to change their genitals to be more clearly male or female. Unfortunately, these surgeries cannot be undone, and there have been many cases in which these babies grew up and found that the surgeries hadn't been needed or that incorrect assumptions had been made about their genders. Some said they had been assigned the wrong gender while others had endured severe complications, including sexual dysfunction and infertility.

Personally, I have no interest in being genetically tested because I don't think it matters. I could be most any of the variations, and the fact still remains that there was a disconnect between my inner truth and my external reality. With my knowledge of myself, the complexity and variations highlighted by intersex people, and the totality of my research of all those elements that *didn't* define gender, I was left to accept that the answer to my original question, "What defines a woman?" was another element, which was backed by considerable scientific evidence. That element was gender identity. I added it as the final slice in my analysis pie.

> **Gender identity:** Merriam-Webster offers multiple definitions for the adjective *female*. The first is "of, relating to, or being the sex that *typically* [italics added for emphasis] has the capacity to bear young or produce eggs." The second definition is "having a gender identity that is the opposite of male." It defines the noun *gender identity* as "a person's internal sense of being male, female, some combination of male and female, or neither male nor female."

Every individual—everyone—has a gender identity, regardless of whether they've consciously thought about it or not. The concept of gender identity was new to me, and after I'd come to understand all those other elements that do *not* define gender, it resonated loudly. It was the missing piece of the puzzle that brought so many other confusing things into focus, like my relationship with my own body. Growing up, I had heard on talk shows that transgender people frequently said that they were born into the wrong body. That never reflected my experience. I was born into *my* body, and I felt comfortable with much of it. It was the right body. There were elements of my body that I didn't care for, but doesn't everyone have parts they wish were different—bigger breasts, smaller breasts, thinner, shorter, taller, smaller nose, etc.? My body is sacred and a gift. Only one part of me was truly wrong, and that was my malformed vagina. To simply state that I'd been born into the wrong body would inaccurately represent the complexity of the truth that my gender identity didn't align with how the world engaged with me and how people failed to see me as a feminine and female being. That was my truth, and that was the issue for me.

Merriam-Webster's definition doesn't include any science to support the existence of gender identity as separate from chromosomes and other elements, and current research doesn't shed much light on their relationship, either. However, the American Academy of Pediatrics and the Endocrine Society, both well-respected organizations, indicate that gender identity in children is formed as early as age three or four. Other research has tried to explain that the sources of gender identity fall into either one or both of two camps: nature and nurture. I don't believe that my upbringing informed my gender identity. I believe my gender identity is my nature, and I believe its source is perfectly aligned to Merriam-Webster's definition of "internal sense." My internal sense is my soul. It's my spirit and my mind.

With my therapy experience, my gender analysis, and my growing self-knowledge, I began to accept that my gender was, indeed, female. I'd lived with severe confusion and incomprehension for more than forty years, and with this realization, I could finally sense freedom. My gender identity didn't match how the world perceived me. I have come to believe that the disconnect between my gender identity and how my sex characteristics evolved is the result of a birth defect, a congenital abnormality. I accept it for having unfolded as it did, but that doesn't negate the fact there was an issue with either hormone effectiveness or chromosomal variation as part of my conception, early gestation, or both. I'm not a scientist or a doctor and am unable to explain how or why it happened, but I know it was a birth defect that needed correcting in order for me to find peace and be able to live a fulfilling life.

It's worth noting that, although I believe my lower part to have been a birth defect, I'm not negating the experiences of others whose sex and gender identity don't conform with expectations. There are many transgender people whose gender identity doesn't match their sex, and the difference feels right to them. I don't believe it to be a flaw, a problem, or an imperfection for those transgender people who don't want surgeries to fix something that they don't feel is wrong.

Going into therapy, I hoped to gain clarity about whether my gender disconnect had always existed or was something new in adulthood. Once I started doing the work, I had some aha moments, and it became obvious my gender disconnect had always been present. This did not become clear to me until deep into the therapy journey. I had done an excellent job suppressing the bathroom memory—or dream, as it might have been. I had failed to grasp the significance of the Green Dream or of my visceral reaction to that initial encounter with Mr. Leather. I had done no work to really understand my inner feelings, my mind, my soul. It had been the strangest experience to witness myself reacting to things with jealousy (e.g., other girls) or to feel consistent sadness and anger at not being seen and treated for who I was and yet fail to register why I had been feeling that way. Ultimately, my subconscious mind knew the truth, and the nasty trio of fear, a lack of understanding about gender, and a narrow-minded viewpoint had been holding the truth back. I will forever be grateful for those years of therapy that finally exposed all of that and allowed my subconscious feelings to rise to my consciousness so I could understand and accept that my mind, my soul, and my spirit were female. I am also grateful for the Green Dream and for the memory of my frustration in the bathroom as a five-year-old, both of which helped me understand my disconnect. These led me to my truth, and that was all that mattered.

It was a critical revelation, and I was grateful to have it. And at the same time, the consequences felt terrifying. If I were to be true to myself and do something to escape my never-ending sadness, I would need to continue to do the internal work to move from fear into acceptance so that eventually I could be in a better place. It felt daunting until I remembered my promise to myself to take it one step at a time without determining, committing to, or worrying about any next steps. I owned my own destiny.

6

JUST THIS STEP

It was now mid-2013, and after half a year of gender-specific therapy, I'd found some clarity and was making progress. I'd pushed beyond my misconceptions and confusion about what it meant to be transgender and better understood that I could be a woman. Despite my growing knowledge and my personal experiences, I still found it hard to understand how one's gender could differ from their sex at birth. I also had to contend with a new set of fears, including the potential for negative reactions from my family and friends, rejection or harm from society in general, and the impact this might have on my ability to find someone I could love and who would love me.

If I were to move forward with an emergence, I'd want to be seen for who I was: a woman. I didn't think it would be worth it if I'd still only be seen as a man or someone who fit somewhere else on the gender spectrum. I was terrified of being seen as simply a man in a dress. I had grown up witnessing my dad's ridiculing of cross-dressers and transgender people; I could still hear his insults and derision. The possibility I might still be seen as a man after emerging felt like it would be the ultimate rejection of who I was at my core. Would that possibility negate the effort and risk of going through an emergence at all? In that scenario, I would not only still be seen as a man; I would also be seen as something that the likes of my family and many others didn't respect, let alone understand. I didn't know whether I had the emotional or mental strength to handle the possibility that I might still be seen as a man after all the work of an emergence. I wanted to be seen for who I truly was, but these fears had the potential to overwhelm me.

The other option—remaining as I'd always been—was a worse fate. Despite all my fears, I couldn't allow myself to remain in a perpetual state of sadness and hopelessness. I'd endured it for more than forty years, and I could not bear the thought of another forty like that. So I began to take small steps to test my emergence while working on self-acceptance and my own emotional readiness. I would not need to consider truly meaningful changes—like hormone replacement therapy (HRT) or lower surgery—until much later, and only if I ended up choosing that entire route. Many women opt for hormone therapy but not surgery, and many others opt for neither. I still couldn't give myself permission to dream that my lower part might someday look the way it was intended to, but I did decide early on that the two would go hand in hand. If I ever got to the step of starting hormones, then I would plan to have my lower surgery as well. Well before I reached that stage, though, there were some smaller things I could try. As I had done with psychotherapy, I would explore one small step at a time. Only once I'd fully explored each step would I allow myself to move on, and only if it made sense.

I hoped for one goal with my emergence: to be a little less sad.

I would use that goal as the measuring stick to evaluate each step and determine whether I wanted to go any further. At each step, I'd ask myself, *How does this feel? Am I feeling a little less sad? Do I feel like taking another step? And if so, what feels good?*

My first step was just what my first therapist had suggested a year and a half earlier: growing out my hair. I was ready for it now, and glad to do it. I had always kept my hair short, and with my wild curly Jewish hair, the pace of change felt glacial. It took about six months to go from a crew cut to a few inches. It wasn't dramatic to others, but it did feel different for me because I'd never had my hair that long. I thought it made me look less rigid and a little softer, and I liked it. Soon, I saw that I'd need some help to keep it from turning into a shaggy mess. Ryan came to the rescue once again and recommended a superb stylist for women whom he felt I could trust with my journey.

When I walked in that first time, I was quivering with an unexpected juxtaposition of excitement and nervousness. It felt scary to talk about my journey and the stylist's role with my hair, but it felt right. He received me with openness and compassion and shared his vision with me, which included a plan to deemphasize my receding hairline. It had been a source of anxiety; I worried that my hairline might impede a feminine hairstyle, but the stylist scoffed at that, confident my hairline was a nonissue. I wasn't convinced but was ready to find out. Over time, the visits became less nerve-wracking, and slowly, with each subsequent visit, I began to look forward to them.

I was grateful that my legs and arms weren't overly hairy, but another hair challenge, also due to my Jewish genes, was that my entire upper body was hairy. I'd been waxing my back since my teenage years, which had been an easy routine to implement emotionally because Papa waxed his back, too. Hormone therapy reduces body hair, but I wasn't ready for that yet, so a few months after my first trip to the stylist, I started with laser treatments. It was low-risk, and since I wasn't dating or involved with anyone intimately, it also would have no impact on my perceived gender. I began with my back, which didn't feel like much of a step since I'd already been waxing. From there, I moved to laser hair removal on the rest of my upper body, which was definitely a new step. Since my hair was dense, this was particularly painful, but again, it felt like the right thing to do. I was liking the slightly longer, more feminine hair on my head, and it encouraged me to keep pushing forward.

I'd been treating myself to manicures for quite some time but had never before had color applied and rarely received pedicures. Now I had a desire to treat myself to pedicures more regularly, and more importantly, I wanted to try adding color to my toes: red. I wanted red. So I got a pedicure, got my toenails painted red, and *loved* it. My toes have never been without some shade of red since that first visit. In fact, my toenails carried me right into my next major step.

We were driving out of Boston in my car, headed for a day of outlet-store shopping and a beach visit in Ogunquit, Maine, about an hour's drive north. I was at the wheel, with Ryan in the passenger seat and our friend Bill in the back, and at that point, my red toenails were quietly tucked away inside my shoes. Ryan knew I was exploring a possible emergence, but he had no idea I'd painted my toenails. Bill didn't know about it either. He himself presented as masculine and metrosexual, as did Ryan and I, and nobody in our immediate friend group had dabbled in any kind of feminine-leaning presentation before, at least not publicly. I'd be breaking new ground once we hit the sand, and I was a little nervous and a lot excited.

We parked, made our way to the beach, staked out a spot, and then I casually took my shoes off. Bill's shocked reaction was comical—his head went back, his eyebrows arched upward, and his eyes bugged out. "Wow, look at those beauties!" he exclaimed.

Ryan was equally surprised, but he knew more about the context.

He could surmise what I was doing and why, and he knew how my toenails must have been landing with Bill and how Bill's reaction was landing with me. It all turned to shared laughter, and the whole time, my red toenails waved proudly in the sun, basking in the attention. It was an affirming moment; I felt seen and chuckled nervously, albeit joyfully, along with them.

Bill brought my toenails back into the conversation several times that day, each time with humor, and we'd crack up all over again. On our drive back to Boston, he was getting impatient with my lack of speed and shouted from the back, "Girl, would you please stomp those juicy cherry-red toes to the metal so we can get home already?" We laughed so hard, I had to fight to stay in my lane. The experiment had been a resounding success. It was a small physical detail, but it was totally, unabashedly feminine, and I loved it. It felt like the true me, finally beginning to emerge.

At about the same time, I changed my name back to my original given name. My parents had named me Benni after my dad's father, who had passed away so young, shortly after the war. By the time I turned thirteen, that name had come to feel childish to me, and I requested that everyone call me Ben. I'd been Ben ever since, but now, in my early forties, I discovered that Benni felt much better suited to me and decided to try it back on. I was grateful it was spelled with an *i* instead of a *y*, which made it more feminine, by American conventions, and I even thought it might be perfect as my forever name were I to fully emerge.

I asked my friends to start calling me Benni and had it officially changed at work, which was easy since all the official documentation carried my full given legal name. The reason I gave for the change was that I wanted to feel more connected to my grandfather and to honor him. Although my reason was a white lie, the story was true, and I was glad to be able to speak about him and pay homage to his impact on my family.

Another small step I took in those early stages was to explore community. While in the midst of the hair-removal phase, I joined a local support group, and though I found the facilitator to be competent enough and the women in the group to be warmhearted and welcoming, I didn't have much in common with the group. The overall feel was negative and sad, which wasn't a good fit.

All of the other members were significantly older than I was, in different phases of life. They almost all identified as lesbians, and most were married with kids. A good number struggled with health, weight, finances, discrimination, or relationship issues, and some had serious emotional challenges. I wasn't struggling with those, was in a different phase of life, and was straight. Even though I didn't fit in, the group made me feel grateful for my own situation and, ironically, hopeful about my emergence. There were lots of ways the emergence journey could go awry; I was hearing about them all in our group sessions. From their cautionary tales, and with what my own intuition was telling me, I was figuring out how to move forward if I chose to do so. I knew I had the resources and support to do it, for which I was grateful.

I found myself providing support for the others during group meetings, but at the same time, I often left feeling weighed down and pining for women my age who were straight, with professional careers. Ultimately, though, the group was a positive experience. It gave me meaningful visibility of transgender women, which helped improve my understanding of transgender people, fostered my compassion, and helped further erode my own transphobia.

Continuing my search for community, I attended First Event, an annual conference hosted by the Trans Community of New England (TCNE). TCNE is a Boston-area transgender support organization and First Event is one of the longest-running conferences in the US for transgender and gender-expansive people and those who love and support them. The conference runs over the course of a week and includes workshops, speakers, and social gatherings. A vendor area offers attendees the opportunity to connect with helpful businesses. I was nervous but discovered the conference to be welcoming and educational. I made new friends and gained insight into the possible journey ahead of me. I loved the opportunity to meet local hair-removal specialists as well as surgeons, who'd flown in from all around the country to discuss their approaches and experiences with lower surgery.

At that point, it had been about a year since I'd chosen to start taking small steps toward a possible emergence. I'd apprised Ryan of my progress and occasionally updated Amalia about hair-removal activities, but otherwise, I'd kept the entirety of the process to myself. I wondered often how Mama would react to knowing all this, but I wasn't ready for that yet. As for Papa, we were still not in contact, now three years beyond my Palm Springs birthday, and my grief and anger remained—not just because of the loss of my relationship with him but because of how it affected the rest of the family. Previously, when I'd lived on the opposite coast, I'd try to see them two or three times a year, typically on Thanksgiving and around birthdays. He'd refused to attend another Thanksgiving, however, and directed protracted anger toward Mama when she didn't sit out with him in solidarity. He'd effectively broken up the family—my visits were reduced to once or twice per year at most, and they were strained and difficult, with me trying to visit with Mama apart from him, and her caught between her loyalties to me and to him. I still had no idea why he'd rejected me.

Mixed in with my sadness and the complications of my visits, though, was a bit of peace. His unreasonable, unnecessary reactions could be wearing, and though I had lots of unresolved questions, I didn't miss the drama. I had other more personal matters to think about.

I was feeling really good about my name change, my happy toenails, my longer hair, and my body hair removal. With excitement and newfound optimism, I decided to take a bigger step, one that would not only be visible to the outside world but also irreversible: facial-hair removal. The method, duration, and complexity of facial-hair removal is completely individual, as it's dependent on hair color, skin color, and the strength and volume of the hair. I soon discovered that I presented the worst-case scenario in all categories. Laser removal is quick and effective, but it doesn't work well for light hair, like mine. I would have to combine laser treatments with electrolysis, a laborious and painful procedure that made the upper-body-hair-removal process seem like child's play. In electrolysis, a conductive needle plunges into the root of each individual hair follicle and delivers an electric current. The needle retracts, and tweezers pull out the hair. If the current isn't strong enough, the hair resists, and it's breath-gulpingly painful. The needle then needs to be reinserted for another electric shock. Once removed, a follicle could come back half a dozen times, or even more. There are several variables in the process, like frequency and duration of visits, color of hair versus color of skin, and follicle density, so there's no way to know how long it will take before the hair is gone for good. For most people, it takes years. It's also expensive, and at the time, my health insurance didn't cover it. Many insurers still don't cover it, so it can be a significant barrier to self-expression for women who can't afford it. This is an issue that has much more to it than cosmetics or even self-expression; facial hair is often a trigger for transgender women to be harassed.

I was fortunate to be able to commit to the process and developed a plan to go as frequently as I could for as long a duration as I could each visit. As with therapy, I had a few false starts—either I didn't feel connected to the technicians, or the pain levels made me suspect their skill. Given the expense and probable multiyear commitment, I wasn't prepared to settle and kept searching. I'm infinitely appreciative for the one I eventually found.

Lee had been recommended to me at the First Event conference. She had a masterful hand, balancing my discomfort and what my sensitive skin could handle with maximizing electricity to reduce regrowth. She also had a plan for the sequence of treatments so my facial hair wouldn't look strange over the years before I emerged. We were also a good fit personally. I liked her, and we developed a friendly, connecting energy, which was crucial.

I settled into a routine of two hours every Tuesday afternoon; that was all my face could handle. The process was excruciatingly painful, and the skin on my face never failed to swell and brighten to a bright strawberry red for a few hours after each visit, despite my preparations. At home before each visit, I took Tylenol and applied a thick layer of prescription numbing cream, which contained lidocaine and prilocaine. Lee taught me to cover the cream with plastic wrap to ensure maximum absorption, which also reduced drips. Once my face was covered in cream and plastic wrap, I had to make the thirty-minute drive to the appointment, which began with me peering out my front window to make sure nobody was around before I made a mad dash from my front door to the car. Once I was away from my neighborhood, I relaxed. I didn't care what other drivers might think about my face, but I did feel bad that I may have unintentionally startled some kids. As painful as it was, I always looked forward to the appointments, as I knew I was making progress toward emerging as myself. Through our conversations, Lee and I got to know each other well, and she eventually became a friend and a helpful ally on the long course of my journey.

Meanwhile, in therapy, I continued to focus on accepting that I was, in fact, headed down the path of emergence and likely headed for hormone replacement therapy and surgery. Part of that process was asking all sorts of random questions, like whether my dog Bosco would still know me, since my smell would change in the likely course of HRT. Bosco was a little over a year old at the time, and I didn't want him to be confused. My question was serious, but I think my therapist had to force herself to keep a straight face. She took a long pause—likely to compose herself—and told me earnestly that she hadn't been asked that question before and hadn't ever heard of it being a problem. I can join her silent laughter now. The physical changes, like smell, are so gradual that of course my concern turned out to be a nonissue.

With progress in therapy and hair removal underway in earnest, I was ready for another step: makeup. I'd never had any interest in it, but I felt that if I were to emerge, I'd likely want to wear some, and my curiosity about it was growing. With zero guidance or experience, I went to the drugstore and bought a couple of shades of eye shadow I thought might look good: coral and green. I went home and tried to put them on, and it was a complete disaster. I had no clue what I was doing, and by the end, there was more eye shadow in the sink than on my eyelids, and what color did make it onto my eyelids made me look like a clown. *Fuck, this sucks*, I thought, heaving a big sigh at my reflection. I would have to take some lessons if I were moving forward. I hoped to God my face would become more feminine and that I could figure out how to do this. I wanted to take that makeup off immediately—but soon discovered I had no clue how to do that, either.

———

One afternoon, I was sitting in the electrology waiting room, waiting to be called into my session. As usual, I had my face covered in plastic wrap and was anxious to get started. Those waits always pulled me in competing directions. On the one hand, I hoped the numbing cream had been there long enough to alleviate some discomfort. On the other hand, my wrapped-up face made me feel ridiculous, and I was in a hurry to get underway. I didn't want any attention and dreaded a conversation with a stranger about why I was there.

That Tuesday, a large-framed, strong-looking, middle-aged woman was sitting in one of the chairs near mine. She made eye contact and said hello. Her frame and her voice made me think she was transgender. I stiffened. She clearly wanted to have a conversation, but I just wanted to be left alone. I was embarrassed about my face. My emergence journey was still full of question marks, and I wasn't ready to associate publicly with anyone who was transgender. She was persistent and congenial, however, and introduced herself as Michelle. As feared, she asked questions which I begrudgingly found myself answering. It was nothing involved—just basic get-to-know-you questions like where I was from, what I did for a living, and so on.

Even though I was uncomfortable for the entirety of our interaction, it was hard not to like her, and our eyes and smiles connected. She was kind, optimistic, smart, genial, and bubbly. After a bit of chatting, a man came out of one of the rooms, and she proudly introduced him as her husband. He was there to have some hair removed from his back.

By now, I was paying close attention. This was a transgender woman, close to my age, married to a man. I hadn't heard or seen that before and was intrigued. As they were leaving, she gave me her card and encouraged me to reach out. I could see being friends with her. When I got home, I put her card on the foyer console table. I couldn't get her out of my mind, and about a month later, I sent her an email and suggested we get a drink. We met for drinks, had a fun and connecting conversation, and set a time to meet again. It was the start of a dear friendship, and soon I brought her into my confidence and began talking more about my journey. With her own experiences and wisdom, she provided me with tremendous support and understanding, for which I'll be eternally thankful. In general, my journey up until that point had been lonely, and many moments along the way had brought trepidation and uncertainty. It was delightful to have a new companion.

By this point, my deliberate, careful steps were adding up and carrying me in a direction that felt authentic, but I was coming up against a much bigger decision than I'd had to grapple with before—the decision of whether or not to begin HRT. I struggled with the idea that if and when I were to begin hormones, my journey could potentially become visible to the outside world before I felt ready to come out about it. If I did choose to go down that path, I would do everything I could to time my coming out so that others would know before the impact of the medicine became obvious. It was a momentous choice, and at times, the prospect had begun to trigger some constriction, but I'd always been able to remind myself that I never needed to take a path I was uncomfortable with. If I were to choose to take them, it would be because I was absolutely certain that I needed them to be happy.

By the time I reached the one-year mark of facial-hair removal, I'd reverted my name back to Benni, continued exploring my gender identity in therapy, and done some experimentation with feminine presentations. My hair was getting longer, and I had a better understanding of who I was. With all that, the journey became clearer, and my resolve strengthened. I recognized I would undergo hormone replacement therapy and see this emergence all the way through. I don't remember the exact moment of the decision; it arrived piecemeal. Given my conservative, slow, and introspective approach, there was zero doubt about it. The decision itself had been a nonevent—exactly as I'd needed it to be. That was perfect, and I was grateful for it.

I wasn't ready to jump right into it yet, though. I had numerous preliminary steps to get through first. I didn't want changes in my body to be visible until my facial hair was mostly gone. I also desired a thoughtful plan for my work emergence. It typically takes three to six months before changes from HRT become apparent, which meant I'd want to start hormones that far in advance before I could show up at work as myself. Before then, I'd open a confidential conversation with trusted leaders to confirm their support, understand relevant company policies, and develop a detailed plan for my emergence. I would also need to decide how to come out to Mama and Papa to give them time to get used to the idea before my body began to change. I was still not in communication with Papa, but I was determined to do everything I could to bring my loved ones along with me before emerging.

I also embarked on the slow and tedious task of deleting all the photos of me from every social media platform. This would help me maintain control over my own narrative and reduce the likely shock that could come from a possible fixation on my changing physical appearance. I didn't want my story to be about the exterior changes.

I have since learned that there was another important reason for me to have removed pictures from social media. It feels highly personal for others to see my photos from prior to my emergence. Those photos don't reflect who I am, nor do they represent me in the past, because my outer appearance didn't represent my inner truth. Having them publicly available would encourage some to see me as a man rather than as the woman I am. I'd once believed that a woman who has a transgender medical history couldn't be a woman, and many people still believe that today. Some might argue that it shouldn't matter what others think. I would agree with that, but that doesn't address the full extent of my reasoning. This was a step I took for myself, not for others. I walked the world for more than forty years as a man, and I had no desire to relive even the tiniest element of that pain. Sharing those photos is intimate and vulnerable and something I reserve for close friends. With those friends, when I feel safe and know they see me for who I am, I feel pride and excitement to share those pictures.

With my painstaking task of scrubbing myself from the internet underway, it was time to tell close relationships I would be starting hormones. I began with Ryan, who gave me his full support. Next, I told Amalia—making sure she was sitting down first. We hadn't discussed the topic much since the Thanksgiving StairMaster conversation three years prior, and during that conversation, I had been full of uncertainty. With my announcement this time, she was supportive but said that it was hard for her and that she would need time to adjust.

Soon after that, I told Mama, who received the news with some shock and lots of confusion. She wondered whether I was doing the right thing and expressed some doubt, which was understandable, since she didn't know I'd been struggling with a gender disconnect. She had no memories of any signs or signals from my younger years— including the bathroom scene in our home in the Netherlands—that might have indicated this for me. I'd never had any interest in girls' clothes or dolls, and this all made it harder for her to understand. But her confusion was overridden by her love for me and her desire to see me happy. She'd known for a long time that I'd been sad, and she sincerely hoped this was the right thing for me and that it would turn things around. She also appreciated that I was giving her lots of notice. After our talk, she did some follow-up reading and scheduled a time to talk to my therapist to learn how she could support me. I never once felt her pull away; her love and warmth remained constant throughout. I am forever grateful for how she supported me at that pivotal time.

By then, it had been almost four years since Papa had stopped speaking with me. I had given up on contacting him, and I was resigned to living with the mystery of whatever had set him off at my 40th birthday and with his complete absence from my life. But I didn't want him to find out about his child's dramatic external change from other people. I had not lost my love for him and wanted him to hear it from me. I also wanted him to have plenty of notice. A few months after I told Mama, I decided I'd call and, assuming he wouldn't pick up, leave him a voicemail.

I wrote, rewrote, and rewrote again what I would say. It ended up being intentionally short—a two-minute message where I gave him the basic facts. I reminded him that I'd been extremely unhappy and that I had done a lot of work to figure out why. I told him I was a woman and that I would be starting hormones and eventually emerging as myself. I didn't ask for his support, didn't ask if he had questions, didn't request he return my call. I said what I needed him to know and let it go, figuring there was a fifty-fifty chance he'd take it well.

Mama was in the kitchen with him when he heard my voicemail. She told me that he'd hung up, turned to her, and told her he had some news from me. Then, before telling her the specifics, he told her that it was nothing to get upset about and that she should accept my news. He didn't reach out to me himself, but I was grateful to hear that he had received my news with openness. Later, Amalia told me that about ten years earlier, he had told her that he had another daughter. Amalia recounted that she had been confused and upset, interpreting Papa's statement to mean that he had fathered a daughter with another woman. Papa didn't deny that at the time, and he didn't explain what he meant. He told her that someday she would know more, and he left it at that.

I was elated to hear that he'd had an intuition about my gender identity. Years later, he validated that he'd always known, but he didn't offer more information to help me understand his actions. Maybe his treatment of me had come from his fear of the unknown. Maybe he'd been trying to change me as a reaction to his fear of how the world might view me—and to his own phobias and misconceptions. I didn't know for sure, and I figured I never would. I'd learned not to try to make sense of it but just to accept it. I was grateful that he wasn't going to create difficulties for me and that he seemed to understand and accept the news.

After coming out to my family—for the second time—I was reminded not only of our deep love but also of the way we will always be there for one another at crucial times, despite the drama and dysfunction. I had planned to move forward with or without my family's support, but knowing I had them at my side gave me great strength. Many men and women who have had a similar journey don't have that benefit, and I can't imagine the pain of that rejection or the exponentially more difficult emergence they have to undergo without the love and support of those closest to them. With my family's support, it was time for me to turn my attention to the biggest step yet: hormone replacement therapy.

———

The first to-do was to find an endocrinologist, one who had a lot of experience treating transgender patients with hormone replacement therapy. Specifically, I wanted one who had experience with what is described as male-to-female patients, otherwise known as MtF or M2F.

As with some of the other language related to the transgender experience, *male-to-female* is inaccurate and misleading. It's an uninformed, archaic, and inaccurate description of the reality of what transpired. I was not male. I have always been female and was born a transgender girl. I did not go from male to female. I went from transgender female to female. The entire point of hormone replacement therapy was to medically fix something that went awry during my own development, starting from conception or gestation. I did not medically change my gender, nor did my gender change. Rather, hormone replacement therapy finally provided my body with the right hormones, which I've needed since birth. As the US Declaration of Independence rightfully posits, everyone is endowed with unalienable rights, including the pursuit of happiness. HRT is not only a medical necessity; it is my right to have the opportunity to live a happy and fulfilling life, walking the world and presenting as the gender in which I was born. Hormone replacement therapy would provide that for me.

Unfortunately, HRT is not an exact science, and the field needs more research on the mix of hormones, approach, and dosing. I spoke to numerous endocrinologists in the course of my research, learning about the process and searching for a good fit. I wanted a conservative approach that would result in an appropriate female hormone range with the lowest possible dosage. This meant that I would start at an unusually low dosage and only gradually step it up. It also meant it would take longer for me to feel or see the impact, but I was comfortable with the trade-off. Taking hormones over an extended period comes with risk, as with any medicine or supplement, and my gradual approach would mitigate possible negative outcomes.

At the time, in 2015, there was only one endocrinologist in the Boston area with a high level of expertise. The next one was more than an hour's drive away. The hospital system I relied on for my care did not offer any providers with meaningful expertise. It was disheartening to learn that the science was still so young that a major Boston-based hospital system hadn't gotten their act together to serve a needy population. To their credit, they have since put together a program to do so.

I ultimately found a great fit with a highly respected physician, and together, we planned for me to start HRT that April, with the goal of coming out to my colleagues sometime between three and six months later, when I felt that the physical changes in my body had begun to reflect the reality of my female gender. It seemed reasonable to assume that my facial-hair removal would also be in a good place by then. The full impact of HRT, including maximum breast growth and body fat redistribution, takes at least two years and can continue for up to five years. However, it can trigger meaningful physical changes in the first three-to-six-month window, which I hoped would give me the confidence to take the plunge and come out fully.

While researching HRT, I also opened the conversation at Deloitte. Specifically, I came out to a leader in the firm who was also my coach and day-to-day direct manager. I was hoping for her support—and for absolute discretion until I was ready. I also needed the assurance that I'd be able to lead and develop the communication plan myself. I went into the conversation full of anxiety about the possibility of negative judgment from her, and I worried whether she'd still trust me to do my work and whether she'd support my need for an intentional and thoughtful emergence at work. It turned out that I didn't need to worry. She came through for me, responded just as I'd hoped, and gave her approval for me to work on the communications approach. As a result, I also felt comfortable to begin to investigate the medical benefits the firm offered for emergence.

With those pieces in place, I excitedly began my research on lower surgery, as I refer to it. Others sometimes call it *gender affirmation* or *gender confirmation surgery*, both of which I think are fine. It can also be called *sex reassignment surgery*, which I don't like because I think it's misleading. Even worse is the old term *sex change operation*, which is misleading and lands as inaccurate and offensive. Fortunately, that phrase has fallen out of common usage.

Hair removal cost me more than $10k over the years, but I was grateful that my insurance would indeed cover lower surgery, and I was eager to have the procedure as soon as I could. At the time, there were a number of options in the US, a few in Canada, and some good cheaper options in Thailand, where the doctors had a lot of experience. In those years, many insurers wouldn't cover surgery, so Thailand was a great option for many women. Since there were good options in the US, my support network was here, and my insurance would cover it, it made sense for me to have my surgery stateside.

I began to research surgeons. I cared most about experience, the number of surgeries they performed annually, and their success rates based on patient feedback. In terms of success rate, I was concerned about the impact on nearby organs, the ability to urinate well, overall sensation, appearance, depth, ability to orgasm, and an outcome with no ongoing pain or other issues.

I also had to make a decision on which variety of surgery I wanted, as there were a few different approaches. One established procedure was well tested but didn't provide the best look. Another was newer yet proven—multiple surgeons had been practicing and perfecting it for several years. A third option, which provided an increased chance of natural lubrication during intercourse, was even newer and less robustly tested. I opted for the middle-of-the-road proven approach and felt confident since highly respected, well-known surgeons in the field had been refining it for years. There were a number of surgeons offering the procedure; however, there were only two who had been doing it for decades. At the time, they were both in very high demand, with waiting lists that spanned years, but I wasn't going to let timeline be a factor. It was too big a decision to leave to anyone but the best for me. I continued studying their work and planned to reach out to them to set up times for interviews. Everything was falling into place— everything but for one key relationship.

Papa's positive reaction to my news inspired me to reach out again in hopes of mending whatever had transpired. I wanted our family to be able to be together for birthdays and holidays. I hoped to be able to see everyone at Mama and Papa's home when I visited rather than meeting them in hotel lobbies, restaurants, and shopping malls, and I wished for easier phone conversations with Mama. I had gotten used to her hanging up midconversation when Papa entered the room but never stopped feeling a twinge of sadness, hurt, and anger.

Another motivation to mend our relationship was my desire to visit with both parents a few times before emerging. Living on the opposite coast meant I didn't see them much, and even though I had their emotional support, I craved in-person interactions before I emerged. I wanted them to have the opportunity to answer questions I figured they might only ask face-to-face, and I desired the in-person energy of their support and love. I had been unable to reach Papa by phone, so in collaboration with Mama, I made a plan to fly out and show up on their doorstep.

With nothing to lose and an opportunity to at least see Mama and enjoy some Sonoma County sun in February, I flew west. I landed and made the one-and-a-half-hour drive north to their house. Mama wouldn't be there. We'd planned for her to be gone so it would just be me and Papa. I parked around the block, walked up to the front door, and rang the bell, my heart racing.

He didn't open the door. I knew he was home because Mama had told me he was and his car was in the driveway. I rang again, and the door didn't open. I rang once more without luck and then called his cell, and there was no answer. I called the home landline and still no answer. It hadn't occurred to me that I'd fly cross-country just to have him refuse to open the door. I'd prepared myself for a fight or for reconciliation—but not for being left alone on the doorstep. I felt silly that I hadn't considered the possibility.

I stepped one foot to the right to peer through the living room window, and he was standing right there. We locked eyes, and I gave him a two-handed shrug. I stepped back to the left, rang the bell again, and waited. I was a second away from considering the attempt futile and turning around when the door opened.

"Hallo," he said.

Having been in a similar situation about twenty years earlier, I felt a sense of déjà vu when I began, "I love you, Papa. I came because I appreciated how you handled the news of my emergence, and I want a relationship with you." He stood still, listening, and I continued. "I don't know why you stopped talking with me, but if it was because you felt slighted about the coffee invitation, it certainly wasn't intentional, and I'm sorry if you received it that way."

He began to cry. "Okay," he said, nodding, and he invited me inside. He invited me to sit at the kitchen island with him and talk. And talk we did. For hours. He told me that he was proud of me and my emergence. He said that he'd always known and was happy that I had found the strength to emerge and admired me for doing it.

I sat and listened as the distance and the animosity melted away. I inquired why he hadn't said something when he had known, and he responded that he didn't think I would have taken it well and that it wasn't his place to do so. He wanted me to figure it out when I was ready.

I could see the reasoning behind that. I didn't think to ask him why he had been so cruel to me if he had known about my gender. My guess is that he didn't see his actions as cruel. I think he was trying to protect me from the world's cruelty, but I suspect his suppression was more harmful than the intended benefit.

If I'd been surprised by his support and encouragement, I was shocked when he offered to buy me a dress. I was taken aback by the sweetness of it, and it made his acceptance of my emergence feel more sincere. But the offer also created some constriction in my body, as I hadn't even considered that I'd be wearing dresses. Not having had any interest in them in the past, I thanked him and told him, as I had told others, that I wouldn't be dressing very feminine and that I'd likely be presenting in the style of a butch lesbian.

I asked him whether there was any reason he'd stopped talking with me other than the coffee incident. He said no. I asked whether he would do the same thing again, and he said he would. I thought it was ridiculous that he would behave the same way all over again, and I told him such. We agreed to disagree on that point.

He also opened up about some early traumas, including abuse, which had influenced how he lived his life. I'd not known about them. He'd never been to therapy, and he lacked the openness and the communication skills to work on his own pain. I realized that his behavior was not a reflection of me or my actions but rather the result of his own upbringing, his emotional pain and unresolved issues, and his overall mental health. I felt compassion for him and sadness for the pain that he carried. I was grateful that we had reconciled but also recognized that I didn't have it in me to go through another round of drama with him if another were ever to materialize. It had been too stressful. I felt a lingering sense of strangeness about the whole situation. He'd cut me out of his life for four years over the smallest misunderstanding and was adamant he'd do it again. It made no sense to me. But at the same time, I was grateful we were back on good terms and to have his and Mama's support as I entered the most pivotal stage of my emergence. And that's why I'd come here in the first place.

Mama eventually came home from her unusually long trip to the grocery store, and the three of us had a lovely few days together before I flew back to Boston with smiling hope and optimism.

7

THREE TINY PILLS

It seems unfathomable that a few pills of medicine—each only about the size of a grain of rice—could dramatically, albeit slowly, change how I looked and how others perceived my gender. At seven in the morning on March 22, 2015, I stood at the kitchen counter with a mix of disbelief and reverence as I studied that first dose, which lay in the palm of my hand. There were two types of pills. The small ones would provide me with my much-needed estrogen, and the slightly larger one would reduce my testosterone until it fell into a typical female range. I'd be taking a variation of that dose every day for most of the rest of my life.

The journey had been underway for three years, beginning with those first explorations into therapy. Recently, I had found a new therapist, a social worker who specialized in gender identity, to support me during my emergence. The new therapist had written my endocrinologist a letter in support of me receiving hormones, which, at the time, was a prerequisite to undergoing treatment. I had done all the preliminary work, and now one of the most physically impactful moments had arrived.

I was ready and excited to take them without any reservation or doubt. I had done all the hard work and preparation, and now it felt perfectly anticlimactic to take this step. Although the moment might have called for trumpets and fanfare, it passed in a flash—the motion of my arm, a drink of water, a swallow, and it was done. In a few months, I'd see the first small changes. It would be years before the changes would be fully expressed.

A few days later, I started working with Brenda, a voice coach. My voice wasn't very deep, but it was clearly coming from vocal cords that had thickened from a testosterone wash during puberty. No amount of estrogen could reverse that. For transgender men, it's a different case: one of the early effects of testosterone HRT is the deepening of the voice. For transgender women, the challenge is much greater. Some opt for surgery on the vocal cords, but this can lead to complications, and results can be mixed. Sometimes it leads to a high, squeaky voice, a bit like Minnie Mouse's. Due to the varying risks, and because I could make significant adjustments with practice and training, I opted not to have surgery and began voice training.

There are numerous elements that inform a voice's perceived gender, including pitch, resonance, inflection, speed, breathiness, and clarity. My first task was to find and practice a voice that was not only sustainable given the physical characteristics of my voice box but one that also felt authentic and aligned with my personality and presentation. Brenda and I played around with various voices and eventually landed on something that I felt could work. She gave me daily exercises, which I practiced in the car, on my daily morning walks with Bosco, at work, and in various other cases. I had lines to practice such as, "Good morning," "Bosco is a good boy," and "Does anyone have anything else to add?" The key for me was to speak from my upper throat rather than from my lower throat or from my chest. It was difficult, and I wasn't sure how well this would all turn out, but it also felt right. It was another front in my battle against the sadness of the disconnect that had plagued me my whole life.

Exactly a week after I took that first dose of hormones, I moved out of Boston's South End and into an apartment on the other side of the Charles River in Belmont. It was a great location right at the intersection of three towns: Cambridge, Watertown, and Belmont. A confluence of reasons had led to the move, one of which was my motivation to live in an area where people didn't know me.

I was terrified that someone at Deloitte would find out about my emergence before I was ready to come out. I can't overstate how important this was to me. My day-to-day work was tied in with so many different people in the organization, both vertically and horizontally, and in order to continue doing my job well, I felt I would need meaningful acceptance from my leaders, peers, collaborators, and internal clients. I'd need my leadership to continue to be accepted. I was concerned that one problematic person or relationship could potentially have a big impact on my effectiveness, which in turn I feared could possibly affect my performance evaluations, my compensation, and even my ability to stay in my role. My financial livelihood was at stake. Even if the potential problems did not become that serious, I was also worried about smaller conflicts. Possible microaggressions like misgendering or talking behind my back could add up and result in frustration and long-term discomfort. I couldn't control reactions, but I could control the timing and messaging to create the best possible chances for a smooth emergence.

At that point, I had only discussed my journey with two people at Deloitte. The initial conversation with my manager led to a few additional deeper conversations for her to understand my needs and initial thoughts on the timing and approach of my emergence. With my agreement, she also had engaged one person in Talent who had experience with employees who had emerged in the workplace. Both individuals reiterated that my information would be kept confidential until I was ready to move forward. That and their initial approach to understanding my needs and their expressions of Deloitte's support gave me a strong feeling of psychological safety. Also, I was fortunate that I was mostly working from home and video calls were not yet the norm. This gave me the privacy to begin my physical emergence without having to come out at work until I was ready. The move to Belmont gave me further privacy and the confidence that I was doing all I could to retain control of my own narrative.

With my emergence underway in earnest, I returned to the question of what clothes I'd wear. Since neither my disconnect nor my emergence had been informed by clothing choices, I hadn't thought my presentation would change much. I imagined an appearance that would be decidedly female but with hair and fashion choices that were gender neutral or even masculine leaning. Feeling nervous, I took a trip to Newbury Street, the center of Boston's swanky retail district, which was full of high-end boutiques and restaurants. I pushed through my nerves and reminded myself of the attitude that had gotten me this far—just take one small step at a time. Determined, I went into some shops that carried styles I liked and requested help finding women's jeans. The day was a big success. By the end of my trip, I'd found a few pairs of jeans and some tops that were gender neutral or perhaps just a little feminine leaning. They all fit me well, and I liked how they looked on me—more feminine but not too much of a departure from what I was used to.

While my wardrobe was evolving, I also made another foray into the world of makeup. I didn't want my femininity to be defined by whether I wore it or how much, but I wanted to be able to use it to highlight my features, and I was determined to learn as much as I could. After my first experiment, I knew I could benefit from some support. I didn't have any friends in Boston who could help me. Mama and Amalia, in addition to being on the other side of the country, were still getting used to the idea of my emergence. I watched some tutorials but quickly recognized that I'd benefit from in-person, one-on-one lessons from someone who could give me immediate, specific feedback and guidance. I began visiting makeup stores and counters, where I paid rapt attention and eagerly sponged up tips and tricks. I discovered there were classes and private lessons I could take, and I set out to learn what I needed to know.

As part of my emergence, I also had to update all my paperwork—and I do mean *all* of it, everything I could possibly obtain and correct. I wanted everything to reflect both my correct gender and my name. I'd been planning to retain my name as Benni, but both Ryan and Amalia advised me that they thought it would be cleaner and easier if I were to change to a clearly feminine name. After some thought, I realized they were right, and my name became an open question. I needed a clean break and a new name that represented my personality.

Mama asked me to choose a name that started with a *B* as a nod to my given name and to make it easier for her and Papa. I wracked my brain but couldn't come up with one that felt right. I slept on it. I sat with it. I tried on some names and gave it a few months, without success. The clock was ticking, and I needed to make a decision.

In mid-June, I was having dinner and a delicious cocktail at a favorite Italian restaurant, Il Casale, when I gave myself permission to consider names that didn't start with a *B*. Immediately, *Ella* dropped out of the sky and into my slightly buzzed head, and I knew it to be me. I liked that it was two syllables, and it felt right. I did a quick internet search to better understand its various meanings and to make sure it didn't translate to something unfortunate in another language. It didn't, and my search only made me like it more. I decided my name would be *Ella* and that I'd retain *Benni* as my middle name.

While sitting at the restaurant, I called Amalia and told her I had chosen a name, and I wanted to make sure it landed well with her before I committed fully. She always had a strong opinion, and I trusted her to tell me whether she thought it suited me. I told her, and without hesitation, she told me that she liked it. That cemented it.

I called Mama the next day to tell her I'd chosen a name. I set it up by reminding her that I'd tried *B* names with no success, that I had something I loved, and that I would only consider something else if she absolutely hated it. She took the setup in stride and inquired what it was. I breathed a sigh of relief when she shared that she also liked it. She was happy that I would be keeping *Benni* as my middle name.

With that important decision made, I moved forward with all the legal and administrative elements of my emergence. I wanted full integration of my past with my present and resolved to have every possible document reflect my actual gender and new name. My goal was to update all inaccurate records and paperwork. I prioritized my driver's license, bank accounts, US passport, health records, insurance records, and Social Security. I requested and received a court order for a name change from the court of the Commonwealth of Massachusetts and also requested and received letters of affirmation of my gender from both my endocrinologist and therapist. A combination of those three documents and in-person appointments sufficed for almost all fixes that needed to be made. It would take additional steps and an extended period of time to fix my original birth certificate in the Netherlands and subsequently my Dutch passport. In parallel, I went to work fixing all my online accounts, memberships, magazine subscriptions, utility bills, etc. I also requested corrections to all school records from high school through graduate school and received corrected diplomas for all of them. There were hundreds of accounts and records, and it would take months for me to update them, but I was determined to avoid any possible confusion or administrative headaches in the future. More importantly, this would reduce the likelihood of an emotional trigger at some unsuspecting moment in the future. That peace of mind would make my efforts worthwhile.

———

After a few months, I began to notice the hormones' first effects. I felt different—more grounded, more relaxed, more alive. It's hard to describe, but I liken it to turning on a color television after having only ever looked at black and white. Another analogy is turning on the lights after having only ever walked around in the dark. It was like changing from a radio station that had made me cringe to one I could vibe with. Described yet another way, it was like there were internal sine waves that had been out of sync that finally fell into place and allowed me to flow effortlessly. Instead of frustration, flatness, and sharpness, I now felt a more rounded, spongy ease. I hadn't yet had my much-needed lower surgery; however, I was beginning to feel more like me, and it felt better. I physically felt better and emotionally and mentally felt more comfortable, less frustrated, and generally able to ease into a more relaxed version of myself. Although subtle, life felt more dynamic, more hopeful, more meaningful than it ever had.

The physical changes took a little longer and began quite subtly. Initially, my skin got softer and more sensitive. Soon after, during months three to six, I noticed the early stages of breast development. There were annoying changes, too—the testosterone blocker was also a diuretic, otherwise known as a water pill, that faithfully interrupted my nightly sleep and would do so as long as I took it. Those who hadn't seen me in a while did notice the first hints of feminization in my face. When I inquired, they said that they'd noticed a general softening—nothing dramatic, just a slight shift. I knew it would be a long game, and I resisted the temptation to look for changes in the mirror every day.

By the end of spring, I began walking the world more as my true female self. My haircut was slowly becoming more feminine, and my body and facial hair were disappearing. I didn't consciously change my affect, my presence, or my walk, but I think that with the hormones, with the full acknowledgment of who I was, and with my declaration to my family and their acceptance, I had subconsciously given myself permission to let go and be myself. As a result, my inner woman stood up and took control of the reins. My emergence continued slowly and compounded over time. However, there was a change that happened in the first few months as I started to fully live in my born gender as female. I shifted from walking deliberately and with no hand movements when speaking to a softer gait with a more traditional feminine way of movement. These weren't conscious choices, but I noticed them, and they felt good and right.

When I had conducted my crude analysis of the various elements that might define a woman, I concluded that affect is a social construct and a learned behavior—not something tied to gender itself. Now that I'm on the other side of my emergence, my experiences confirm this, and I've also learned how affect comes naturally, without conscious thought or intention. My femininity is a part of my being, separate from my gender identity. There are feminine beings who are male and masculine beings who are female. I could easily have been a woman who was butch and had a masculine way of being. In my case, it turns out that I am a feminine being who, when living authentically, moves through the world with a lighter and softer touch. The way I move now comes with ease and is me without cover or guard rails. Before my emergence, I was subconsciously hiding my femininity to fit in and avoid conflict. Now that I was emerging, my feminine affect felt safe to come out.

With the hormones working their magic from the interior, I continued with my slow, steady work on the exterior. I was two years into my electrolysis marathon, and though I still had a long way to go, I was making good progress and wasn't far off from being able to taper down to biweekly sessions. Most of those sessions blurred together, but there is a memorable one seared into my mind. Lee was working on my upper lip, the most sensitive area on the face. There was a particularly stubborn hair that just didn't want to come out, so the electricity had to be dialed higher. The shooting pain reached so deep into my body that it made me lightheaded. I had no bodily reaction other than the slow drip of involuntary tears from one eye. I nearly passed out. I remember thinking, *I am fine. I am grateful to be here, to be doing this, and I know this will all be worth it. This is nothing compared with what life has been like, and I am doing something to fix it.* I smiled through the pain, happy to continue the process. *Keep going,* I told myself. *Keep going. Get it all out. As long as it takes. Keep going until it's gone.*

One gorgeous morning in early July, on my way home from the gym with not a lick of makeup on my face, I pulled into a full-service gas station and rolled down the window to ask the attendant to fill it up. Before I was able to get the words out, he said, "What will it be, ma'am?"

I just about died. I gulped and told him what I wanted and just sat there, feeling stunned and filled with glee. I looked in the rearview mirror. Nothing looked different to me, but clearly the hormones were doing something. Even after our conversation, after he'd heard my voice, he thanked me with a cheerful, "Have a great day, ma'am." My smile was stuck to my face for the remainder of the day.

Soon after that, I took another trip west to visit with my parents for a long weekend. Amalia would be coming down from Oregon as well. My body and face were changing, and I hoped that by seeing me as often as possible, it would make it easier for them to get used to my emergence as their daughter and sister.

I arrived first and settled onto the back patio with Mama and Papa for some drinks and snacks. I was wearing open-toed shoes, and Mama dove right in.

"I see your nails are red," she said. "I like the color!"

All eyes were on my toes now, and I was feeling both elation and some slight discomfort. "Thank you," I said, with a smile.

Papa joined in and commented, with much neutrality and no judgment, "It looks like you're developing breasts."

Now everyone was looking at my chest. My discomfort went up a notch, but I was also happy to hear that the change was noticeable. "Yes, I think so!" I said.

It was all very matter-of-fact—very Dutch—and we soon moved on to other topics. It had been a quick and simple but incredibly affirming exchange, and it meant a great deal to me. Amalia arrived soon afterward. Together, the four of us had a terrific weekend, but I did notice a bit of coolness coming from Amalia. There was nothing overt about it—just a slight sense of distance, a little less warmth than I was used to. I wondered about it, but I didn't ask, and it didn't stop us from enjoying the weekend.

The night before I was to depart, Papa treated us to a nice dinner at an acclaimed local restaurant that was nestled in a vineyard and famous for its California cuisine. The weather was idyllic, and we were on the patio, enjoying the atmosphere and our dinners, when I volunteered my research progress for my lower surgery. I still hadn't figured out which of the surgeons I'd go with but was getting close to a decision. The topic piqued everyone's attention.

"How does that work?" Papa asked. "How is it done?"

"It's not how a lot of people might imagine," I said. "They don't just cut it off." There were videos of the surgery online, but my squeamishness had kept me from watching them. "Basically, the surgeon reverse engineers what went wrong in the womb when testosterone changed the original vulva and clitoris into the testes and penis," I continued, vaguely wondering whether my words were carrying to any of the neighboring tables. I didn't much care. "The surgery is quite elegant. She will use all my existing parts to recreate the parts that were originally intended for me."

He digested all that for a time and then deadpanned, "Will you have a starter button?"

I wasn't sure whether I'd heard him right, and I stared at him blankly for a few seconds, confused. Mama and Amalia were also watching me, awaiting my answer. And then it dawned on me. I reddened, chuckled, and with a nod of my head, I responded, "Yes, I will have a clitoris. I just hope it will actually work!"

"Hmm," was all he said in response, still digesting the information. Amalia and I shared a laugh, and the look on Mama's face made it clear she wanted to talk about anything in the world besides my clitoris.

Back home in Massachusetts, I started thinking about using the women's restroom. My body was changing, my features were softening, and I began to feel a little concerned about my safety going into the men's room. I was keeping my head down, trying to get in and out, but I knew there would come a point when I needed to make the switch. It was nerve-wracking, and I was scared to make that change, but I knew I had the right and that the women's room was where I belonged. And I was determined. However, I was also concerned that my presence there might cause others some discomfort, and I didn't want any trouble. At the time, there was no middle ground on this decision. It was one or the other. Regardless of the bathroom I used, my only objective was to pee, wash my hands, and get out of there safely without confrontation, drama, or harm.

At some point that summer, I made the change. I walked in with hurried intent and kept my head down, avoided eye contact and conversation, and tried to communicate with my posture that I belonged there and wasn't seeking permission. I was conscious of my pee stream, as I didn't want a different sound to cause an issue. I wanted it to sound no different from the other women peeing and made sure my pee hit the water in the bottom of the bowl rather than the side, just above the water. I washed my hands and quickly exited, happy I'd accomplished another milestone.

With that behind me, it was time to make the switch at my gym. The changing rooms weren't an issue for me; I always dressed to work out at home and came home to shower, so I only used the locker room area for the bathrooms. I'd been attending that particular gym for a while, though, so the change of bathrooms required a little more groundwork. I went in and asked to speak to the manager. I hoped that by discussing it with him, I'd create the opportunity for him to remind staff about their policies and reduce the risk of unintentional mishandling by staff at the front desk. The entire conversation and computer system update lasted less than five minutes and couldn't have gone more smoothly. It was the epitome of a nonevent, and I was grateful for it.

It was a start, but it would take me years to feel fully comfortable in the women's restroom. When I first made the switch, the US political climate did not prioritize safety for people like me. Transgender men and women have disproportionately been the targets of violence, for no reason beyond their gender identities. With a pragmatic approach and some luck, I navigated the switch so that I never was on the receiving end of any verbal or physical trouble, neither in the men's room nor in the women's room. I am lucky and grateful for it, but it remains a systemic problem, and others have not been so fortunate.

Bathroom usage is just one of many areas where transgender people need public protections. My work took me back and forth from Boston to Atlanta, so I began looking at their respective laws to better understand where I had support and where I didn't. Fortunately, Massachusetts had statewide protections in place for employment, housing, education, and health care, and the city of Boston had additional policies in place. Georgia lacked these statewide policies, but the city of Atlanta had passed local ordinances to address discrimination and support inclusivity. I began to see how my well-being could be influenced by a patchwork of federal, state, and municipal laws that could vary greatly from one place to another, giving me something else to consider.

Now that my emergence was gathering momentum, I felt ready to share it with a small circle of close friends. I'd continued to work on the communication plan at work and wanted to come out at Deloitte before I came out to the majority of my friends; in this way, I could reduce the risk of information leaking from my friend network to my work network. But there was a small group I trusted, and I wanted their support, so I reached out to about ten people individually and had lengthy, connecting, and supportive conversations with each of them. I told them the news, asked for their assistance with confidentiality, and told them I'd eventually make a broader announcement via social media but that I wanted them to hear it directly from me, in advance. I trusted them all and knew I'd need their support and love during the coming months.

I also joined another support group and discovered it to be similar to the one I'd attended the previous year. I was grateful for opportunities to spread positivity, to meet some new people, and to learn a little more about the transgender community. As before, however, I didn't feel a meaningful connection to the group or any of its members because of our different life experiences, phases, and interests.

The group didn't provide me with much support, but I was spending more and more time with Michelle, who introduced me to her network of lovely friends, some of whom were transgender women. These women were significantly older than I was and were lesbians who were married with kids. Although we didn't have a lot in common, I appreciated that they were each successful in their careers and generally happy, and it was affirming to be surrounded by people who understood my journey and who showered me with love and helpful tips as I marched into fully emerging as myself.

Michelle herself was an effervescent force, and we became very close. She had a tall, strong presence, and she moved through the world in ways that many would associate with men. As a transgender woman, she was proud of her journey, and she owned it with her head held high. She had no desire for lower surgery. She was the only other woman I met during my journey who was straight and who'd emerged later in her life, after having presented as a gay man. She could relate to my experiences of dating men while presenting as male, and we had much to discuss. In her case, she had been married to her husband for a few years before she had emerged. Her husband was a gay man who suddenly found himself married to a woman, which presented its own challenges. It was difficult for him, and it strained their relationship, but they were working on it.

It was Michelle who helped me shed my last vestiges of transphobia. One evening, we were out to dinner at a popular local steakhouse, Boston Chops, in the South End. We sat at the bar, as we always did there, and she rose to walk to the bathroom. I watched her go and couldn't help but notice how masculine her walk was. I noticed my own discomfort with it but also realized I was much less uncomfortable with it than I used to be. I saw how useless my remaining discomfort was. Her gait was just a part of her. It wasn't a good thing or a bad thing. It didn't define her gender, and it wasn't a reflection on me or anyone else. It didn't matter. I cared less and less what others might think about her or my association with her.

When she came back from the bathroom, I smiled and said, "Girl, you walk like a male cowboy who means business!"

She laughed. That led to a conversation about how it was a good thing that she was so comfortable with who she was and that her height, walk, and identification as a transgender woman all felt very right for her. We talked a bit about how my presentation differed from hers, and, even though I had some way to go in my emergence, how my movement, my desire for lower surgery, and the other changes to my appearance fully aligned with the stereotypical understanding of what it means to be a woman.

"In fact," I said, "once I have my lower surgery, I think I'll drop the 'transgender' label entirely." This felt like a daring position for me to take, and I was unsure how she would react, but the stance felt correct and appropriate. After the surgery, the disconnect would be gone, and I'd be a fully aligned woman, on the inside and the outside, with no modifiers needed.

Michelle understood immediately. Without skipping a beat, she gave me her full-throated acceptance and understanding and made me feel I had permission to own that truth. That felt powerful and empowering coming from another transgender woman. She was the first to provide me with that validation, for which I'll always be grateful.

Meanwhile, I continued meeting with Brenda, my voice coach, a few times each month. It required a lot of practice to be able to fully shift into my new voice, and it became harder to maintain when I was tired or had been talking a lot. I found the exercises to be exhausting emotionally, mentally, and physically, and after seven months of daily practice, I became satisfied with my progress and stopped consciously practicing. I didn't consider it a resounding success, as I'd wanted a more feminine-sounding voice. However, my voice had changed enough that most of the time, it seemed to register as female.

Today, the voice I automatically use, without thought, is authentically my voice. I'm rarely misgendered on the phone, but in those early years, this did happen about 25% of the time. As the years progressed, it became easier and more natural for me to use my voice, but misgendering still occasionally occurs today when my voice drops a little, which can happen as a result of exhaustion, after I've been talking all day. Whenever this happens, it brings a painful, dysphoric twinge. I continue to be conscious of guarding my voice when on the phone with someone new. I know there are women *without* my medical history who also get misgendered on the phone, either because they have naturally deeper voices or because of years of smoking. But for me, misgendering rushes back painful memories and feels constricting. I know it's not intentional and have learned to let it go right after it happens. I also recognize that the innocent mistake doesn't define my womanhood. At the same time, I do correct unintended misgendering.

I don't love my voice when it leads to misgendering but am

practicing loving it and take comfort knowing that I'm not alone in this respect. Many people don't love their voices. Every once in a while, however, someone I've just met for the first time in person will tell me that they love my voice. They say it has a calm, soothing, sultry vibe. That lights me up whenever I hear it. Overall, I consider my efforts with my voice to have been enough to make me glad I didn't risk surgery. And I am also glad for the friendship that came out of the work. Every year for Bosco's birthday, I take him to the beach and to eat a burger—Bosco's Beach and Burger Birthday Bash. It has become a tradition that Brenda joins our little party.

With fall and my public emergence approaching, I needed to make some decisions about other surgeries. I'd opted out of vocal cord surgery, but there were other procedures to consider. Many women with transgender medical history have breast augmentation, facial feminization surgery, or both. Facial surgery can also include a tracheal shave, which reduces the size of the Adam's apple. I did some preliminary research on both. Most women who emerge later in life don't have the full breast development that would have occurred had they emerged in their teenage years. As such, most opt for breast augmentation. However, some do develop a lot of natural breast tissue. In regards to facial feminization surgery, I was concerned that it could change my appearance too much. I still wanted to look like me. Many plastic surgeons advertise just that—a focus on ensuring the retention of one's familial look—but the risk still concerned me. I was also worried about a botched surgery that would leave me looking different than intended.

I determined I wouldn't consider either seriously before I felt the full impact of hormones, which would take years. All surgeries bring risks, and I was willing to be patient with the hope that I could avoid the operating room as much as possible. Natural breast development and natural facial feminization vary by individual and are based on genetics, health, and age. Since the women in my family are quite well blessed topside, I held out hope that my natural breast development would suffice for my own internal sense of peace. My barometer would be to be seen as myself, for who I am as a woman. If the hormones didn't lead to that, then I would choose to have one or both surgeries.

Now that my immediate family and close friends knew about my journey, it was time to come out to my extended family in the Netherlands. Unlike the last time, when my parents broadcasted an all-points bulletin about my sexuality to the whole family, I insisted that this time I be the one to share the news. My grandparents had all passed by that time, but Mama had one sister and Papa had two brothers there, along with their families. Over the many years since our immigration, I had visited my Dutch family numerous times in an effort to stay connected. Now, I reached out with phone calls to my aunts, uncles, and cousins and was relieved to receive acceptance and unwavering support. Like many people at the time, they didn't really understand gender identity, but the Dutch social fabric was beginning to see more transgender people, and there was some positive visibility in the Dutch media.

One of the questions they had was when they should start using female pronouns. Mama had also asked me about that. I've had a complicated relationship with pronouns. Early in my emergence, before I started hormones, I didn't care which ones were used. I liked being referred to in the feminine, but I didn't expect those around me to remember to do so and didn't ask them to. Also, it felt a little funny since I still presented as male. Michelle and her circle of friends were the first to regularly make the switch to *she* for me, and though it felt jarring initially, it was also affirming. It made me feel seen and accepted for who I was. Ryan began to do so as well, and it made me inwardly smile when he did. I decided that a good demarcation point to switch pronouns to *she/her* would be once I had started taking hormones and once someone knew about my journey.

It didn't bother me if someone slipped early in my emergence, as old habits are understandably hard to break, especially for those who had known me the longest. It takes conscious effort by the most well-intentioned allies to adjust their concept of someone's gender. I didn't mind mistakes as long as they were attempting to get it right. At the same time, and particularly as time went on, I believed it was appropriate for me to discreetly and kindly remind someone when they unwittingly slipped, even if this was a little irritating, as was frequently the case with my family. Misgendering can feel like a sign of rejection, and I knew it would take some time and effort before the slipups would fade away. I strove to remember one of the guiding principles of my emergence—to approach those around me with patience. I know their slipups were accidents; however, I found them frustrating because they landed like a reminder that they didn't see me for who I truly am. I felt that my own feelings of acceptance were well worth their irritations.

Sometimes, my family accidentally used my old name, which is sometimes referred to as my *dead name*. I don't like that terminology. No one died, and the same person is still there. It feels disrespectful of that lived time. It's just my *old name*, my *original name*, or my *given name*. At the same time, it's hurtful to address someone by their former name purposefully. Usage of the former name outs its owner, denies who they are at their core, and reminds them of a period that was likely painful. The purposeful usage of that former name or the lack of effort to shift to the new name is inconsiderate, jarring, and possibly even harmful. It can even be physically harmful if the usage of the former name outs the person around others who are not accepting and who seek to harm transgender people. Although it became frustrating when those close to me slipped up, I understood it would take time and all that mattered was that they were trying.

————

At about that time, in the late summer of 2015, I completed my research on surgeons. I'd had the opportunity to interview both of my short-listed candidates, and a clear winner emerged: Dr. Marci Bowers, who was located in San Mateo County, just south of San Francisco. She was a woman with trans history herself and had the most experience. I found her to be sex positive, and she spoke freely about her goals to give me adequate depth and to ensure I could orgasm. She focused on aesthetics and reduced scar visibility, and after talking to her, I was confident that she could give me the vagina I'd always known was rightfully mine. Her location would make it possible for my parents to visit me in the hospital, and I'd be able to recover at their home, too, which were big benefits.

By the time I had completed the voluminous paperwork and checklist items, which included letters of support from therapists, her waiting list was almost three years long. My surgery wouldn't be until February 2018. It was disappointing that I'd have to wait so long, but in the grand scheme of my life and my emergence, I was grateful to have come as far as I had and accepted the timeline, thrilled that I had a date.

However, now that I was on hormones and the surgery decision had been made, the dysphoria and conscious revulsion for my malformed vagina became more acute. That summer, I had begun to wear tight compression underwear called gaffs that made it easier for me to look at myself when dressing and when in front of a mirror. Gaffs are extremely tight and constricting and are designed for people who want to tuck their private parts to hide them. Tucking wasn't an option for me—I wasn't that large, fortunately—but the compression was still quite uncomfortable. The discomfort was better than the dysphoria, however, so I resolved to wear them or similar articles until my surgery. I also managed my dysphoria with clear communications. When I had the rare opportunity for physical intimacy with someone, I was up front that I didn't want them to touch my lower part or give it any attention at all. It was empowering and affirming to recognize and communicate that boundary.

February of 2018 couldn't come soon enough, but I focused on work, living life, and happily obsessing over the elements of my emergence. With surgery scheduled and the hormones' effects becoming clearer, it was time to prepare for coming out at work and subsequently to the rest of my friends and the public in general.

8

CLAIMING MY TRUTH

Even though I worked primarily from home, my business unit met in person every month in Atlanta. Hundreds of us descended to colocate for a week full of meetings, events, and fun. Earlier that summer, at one of the gatherings, a senior leader, who was not yet in the know, had seen me across the open-concept working space. He gave me a big smile and innocently hollered, "Benni, hi! Every time I see you, your hair is getting longer!"

I gave a forced chuckle and said, "Ha, yes, it is," with considerably less volume.

It was a wake-up call for me to step away from those get-togethers for a couple of months. My body was changing, and I was running the risk of outing myself prematurely. I needed some time away from the in-person meetings for the hormones to take further effect and to finish and execute the communications; then, I could return as my true self. Fortunately, my primary leader, who knew about my journey, agreed to exempt me from the in-persons until I emerged.

Although Deloitte had supportive policies related to transgender people and their emergences, it did not have standardized communication protocols at the time. I wasn't sure exactly how it would all unfold but knew my communications had to be succinct and positive. I would limit them to relevant information and include reminders about the policies. Through the connections I had made at First Event, the conference for the transgender community, I gained access to some communications that others had used elsewhere and used them as fodder for crafting my own messaging.

There was much in that tranche of documents that didn't align with my communications objectives. I noted that their authors had attempted to garner support by emphasizing what felt to me to be sob stories. The communications aimed to educate about a medical condition, and the tone tilted toward apologetic. Thematically, the communications seemed to hope for acceptance by pulling on heartstrings. I also noticed that some of them didn't have a cohesive, clear, or timely plan, an omission that left space for office gossip and confusion, and would lead to a vacuum in regards to how colleagues were supposed to react. A communication plan that didn't clearly indicate expectations about proper name and pronoun usage and bathroom policies left the door open for uninformed people to behave inappropriately, which could ultimately put the emerging person in a bad position. I was lucky that Deloitte had some clear policies and gave me the flexibility to shape my own communications. I still wasn't sure exactly when the right time would be, but knowing how important this was to get right, I had begun crafting the plan earlier in the year, after the first few conversations with my leader and Talent.

In the spring and through the summer, they engaged with me in a number of working sessions in which they provided guidance on my proposed communications approach and tactical plan. Together, their thoughtful input and expertise were not only instrumental in building out and shaping a stronger plan, but they also helped me to refine the details and ensure that the firm was fully on board with all of it.

My primary objectives were threefold. First, I wanted to own the story and to ensure that everyone would learn it via official communications rather than through office gossip. Second, I needed to demonstrate unequivocal support from my leadership. Third, I wanted to focus the messaging on the facts and the associated impact on the audience. I hoped my communications would leave no doubt regarding the firm's policies and expectations about appropriate behavior. As such, I felt it important that the message come from senior business and office leaders. For some people, I would follow that up with a personal email providing just a little more information.

Deloitte is a huge firm; my audience was too large and varied for a one-size-fits-all approach, so I divided everyone into different groups and developed a communication plan for each of them. My first step was to create a recipient list that ensured my communications would go out only to those who needed to know about my emergence. Next, I considered three factors for each possible recipient: how closely I worked with them; the nature of my personal relationship with them; and their level within the company, which determined how much influence they had. With these groupings and a bit of subjectivity, I assigned each individual a communication category: low touch, medium touch, and high touch. My colleagues in the low-touch category would receive an email from senior leadership and nothing further. Those in the medium-touch category would receive the email from senior leadership, which would then be followed by a note from me—either a generic message or a highly personalized message. The high-touch group was more complex and included a varied mix of leaders, close work friends, and members of the teams that I led. Some in this group would receive a day's advance notice from me or another leader before the mass communications, which would give them time to prepare for questions that could come their way from their teams. Some in the high-touch group would also receive an additional email of support from other senior leaders who would reinforce the central message. My own teams would also have the opportunity to chat with me right after the communications went out for any follow-up questions they might have.

To some, my plan might sound like it was over-the-top, but I was determined to do everything in my power to minimize the chances of anyone taking issue with me using the women's room or feeling like they didn't have to respect the usage of my new name or correct pronouns. Even worse, there could have been attempts to thwart my ability to do my job by excluding me from meetings and decisions or otherwise working to ensure that I stumbled in my role.

Even setting aside ill intentions, in my experience, I have found that most people simply aren't sure how to respond appropriately, even though they may want to. With my communication plan, I wanted to provide recipients a chance to bring their best selves to the situation so they could respond in a way that was best not only for me but also for them. This would not only maximize the chances of a smooth experience for me but also reduce the risk of someone getting themselves into hot water with the firm. With my plan in place, I just needed to let the hormones work a little more of their magic, and then it would be time to execute.

———

As summer wore on and July became August, I began to set my sights on early September for my emergence at work. We had an in-person gathering in Atlanta scheduled for September 8, just after Labor Day, so after consulting with leadership and Talent, I decided to send out my emails on September 1. The next morning, I'd post an announcement on Facebook for my network of friends. Then, on September 8, I'd walk into the Atlanta office as myself, as Ella, after I'd provided everyone with a week to digest the announcement.

I'd always assumed my presentation would be fairly gender-neutral, but now that it was almost time for my public emergence, I wanted to challenge that. I wanted to be sure, because I wanted to show up at work on day one presenting as myself. I had one chance to make that statement, and I wanted it to be both genuine and confident.

My body had changed a bit more, and I was curious how I'd look and feel in a dress, so I took another run to Newbury Street to try some on. Again, feeling nervous, I approached it with my usual one-foot-in-front-of-the-other attitude. I chose Banana Republic as a starting point, with the simple objective of trying on one dress, and was soon lost in the sizing of women's clothes, which differed so drastically from men's. Some manufacturers used small, medium, and large, and others used numbers. It was a learning curve that would take me some time to figure out, but over the next hour, I examined many dresses and tried on a number that I liked. I surprised myself; I had a pretty clear opinion of what I liked and really loved how three of them looked on me. And I was lucky: my size-six frame provided me with many options. Most everything fit well, and I loved the feeling of femininity. In the end, I walked out with three dresses, my plan to present like a butch lesbian having gone up in smoke. I had found my style. Later, a fabulous gay friend who lives and breathes haute couture put a smile on my face when he declared with authority that my style was "feminine elegant chic." He was right, and I love it. I'm grateful I challenged myself to go to a store and try a few pieces. Since then, I've come to love buying new clothes and adore going clothes shopping with friends.

I was also making fast progress with makeup. By that August, I'd attended a class and two private lessons and had absorbed a great deal from the technicians at various shops and counters. I landed on a low-key look that felt natural, with just a little bit of eye shadow and mascara. I tried foundation, which all the technicians seemed to push, but it didn't make a big difference for me, and worse, it made my skin itch. That wasn't for me. I learned that I love wearing lipstick, and today, I almost always have some on. It's easy to apply, and it makes me feel beautiful and sexy. I have a bunch of almost-empty lipsticks that sit by the front door, just for my morning walks, and some light pink ones that stay in my gym bag. During the COVID-19 pandemic, I wore lipstick every day under my mask. Because why not.

———

That August, in the lead-up to fully coming out, I was feeling nervous and overwhelmed. My name change was complete. I'd begun wearing some light makeup along with my women's clothes, and I had begun wearing a bra. The bra felt tight and uncomfortable, and I was self-conscious about my voice, but I liked being dressed as myself and generally felt good about how far I'd come. With my nerves on edge, I toyed with the idea of pushing the announcement out another month but decided against continuing to live in limbo, where only a small number of people were aware of my emergence. It was time.

On August 31, a targeted group of high-touch work friends and leaders received the preliminary email. The next morning, I was a taut bundle of nerves, fear, and excitement. Once the announcement went out, it would be out, and there would be no going back. But I was ready. I knew this was right for me. It was my truth.

Early in the work day, my phone rang. It was the administrative assistant of the senior leader who would be sending out the first mass email. "Are we doing this?" she asked. "Are you ready?"

In that moment, I imagined myself poised atop a high dive. I took a breath and said, "Yes, I'm ready. Please send." I felt the jump in my body; my stomach dropped. In that moment, I—Ella—emerged.

The email went out to hundreds of recipients. It stated with concision that I was emerging, provided my new name, and indicated to refer to me as such. It provided correct pronoun usage and outlined expectations of how to refer to me while leaving room for unintentional mistakes. It stated that my emergence would be gradual in terms of physical appearance and that the firm respected my right to use the women's bathroom. It mentioned the firm's policies and included links to resources for information regarding emerging in the workplace. As soon as I saw it land in my inbox, I sent my follow-ups to each list, stating that I was more happy and peaceful as Ella than I had been as Benni and that I understood it would take time to get used to the changes to my name and pronouns. I told everyone that I was open to talking about it and to reach out anytime. It was done.

The plan unfolded perfectly. There had been no time for rumors or the gossip mill and no sob story. Everyone knew only what they needed to know, as it pertained to them. The landing from that high dive and into the water was a perfect ten. I felt safe, physically and emotionally, and extraordinarily happy to know that I had managed to maintain control of the narrative all the way through. I was really proud of how it had unfolded and of my part in creating and leading it.

———

My news was received well, and it triggered an unexpected outpouring of love, support, and validation, which flooded in via calls and emails.

Some people opened up to me with stories of their kids or other family members struggling with gender identity, and they told me that it had given them hope to see the emergence of someone at my level who was happy and thriving. Others shared that my emergence had opened their eyes to something they had only ever heard about but had never encountered personally. Still others shared that they were struggling with different things in their own lives but that my confidence and courage had inspired them to tackle those challenges. There were messages that expressed pride for Deloitte and how well it was handling my emergence. Many affirmed their allegiance for the company and expressed joy at how Deloitte clearly cared for and supported its people. My announcement and the reactions filled me with adrenaline, and I was amped up for the rest of the day.

For months, I'd been afraid that my emergence at work would result in negativity, confusion, and a backlash against me and my career. That's a reality for many who emerge in the workplace. Just the opposite happened for me. I received full acceptance and a full loving embrace. I'd be naive to believe that no one had an issue with me or my emergence. I'm sure someone did somewhere in the firm. However, none of it bubbled up to me. In the months and years that followed, I had no issues at all in any of the areas I'd worried about. There were no bathroom issues, no weird vibes or interactions, no negativity, and no pronoun issues other than the occasional early slip by a small number of people, to which I strove to respond with grace and patience.

I attribute this success to numerous factors. First and foremost, Deloitte is known for its inclusive culture, and its handling of my emergence showcased that. Beyond their policies and processes, many people came together to execute the plan so positively and effectively: Talent, IT, my manager and the rest of my business unit's leaders, my local leadership, the services team, my peers, and my team. Second, the communication plan was deliberate and thoughtful. Third, I had worked hard for the organization for five years by that time and had earned respect and a reputation for delivering impactful work and being dependable, consistent, trustworthy, and reasonable. I supported my colleagues and had strong personal connections. None of those things would change, and in a professional environment, that's what mattered most. Although I didn't realize it at the time, today, I recognize that I strengthened my brand—as a human and a leader—by showing the human side of myself with authenticity and courage.

———

Flying high from an atypical and momentous day, I went to bed knowing that I'd wake up in the morning and come out to all my friends online. Almost all of my friends were on Facebook, as was a large circle of acquaintances—I had more than 500 connections. I had prepared my post in advance, and the objective was similar to my communications for Deloitte, but given the more personal nature of my relationships on Facebook, my message would provide a bit more reflection and explanation. As soon as I got up the next morning, September 2, 2015, I uploaded a pair of photographs that Michelle had taken of me a few weeks prior, along with the following message:

> Dear Friends: Gender identity is something that most people don't ever think about; for some folks—including myself—their internal gender isn't congruent with how they are perceived and can have a pretty negative impact on one's overall well-being. I'm glad to finally be able to tell you that I've been working on aligning my outer self with my inner female self. I actively began to tackle this about five years ago and in earnest a few

years ago. I've taken a deliberately slow approach, taking it one small step at a time, allowing myself space to experience each step before making decisions about what comes next to ensure I'm doing the right thing. I can unequivocally tell you that it is and have found myself to be more peaceful and happier. At this point in my emergence, I ask that you call me Ella and refer to me using female pronouns—which reflect and respect my gender identity. I'm grateful for your support and am excited for the next chapter!

I'm no longer on Facebook and have had mixed feelings about whether that network adds a net positive value to humankind. However, on September 2, 2015, it was invaluable to me. By the end of that day, everyone knew, and they knew it from me. I loved it and was grateful for it. As with coming out at work, the support and love from my friends and extended network of acquaintances were positively overwhelming.

Since my early twenties, I have made a hobby out of creating a physical photo album at the end of each year. It's a fun way to reflect on the year and create something I can hold in my hands. I know I'll be able to look at them with a smile in the future. Ryan and I joke that I'll be looking at them when I'm gumming it in the old-age home in fifty years. At the end of 2015, I memorialized all the wonderful messages of love and support that came back to me after my post.

9

MORE THAN OKAY

After my public emergence, it slowly became clear that my biggest fear—negative reactions and the loss of my friends and family— would not transpire. All of my relationships continued, with the natural ebbs and flows of life. I am endlessly grateful for it and consider myself to be extremely fortunate that I was able to emerge with such blessings.

There were subtle changes in my interactions with others that slowly evolved over the years to become significant and positively meaningful. At the root of the subtle change was me and how I conducted myself. I was the same person at the core—the same dependable, pragmatic, inquisitive, loving, food-oriented, healthful, calm, strong, quiet, quirky, funny-to-some-people person. In the months and years following my emergence, I became lighter, less distracted, and more capable of connecting and caring about others. My sad cloud had lifted, and now that I had lost a big part of the heavy weight and distraction of the disconnect, I was also able to be more authentic—a better, more easygoing version of myself. Within that first year, both Mama and Ryan remarked that I was unequivocally a happier person. It was satisfying to receive their recognition of the positive impact of my emergence.

I discovered that a number of my friendships grew more intimate. With my newly available authenticity, friends felt like they could open up more to me and share their challenges and struggles. Ryan told me that he'd had some fears about the impact of my emergence on our friendship, but instead, he'd found that I'd become a better friend—a surprise gift he couldn't have imagined. My relationship with Mama was much the same as it had been before, but now our conversations were lighter and more connecting. Ironically, Amalia leans tomboy, so my mom finally had a daughter who enjoyed clothes shopping. Mama and I share similar tastes in clothes, so it became fun to go shopping together, something we never did before I emerged. When I visit, there's always at least one trip to shop on our to-do list.

On one such outing, I asked her whether she had arrived at the point of recognizing me as female. I knew she loved me, accepted me, and was using the correct pronouns, for which I was grateful, but I was curious whether her love and acceptance came from her truly seeing me for who I am as a woman or whether she was simply showing support for her offspring. Her response was sweet at its core—but also surprising and mildly disappointing. She said she doesn't see gender in either of her kids; she just saw her child. She added that she thought I had done the right thing. She knew I was happier, and that was all she cared about. She didn't say much more than that. It should have been enough, but it landed flat. The feeling I got was that she loved me *in spite of* my journey. I was grateful to have her love, but this didn't make me feel truly seen or celebrated for all I went through to honor my truth. I wish there could have also been a sincere recognition and some happiness and pride for that, but that's a gift I didn't receive.

Ryan, who had known me for more than twenty years by that

point, is one example of my many friends who, after conscious effort in the beginning, had no issue switching pronouns. He rapidly internalized my womanhood in his heart and mind, which was incredibly validating. I did experience some superficial changes in my relationship with him and with other local gay male friends. Invitations to their parties and large group dinners became less frequent and then reduced to almost nil. That was fine, as I had always felt a bit like a fish out of water at those gatherings, and it was oddly satisfying to not be included. They didn't see me as "one of the guys" anymore, and that felt validating. I still enjoy friendships with many of those men but see them less frequently—and rarely in the context of large events where most or all of the attendees are gay men.

At work, my emergence opened the door for some open, connecting conversations. During one of my stays in Atlanta, I was in the office of my colleague and friend Lynn, having a chat and catching up, when she mentioned that she had been invited to a bar mitzvah.

"Wait," she said. "Didn't you have a bar mitzvah?"

"Well, I did, and I didn't," I said. "I don't refer to it as a bar mitzvah. It was my *bat* mitzvah."

Her eyes widened. "I was just talking to Tom about your emergence, and we found ourselves wondering which name and what pronouns to use when we refer to you in the past. Tell me more!"

"Happy to!" I said, thrilled that someone was taking me up on my offer to discuss the nuances. I'd worked with Lynn for years and knew she cared sincerely about demonstrating allyship for minorities. "My gender has always been female, so it's appropriate to use feminine pronouns for me in the past. So it was a bat mitzvah for me. And since my name now is Ella, it's best to always use that name, even for references to me in the past. Using my former name simply doesn't feel good. Plus, and importantly, it'll be confusing to others who may be around who don't know about my journey. It could invite questions about my personal medical history and possibly open me up to physical safety concerns."

"That's so simple," she said. "I totally get it!" She laughed. "I'm going to tell Tom."

Lynn's confusion was understandable, and her question was a good one. My gender identity is female, and it has always been female. Referring to me in the masculine at any point in my life is incorrect and disrespectful if done intentionally. Even when it's unintentional, it reveals that the speaker hasn't fully internalized me as female. To understand this, it's key to recognize that only my *gender presentation* changed—not my core internal reality. Accurate pronoun usage is not tied to gender presentation; it is tied to *gender identity*. My gender was inaccurately assigned at birth. I was never male. Therefore, my gender presentation was wrong in the past, and my pronouns were also incorrect.

Being referred to by the incorrect pronouns is painful, but it's even worse when it happens in the company of those who don't know me well. This discloses my private, personal medical information, which is horrifying for me and possibly uncomfortable for others. It steals my agency to determine whether and when to disclose my personal medical history.

The change of pronouns was not an easy transition, especially for those who had known me the longest, like my immediate family. I didn't mind mistakes as long as they were trying. For the first few years, Mama and Amalia got it right more than 80% of the time. After the first few years, the slipups began to test my patience, but I tried to deal with each instance with grace. I've made the same mistake on occasion with others who have emerged. Old habits can be hard to change, and after a time, my corrections came to frustrate my family, who sometimes responded to me with annoyance and declarations that they knew but just hadn't fully internalized the changes. This was especially the case with Papa, who struggled to make the transition. It took years, but Mama and Amalia eventually got there. It was validating when I began to notice they were doing it with ease and referring to me as a sister and a daughter, and always with the right pronouns. It made me feel loved and accepted.

In the years since my emergence, my thinking about pronoun use in a business setting has evolved. In 2015, when I first emerged, the usage of pronouns in signature lines and next to one's Zoom name was just entering the consciousness and almost no one was doing it. I didn't want to do so because it felt extremely uncomfortable to be the only one, and by doing so, I would essentially be pointing out that I was the woman with transgender medical history. That felt like putting a target on my back, so I chose not to include my pronouns anywhere. If others had done it in the interest of showing allyship, it would have been a much-appreciated gift. When those who have not had to struggle with gender identity display their pronouns, it's a powerful act of solidarity and allyship. It creates safety and ease for those whose pronouns might not be evident because it spreads the spotlight around.

For many years after my emergence, because my name and gender presentation are obviously feminine, I felt no need to include my pronouns next to my name. After several years, however, I recognized that the *she/her* pronouns next to my name were not a reflection of my medical history but an indication of my own allyship, with the power to provide safety for those who needed it.

———

After my emergence, the responses from my colleagues at Deloitte were beautiful and validating. I was grateful for the opportunities for conversation that followed, but I was still in physical transition and in the midst of an awkward period that would last until I was well past my lower surgery, when I would finally learn to settle deeply into myself. My facial features were still changing and softening and would continue to evolve and settle for another year and a half. My body was shifting fat around, and I was gradually lightening the color of my hair, which was growing longer and longer. Initially, I'd colored my hair a warm chestnut brown, but I felt the brown was too harsh against my skin tone, so I colored it lighter and lighter. I preferred the softer look against my light complexion. I *do* think blondes have more fun. At least this blonde does!

Those who saw me every few months or more frequently didn't notice any dramatic changes. I didn't really see them either. Occasionally, on some mornings when I was brushing my teeth or fixing my hair, I still noticed elements of my former more masculine reflection, which never failed to feel jarring and disappointing. Outside of my family and my local community, I had friends from other phases of life who were spread out across the US and Europe, so it would be years before I could see everyone in person. Many of them hadn't seen me since I'd begun growing out my hair or taking hormones. There was a lot of curiosity about me, understandably, and when I saw someone I hadn't seen in a while, they were sometimes a touch captivated, and my appearance and emergence dominated the conversation. This made me feel like a bit of a show pony, which I didn't mind at the time—I was always curious what changes my friends noticed, and their observations were a boost for my ego and my sense of womanhood. Now that I have fully emerged, however, and don't see Benni anymore when looking in the mirror, it's nice to have the show-pony period behind me and to simply be treated as myself without it being a topic of discussion.

The other dynamic during that time was the remaining disconnect with my lower part. The gaff continued to be an uncomfortable nuisance, and I felt unable to wear the sexy formfitting dresses I really wanted to wear without risking the possible distraction of a bump. I want to make it clear that there are plenty of transgender women who don't have lower surgery and who like to wear close-fitting dresses, which is their business and their right. Nobody has the right to police what others think looks good or doesn't look good—or what's appropriate or not. I celebrate anyone living as their best and most authentic self and dressing how they want to. For me personally, however, the thought of a visible, incongruous appendage made me uncomfortable and reminded me of my disconnect and lack of completeness.

The effects of this ongoing disconnect were particularly acute when it came to dating, which I was doing very little of, although I did stick my toe in the water a bit. Now that I had emerged, my dating pool evolved toward men who didn't identify as gay. That felt like a minefield, however, since I had something between my legs that was the opposite of what straight men understandably expected and desired. Keeping that in mind and feeling a strong sense of self-preservation, I refrained from flirting and continued to shy away from men while out and about. This was no different from before I had emerged—I was good at being invisible.

I did, however, explore online dating sites, including those geared toward men who were interested in transgender women. I found the entire experience to be disappointing and unsatisfying, and it didn't lead to any meaningful dating or connections. There were numerous eye-opening dynamics. Many men who seek transgender women are interested in them because they're looking for a woman with a penis. I believe these men when they say they are not gay. They aren't attracted to the masculine. They are attracted to feminine beings and the feminine form, and they also happen to like penises. Even though I had the part of interest, I didn't see it as such, and the last thing I wanted was any attention on it. So dating those men wasn't an option for me.

I also found that some men who are interested in transgender women do not see them as women to date, get to know, truly connect with, and explore activities with outside of the bedroom. They're only interested in transgender women for satiating a sexual desire, a kink. These men are referred to as *chasers* and view transgender women exclusively as sexual objects, not as whole people. In the course of my online explorations, once a chaser exposed himself as such—which was generally pretty early in the course of a chat—I ended the conversation. Even though I was hungry for romantic connection, it was cheapening in my mind and heart to engage with men who felt that way. I valued myself too much to spend my time on that sort of man, and after everything I had gone through, I was not going to settle for someone who couldn't respect and engage with my full self. Furthermore, I had a real concern about my safety. The media was full of stories about men who had turned to deadly violence toward the same transgender woman they just romanced.

The behavior of some of these men cut straight to the heart of my fear of how likely it would be to find someone who saw women with transgender medical history as actual complete women who were worthy of meaningful, serious relationships. Would I be able to find someone who would value my entire being? Much more time would need to pass for me to get the full answer to that question.

In the meantime, I did meet a few kind, sincere men who were interested in me as a person and a woman and who were content to ignore my lower part. I briefly dated a few of these men, and it was fun, but none of them brought the sort of deep, multifaceted connection I was looking for, so they didn't last long. As a whole, the dating experience at the time was fraught, and it made me more and more anxious to have lower surgery so I could move on with my life. Today, I recognize this to have been an informative time that began my learning curve of dating straight men.

By early 2016, I had been consistently attending therapy sessions for four years and was ready to scale back to sporadic check-ins. The time I'd spent had been invaluable. I had explored all my fears and questions, and over time, I had gained perspective and found answers for all of them. Looking back at my approach, I'm grateful I went about the therapy process deliberately. It gave me full confidence that my only options were either continued sadness or the exploration of my gender. It was comforting to know I had explored all other areas first, and it helped me to communicate with my family that there had been no other paths, that I had done everything I could, and that I was sure. And that surety was all the more powerful because of how hard I'd worked to earn it. I'd come down this path kicking and screaming. I'd been full of fear, confusion, transphobia, and overwhelm. I'd been raised to be transphobic in a transphobic society that had little to offer in the way of positive examples or role models. It had taken me several years to work through the confusion, but I had been determined to discover my true self and had gone the distance to push through to clarity. I had persevered despite the potential for overwhelm I'd felt at the beginning of my journey, when I didn't know where the path would take me. The approach to feel my way into each step without worrying about future steps had carried me through and kept the overwhelm at bay. With much gratitude and reflection, I let go of my regular sessions and kept moving forward with confidence.

By the following fall, a year after having emerged, I had saved enough for a down payment on a home and found a place in Arlington, just north of Boston. It was exciting to be a homeowner again after all these years of renting following my split with Johan, and I eagerly dove into the work of moving and decorating. One day, within a week of my move-in, a pair of technicians from Best Buy were installing a new dryer in my basement. I started down the stairs to check on their progress but took an errant step and fell the rest of the way, landing in an awkward sprawl on the concrete floor, bleeding from my head and with pain shooting from my head and right hand.

The technicians came running over, and one of them called out, "Ma'am, ma'am, are you okay?!"

Despite my pain, I was thrilled. He'd called me "ma'am"! I was more than okay. They'd seen me for who I truly was. And they were gently, chivalrously trying to help me get to my feet and up the stairs to fresh air. I took an Uber to the emergency room, where preliminary results showed that I was fine. Later, however, it was found that I had broken my wrist. I spent the subsequent months in various contraptions with the hope that surgery would not be required.

After that bit of bad luck, though, some phenomenal luck came my way. Right after the turn of the new year and still with just one working wrist, I received a call from Dr. Marci Bowers's office. A spot in her calendar had opened up, and I was next on the wait list. They could schedule my surgery for the following month, a full year sooner than anticipated. To say I was ecstatic would be an understatement. They inquired about my availability and whether I'd be up for having it on February 8. I didn't need to consult my calendar. Whatever day it was and whatever conflict I might have, nothing would stop me from being ready and available that February 8.

The month leading up to the surgery was a whirlwind. I needed approval to take the time off from work, and I needed to prepare to be away from home for at least a month. I had a stack of paperwork, blood work, and tests to get through before I could be officially cleared for surgery. I also needed to pause the hormones, a standard precaution before surgery. I was overjoyed that I'd be able to stop the testosterone suppressant once the surgery was complete so I could get back to nights of sound sleep.

I had some physical preparations to see to as well. As part of the presurgery checklist, Dr. Bowers's office had made it clear that I would need to remove hair in certain areas of my groin to reduce the risk of hair growth inside my vagina. There are steps in the surgery that reduce the risk of that occurrence, but doing hair removal beforehand ensures that it doesn't happen at all. Thankfully, I had already tackled the area with electrolysis. As friendly as Lee and I were with each other, nothing invites increased closeness more than shared laughs while one is naked from the waist down and spread-eagled while the other is designing the perfect vaginal bush via laser and electrolysis.

Bosco and I flew out a few days before the surgery, in plenty of time for my various presurgery appointments and to get comfortable in my hotel room. Although I had been sitting to pee for about two years by this point, I didn't do so in airplanes. Airplane bathrooms are gross, and I took advantage of my ability to stand and pee in a plane for as long as I was able to. As I was sitting on the plane flying west, I smiled knowing this would be the last flight I'd have that perk. It was the only thing I'd miss.

Other than my pure excitement and the tiniest bit of pseudomourning over the coming loss of stand-up peeing in airplane bathrooms, I also harbored some fear. I was afraid that something might cause the surgery date to slip. I had never been so emotionally and mentally ready and excited for something, and the fear of a postponement or a cancellation was deep and real. I wouldn't trust it was finally happening until I was on the gurney, rolling into the surgery arena.

I landed and checked in to my hotel, an Extended Stay property. My suite had a bedroom, a tiny kitchen, and a small, cozy living room. The care plan had me in the hospital for three days after the surgery and then back in my hotel room for the next three days. On day six, I was to return to the clinic in order for Dr. Bowers to remove the vaginal packing and the catheter and to teach me how to dilate. After that, I'd be able to recuperate for a few weeks with my parents, who were a couple hours' drive north.

The next few days unfolded as planned and without fanfare. I gave blood in case a transfusion was needed and completed the unpleasant bowel prep the day before the surgery. The next morning, I awoke to excitement and joy, which were tempered with slight nervousness. It was a four-hour procedure, and there was always a risk of unexpected complications, but I trusted I was in the best possible hands with Dr. Bowers.

My parents met me at the hospital and joined me in the pre-op waiting room. It was comforting to have their support, and I was grateful that my choice of surgeons had made that possible. Dr. Bowers visited and asked whether I had any questions. All my major questions had been answered by then, but I took the opportunity to again request that she do her best to make sure my vagina would not only be functional but also beautiful.

She laughed. "Don't worry," she said. "I've got your back." My parents, sitting next to my bed, were quiet, taking it all in with wide eyes.

With that, I was wheeled away, and the rest of my fear evaporated. It was actually happening. The negative side of my brain jumped in at that point and reminded me that I could die during the surgery. Was this worth it? Was I willing to die on this gurney for this cause? The answer materialized as quickly as the initial thought: yes, absolutely. I couldn't continue to live like this. Dr. Bowers could fix this, and I'd be alive, with a beautiful, working vagina. The sassy part of my brain chimed in, too, with a reminder that I would be out cold, so if I died, I'd never know it anyhow. And with that, it was time for me to stop thinking and let the professionals do their work.

The nurses rolled me into the operating theater and moved me from the gurney to the operating table. Everyone introduced themselves. It was all very civilized and reminded me of the standard introductions and small talk one might have at the start of any work meeting with new colleagues. In this case, it felt a little comedic since I'd soon be unconscious and they'd all be taking a journey deep into my groin, but it was soothing nonetheless.

The anesthesiologist went to work, and the next thing I knew, I was opening my eyes, back in my hospital room, with my parents sitting nearby. I felt a wash of gratitude through my body and heart that I was alive and they were there to support me. Many women who go through what I had just experienced don't have family in attendance, let alone their birth parents. That moment felt like a rebirth. It was perfect that they were there to witness it, just as they had been at my birth.

Mama had expressed concern about serious complications and unexpected issues with nearby organs or urination. I shared the same concerns. It was with much relief that we were informed that the four-and-a-half-hour surgery had been a resounding success.

10

LEARNING AND HEALING

The three days in the hospital unfolded as anticipated. There was a lot of pain, but it was well managed with pain meds. My groin was tightly packed, and I wouldn't see anything for three days, when the dressing would be removed. The time passed both slowly and quickly: I remember many moments of deep physical pain; lots of broken, medicated sleep; frequent icing; walking; and listening to music on my iPod to help pass the time. I listened to a lot of Enya. "Wild Child" and "Flora's Secret" were my favorites, and I played them on repeat. They've become my theme songs, and they instantly bring back those moments of joy and the happiness of freedom. The irony of the names of both songs are not lost on me—I'm neither wild nor a keeper of secrets. Perhaps the universe was telling me something.

I can't describe the emotions I felt throughout my heart, mind, and all the cells in my body during those days in the hospital. They were feelings that had come about at the flip of a switch after forty-five years of buildup—feelings that would be unknowable to most others. I felt a deep, satisfying peace that was borderline spiritual. I relished it, and I cried happy tears, smiling all the while. I finally felt fully born, whole, and complete. And I felt powerful. My emergence had awakened and activated a power that had always been there, latent. I could do anything.

I immediately changed my morning pill regimen since there was no longer a need for the testosterone suppressant. It was remarkably satisfying to let go of that medication. It was physically satisfying because after my bruised bladder fully healed, I would no longer need to pee in the middle of the night. And it was mentally satisfying because my body could now express itself as me, as a woman, without the need for medicine.

While resting in the hospital, I came to learn that Papa had been in fine form. Unbeknownst to me, he'd had multiple conversations with various members of the medical staff before the surgery to cajole them into saving my testes for him as a keepsake. The whole thing was eye-rollingly comical and typical. Thankfully, he had no success in that endeavor, but his joke brought up a question I had faced before the surgery: did I want to preserve my DNA at a cryopreservation facility? I'd decided against it. Although I love kids and there have been times when I would have loved to have had my own kids in the context of a loving relationship, I had no interest in saving sperm to do so. If I were ever to have my own kids, I'd want to adopt or have the sperm come from the father, not from me.

I was disappointed that Amalia hadn't been able to make it down to visit me in the hospital, but I understood. She was juggling a full-time job and the demands of a single parent, so she had her hands full. I connected with her via telephone, and again, I felt that sense of distance that had arisen between us since my emergence. I wasn't sure what to make of it. Perhaps she was simply distracted with the other aspects of her busy life.

On day three, my care team reduced my pain meds, and I was feeling a lot of pain. I returned to Dr. Bowers's office to have the drain and bandages removed, and I had my first glimpse of what I thought of at the time as my "kitty." There was tremendous swelling and a seemingly illegal amount of bruising up and down my inner thighs and lower torso. I'd been well-prepared not to have any expectations just yet; I knew the appearance would change drastically over several months. But the offending part that had triggered such disconnect my entire life was finally gone, and I was thrilled. After the appointment, I returned to my hotel to recuperate for another three days. After that, my catheter and vaginal packing would come out, and then the many remaining stitches would dissolve over time.

The surgery methodology was such that once everything was healed, all traces of the surgery—and the past configuration of my genitals—should be barely visible, and possibly not visible at all. If the scars healed as intended, they would fade away into the folds of my labia and the creases of my inner thighs. It became my personal mission to do everything I could to support the best possible healing outcome. I had very specific healing instructions and followed them with utter care over the coming days, weeks, and months.

Once the packing came out, it would be my job to be more active, get out and about, catch up on sleep, and, frighteningly—get past the constipation. That caused worry because the dilemma would be playing out right next to my freshly stitched, life-changing new gift. The last thing I wanted was to accidentally blow it all open as a by-product of trying to poop. I felt like I had only one chance to get the healing right in order to minimize the scar visibility. I figured that if complications arose and I had to return to the hospital, the final result wouldn't be near as nice as if it all healed well in the first go-round. I was in for several days of concerning bathroom moments, when I felt as if I was going to damage Dr. Bowers's meticulous work. In those moments, I grew sweaty and lightheaded, but each time, I managed to avoid disaster.

My parents, who were taking care of Bosco, had gone home with him the day after my surgery, so it was fortunate that I also had close friends who lived nearby. A number of them dropped by to visit while I was recuperating at the hotel. I hadn't seen some of them for years. We went for walks and drives, caught up, had bites to eat, and reconnected. The days passed quickly. I spent them taking it easy, caring for my kitty, and trying to figure out how to sit down without crippling pain. Dr. Bowers had recommended that I arrange for night nursing care while I was recuperating at the hotel, and I followed her advice. It was reassuring to have someone there to make sure I made it to the bathroom and back without incident. Because of the catheter, I wasn't peeing yet, and emptying the urine bag was complicated, especially when I was sleepy and medicated, with everything feeling so tender in that area.

On the sixth day, I was excited to see Dr. Bowers for another follow-up appointment and an in-depth chat about the surgery. I was curious for her input on the success of the surgery, my vagina, and the healing progress. Upon arrival, I was ushered into a patient room to await a nurse, who would be removing the catheter and the packing and giving me my dilation lesson. All stripes of women need to regularly dilate. This can be for any number of reasons, ranging from physical therapy and recovery from accidents or surgeries to overcoming genetic issues or neglect. I was nervous and hoping the pain would be manageable.

She quickly removed the catheter, which was momentarily uncomfortable. It was an odd sensation to feel the packing coming out of my vagina, but this, too, went quickly. Next, she gave me a mirror so I could watch and learn while she gave me my first dilation. Dilation is clinical and performed with heavy dildo-like cylinders. I had four, each the same length and varying in thickness and color. With the help of a liberal amount of lubricant, she inserted the slimmest dilator, aka Mr. Purple, and showed me how to dilate. Although I could only accommodate Mr. Purple to start, I would need to incorporate the others into my dilation sessions over the coming weeks and months. Mr. Purple was first in line, and then I would move on to the next one in the set, Mr. Blue, which was larger. After Mr. Blue would come Mr. Green, and then Mr. Orange, which looked gigantic compared with Mr. Purple. But one thing at a time.

After that first lesson, the nurse asked me to do it myself. It hurt, and it felt weird, but I knew it needed to be done and was grateful to be doing so. I would need to dilate for fifteen minutes at a time, three times each day, for the first three months, at which point I could start having sex if I so chose. At that point, I would reduce my dilation sessions to twice per day for the subsequent nine months, after which the routine would settle at once daily. After a year, I would be fully healed, but dilation would always be an important part of my routine. Sexual activity reduces the need to dilate but is considered an imperfect replacement, and I would need to continue to dilate at least weekly.

With the preliminary tasks complete, it was time to check in with Dr. Bowers. It was heartwarming to see this woman who had given me such a life-changing gift. Her previous visits in the hospital had been perfunctory, or I'd been under anesthesia, so we hadn't had the opportunity to chat. During this exam, she took her time. She let me know I was healing well and she was extremely pleased with how the surgery had unfolded. She also shared that because of my small frame, she had done the best she could with my vaginal canal and unceremoniously announced that I'd never be able to accommodate Mr. Orange. She went on to let me know that most men weren't that thick and didn't anticipate it would be a problem for me at all. Although I was grateful to be able to dilate, I didn't like the possibility of not being able to receive my eventual guy, so I took her declaration as a fun challenge: I was determined to do my part in ensuring that my vagina lived up to her full potential.

As I was getting dressed and standing there in my panties, she looked at me and exclaimed, "Look, you've got a camel toe!" I looked down, looked back up at her, looked back down, and then we both laughed. I recognized this was likely a standard line she gave many of her patients, but I loved it. Yes, I did have a perfectly cute little camel toe, and it felt awesome. Never shall I have camel-toe shame. With that, I was sent on my way, free to recuperate at my parents' home.

The next few weeks with my parents were nurturing and peaceful. Their home was an ideal haven to continue my recovery. Soon after I arrived, my constipation eased, and my worries about damaging the stitching dissipated. I established a daily routine of dilation, a morning walk, coffee and cookie time, and then my midday dilation. The days ended with one of Mama's delectable meals, an Epsom salt bath, and another dilation. It was awkward to be doing that, as they certainly knew what I was up to when I'd disappear for thirty minutes in the middle of each day. As much as Papa had always joked about body parts and sex, we were not the kind of family who talked about things like that.

I slept a lot the first few days but was soon able to join Mama, Bosco, and my parents' dogs on their morning walks of one or two miles. I started going to the local gym in the second week and got back into a light routine. However, I was still unable to sit without significant pain. I ate standing up and had to have my legs elevated in order to be seated. I'd been told that sitting would get a lot more comfortable after a couple of weeks, and I was looking forward to the end of that discomfort. I had also been warned about the electric jolts and shocks. They began to hit me, which was a good thing: they were an indication that the nerves were beginning to reactivate, connect, and heal. There were other sensations that were surprising and a few that really took me off guard. Altogether, it was a cornucopia of pain, numbness, more pain, electric shocks, occasional pleasurable pulses, and more numbness, followed by more pain.

There were a number of new factors when it came to peeing that would take me a while to get used to. The first was the timing of my stream. My urinary tract had been shortened, and the timing of the pee didn't match the timing my brain expected. There were numerous instances when I started peeing before I'd fully sat down. In addition to the timing, the direction of my pee stream was also a factor. As long as my tissues were swollen, the stream would be unpredictable. Sometimes, it came out in a wide spray and occasionally even sprayed up over the top of the toilet bowl. I was very much looking forward to a reduction in swelling so my bathroom visits would be more predictable.

Passing gas was also a big surprise. It turns out that farts from people with vaginas move upward and escape between the legs when they're sitting. Before my surgery, they'd get trapped down there, necessitating a slight shift to the left or right. This was a funny revelation, and it took me a while to get used to it. Now it always makes me giggle when I share my knowledge about varying escape routes for farts, as dictated by differing anatomy.

As the days went on, it felt disconcerting and frustrating to discover that I had occasional itching in my groin that couldn't be scratched. The itches were inside my body, underneath the skin, and because of the jumbled nerves that still needed to heal, I wasn't able to scratch them. I could bring myself some relief with pressure and rubbing, but I needed to press very hard. Most times, I just needed to give it time for the itch to go away. As I continued to heal, I also discovered that I couldn't feel sensations in some spots on the skin around my vulva. The doctors suspected that everything would be fine and that my brain and eye could reactivate sensation if I looked at the spot in the mirror while lightly and slowly stroking the inactive spots with the tips of my fingers. They advised me to do this a few minutes each day for a month, so I added that to my daily healing regimen as well.

Those weeks of recovery with my parents were a special time, but I was eager to get back home, sleep in my own bed, and get back to my life. I was also cognizant that some luck had played a role in our peaceful time together—and that luck would run out sooner or later. Papa had been in a good mood and avoided potentially divisive comments or topics, thankfully, but I knew how a conversation with him could quickly turn into a misunderstanding and lead to a fight. The political atmosphere at the time didn't help, either. Donald Trump had just been sworn in for his first term the previous month, and the lines that divided the country ran right through our household. Fox News was on a lot, and the potential for disagreements was high. From past experience I knew that having a conversation with Papa about politics quickly became a one-way monologue, which could easily devolve into one-way yelling. When I eventually departed for the airport, I was glad that we had navigated those two weeks without conflict and everyone was still in good spirits. I was excited to get back home, but sitting was still an issue so I popped plenty of pain meds prior to takeoff. I'd brought a donut pillow, but it provided only slight relief, so I stood for most of the return flight.

My care was transferred to a Boston surgeon who specialized in lower surgeries, and I settled into my healing routine. I was continuing to dilate three times each day. My assignment had been for fifteen minutes every session, but I made it a point to dilate twenty minutes each time. Faithfully. I didn't want to risk being personally responsible for any loss in depth, and I was determined to prove Dr. Bowers wrong about Mr. Orange.

Within weeks of getting home, I found myself on another gurney, ready to be wheeled into another operating theater. My wrist had not healed from my fall down the steps, and surgery was required after all. It was to be a relatively minor surgery, but I was surprisingly scared. I felt much more frightened about the wrist surgery, in which the stakes were much lower, than I had about the much more intensive previous one. I didn't want to lose function of my right hand and also was worried about my ability to continue dilation. I was bawling and emotionally shaken before going into wrist surgery, whereas I had been cool as a cucumber and smiling—though I'd been thinking about possibly dying—while going into my lower surgery. Despite my fears, the second surgery also unfolded smoothly, and I found ways to continue dilation even though I was wearing a cast on my dominant hand and wrist.

———

At about that time, I received some crushing news. My dear friend Michelle was diagnosed with a stage-four glioblastoma—an aggressive brain tumor. Even with an immediate surgery and chemotherapy, there would be no eradicating the cancer's spread, and her doctors gave her less than a year to live. She didn't allow her prognosis to alter her attitude and personality. We continued going out to our favorite spots, and she was the same upbeat, optimistic Michelle she'd always been. Her humor and positivity were the same as ever; the only difference was that she'd tire out more easily than she had before, and we'd have to pack it in a little earlier. Other than that, our friendship was unchanged, and I was even more grateful for her companionship.

Meanwhile, I continued to heal. Even though it seemed slow at times, there were many small emergence-related victories that collectively added up and made a big impact. Within a few months, the rewiring of my nerves was complete, and the unscratchable itches disappeared. I was able to sit comfortably again, finally. My brain got used to my shortened urinary tract and the timing of my stream. The mirror training I'd been doing to regain the sensitivity in my skin was beginning to bear fruit: I could feel the faint traces of my fingers, whereas before, I couldn't. I was in awe of the mind–body connection, which had been so present throughout my life.

It was also about this time when I finally completed my hair-removal appointments. Lee had diligently sought and destroyed all the follicles on my face and neck, and with a great sense of accomplishment, after four years, our time together in the electrology room came to an end. By then, I'd been growing out the hair on my head for more than five years, and it had finally reached a length and style that felt just right. The memories of my former presentation were quickly fading away as Ella became more and more distinct and increasingly more confident.

After about five months, my vulva had healed beautifully. Dr. Bowers had delivered on her promise, and then some: everything was stunningly awesome. I wasn't a connoisseur, but based on the reactions of various nurses and doctors, as well as the pictures I'd seen, I couldn't have asked for a more positive result. About a month later, I claimed victory in my quest to be able to fully incorporate Mr. Orange into my dilation routine. He was slightly uncomfortable, but it made it a little easier if I thought of him as Liev, after Liev Schreiber, a crush of mine at the time. I can still feel the elation and satisfaction in achieving that goal.

Although generally rare, there are a number of complications that can arise from lower surgery, such as colonic or urinary complications, wound separation, and infection. I was fortunate to have escaped the truly complicated, problematic outcomes. However, I did have a minor issue. Even after I was able to sit comfortably, I continued to have pain. The pangs varied from a rare shooting jolt or an occasional deep throb to a slightly more frequent snapping sensation. The snap was more of a nuisance than meaningful pain; it felt like a rubber band snapping against my skin. The pain wasn't impacting my ability to fully live my life, but it was bothersome.

I learned from my doctor that the pain was due to three reasons. The first was that nerves were continuing to activate and connect. He shared that it was possible—although unlikely—that some of the nerve pain might never go away. He thought it was more likely it would subside after a year. Deep massage continued to bring some relief, but I wasn't always in a position to self-administer vigorous crotch rubs, and those pangs often managed to materialize at the most inopportune times. I did the best I could with those orders. A second source was organ-related pain that just needed more time to heal. I was still peeing more than before, and it turned out that my bladder had been pushed around and banged up pretty good. The surface bruises that were starting to dissipate on my skin also extended deep into my body. The third source of the discomfort was granulation tissue that had become overexuberant and infected. Granulation is expected; it's an important component of any wound-healing process. However, it can become unhealthy and proliferate, which delays the healing process.

Thankfully, granulation is a minor issue and easily treated. My doctor thought I'd only need a few office visits. The treatment would be straightforward. With the help of a speculum, the doctor would remove the granulation tissue and then dab on some silver nitrate. The silver nitrate would cauterize the infected skin, allowing for healing to resume normally. The pain would be minimal, and it would only take minutes. I scheduled monthly appointments for the treatment and continued with the other facets of my healing regimen.

Now that I had made it through the first few months, I could start exploring other options in the care of my vagina. One decision I faced was whether or not to douche. Most gynecologists recommended against it; the vagina is self-cleaning and develops its own healthy bacterial ecosystem. Dr. Bowers was firmly in this camp, but my local doctor was all for douching. Their clash of opinions left me confused about what to do. I did douche a number of times, but it was tedious, so I stopped and soon found it was unnecessary for me.

I also explored pelvic-floor physical therapy. My doctor told me it would help me get more familiar and intimate with my new parts, improve my mind–body connection, and support pelvic relaxation during intercourse. I found the exercises to be extremely beneficial and highly recommend them for anyone with pelvic floor issues.

The other curiosity that I explored was vibrators. My erogenous zones had shifted around, obviously, and the situation was more complex than it used to be. My challenge was no different from the one facing any other person with a vagina: it required that I take care to learn, tend to, and understand my body. With that mindset, I went on an adventure to buy and test various types of vibrators to help me learn. Although I was overwhelmed by the diversity of options, I began to learn.

11

EMBODIED

Yes! The starter button works. No, I didn't tell Papa.

12

DATING AS MYSELF

I reached the three-month mark, and I was officially in the clear to have sex. I didn't feel rushed to go into it, as there was still too much pain and bruising and there wasn't anyone special in my life. The pain and bruising subsided over the next few months, and by late summer, at around month six, I was feeling eager to try. I was still dealing with the granulation issue, but it wasn't bothersome enough to deter my growing curiosity in sex. Though I hadn't yet resumed dating in earnest, I became a woman on a mission. I was forty-six and not getting any younger, and it was time, regardless of my relationship status.

I had a business trip to New York City on the horizon and figured that would provide the perfect opportunity to find someone. I loaded Tinder onto my phone, set up a profile in which I made my transgender medical history clear, and began to swipe. Soon I matched with someone I thought would be the ideal guy for the occasion. He looked like a bodybuilder and seemed to have a clean, rugged way about him and an irresistible smile. He made it clear he was only on Tinder to have some fun, which was fine with me; my goal that night was to lose my virginity, not to find a boyfriend. We chatted a bit, and I was open about sharing my situation. He was excited and happy to be my first. We decided to meet at a local bar to check whether there was chemistry. I was relieved that not only had he represented himself well, but he possessed a quick, kind wit, and there was a connection.

We went back to my hotel, and I had sex for the first time in my life. Even though I'm unable to get pregnant, I am able to catch STDs, and so we practiced safe sex. He was sweet, validating, and tender when I wanted him to be and not tender when I hoped he wouldn't be. It was exactly what I needed. It was exhilarating and profoundly mentally satisfying. Everything fit together perfectly, and our play felt totally aligned with my mind. There was no disconnect. I had no nausea or thoughts about needing to throw up. There was no fear about him touching or seeing something that would make me uneasy and dampen my fun. I was able to let go and just have fun, and it felt natural and right. I did have a burning question for him, though: the only feedback I'd gotten so far had come from doctors and nurses. What did he think? He told me he thought it looked great, and although I recognized it as one guy's opinion, it was gratifying to hear.

Our connection was strictly physical, and it was perfect for what it was. I had finally experienced sex in a way that matched the wiring of my mind, spirit, and soul. I was finally in a place where I could live a vibrant 360-degree life. I had spent decades thinking this wasn't possible, and the evening left me ecstatic.

Back home in Massachusetts, I began to notice a shift in how I was perceived and treated. I had hoped simply to be seen for who I was, as a woman, but my genes and my lifestyle had come together to grant me a significant bonus, and now I found myself on the receiving end of unsolicited compliments from strangers, such as "beautiful" or "gorgeous." I was no longer the ugliest girl in the world. It was jarring, mind-boggling, and thoroughly fantastic. It would take me quite some time to get used to it. I do recognize that true beauty comes from within. It shines through and manifests as confidence and a connecting heart. I believe I have that internal beauty; however, my journey to acceptance and love has also been supported by my exterior appearance. I love being seen for who I am.

I walked with confidence when I first began to wear clothes aligned with my gender identity, and this grew further as I settled more and more into myself, especially when I no longer had to wear gaffs and could wear dresses that called to me and reflected my personality. By then, I was also having fun exploring the endless world of women's shoes, and I had refined a makeup style and palette that felt like me—natural and feminine. And with two years of the hormones' ongoing effect, my face was continuing to soften, and I was developing curves where I'd hoped.

I began to hear comments about my bearing, most notably after I shared my medical history. I often heard, "Wow, you're so confident!" Occasionally they'd also remark that they hadn't seen such levels of comfort in others who'd had similar journeys. I couldn't speak to other experiences; I only knew that I was rooted in self-knowledge and reveled in showing up as myself, with no pretense. Raw me was also confident me.

Finally walking as myself and with a great start to a new chapter in sex, I was again open to connection and love. Even though it hadn't been meaningfully possible for me before my emergence, my heart and body have always carried an unwavering desire for a deeply intimate and spectacular love story. I had arrived at a place where it all became possible, and I was excited to date as myself. I refer to it as dating *as myself* because I really wasn't myself prior to my emergence and my lower surgery. I had been living an inauthentic life in all ways—mentally, emotionally, and physically. I had been covered up, living behind a façade, disconnected from myself. Being freed from that was life-changing and allowed me to be myself without needing to worry about guarding what would come out of my mouth, how my body would move, how I would adorn myself, or even how I would adorn my home. Not only was I happy, but I also became joyous and carefree about how I was seen and how I interacted with others. I was finally authentic and able to be vulnerable. Those changes would eventually impact all the areas of my life, but nowhere so dramatically as in dating, which became a real and meaningful option for me. In the past, my body had not been aligned to enable physical connection, but now I was finally in a place where it all became possible, and I was excited to date.

Knowing that I was on a journey to love, I became open to the magic around me and began to prioritize dating with an open mind. I welcomed the flirtations of men, whether at the gym, the local coffee shop, or walking my dog down the street. The attention was delightful, and it continued to build my confidence. The drawback of meeting men in real life (versus online) was that they didn't have an inkling about my medical history, and I didn't yet know how to safely and comfortably navigate disclosing it.

Early one afternoon, I was reading in a coffee shop. It was a warm summer Sunday, and I was wearing a casual red cotton dress. A handsome man caught my eye a few times as he passed while coming and going to the bathroom. He seemed to be going to the bathroom more than needed, and it dawned on me, likely a bit later than it should have, that he was flirting with me. On his last bathroom walk-by, he passed me a note. It was a short, sweet message, and it included his number. I texted him and soon found myself intrigued as our rapport developed. He was lean and athletic—perhaps a bicyclist—and seemed easygoing. He was an Israeli Jew; I loved that he shared my faith, and I was excited to get to know him. As our date plans were coming together, I disclosed my medical history via text. Disappointingly, he lost interest. It was the beginning of an important lesson for me: if a guy wasn't okay with my history, then he wasn't for me, regardless of how appealing he might have seemed initially. This realization made it easier to move on. I was grateful for having attracted a seemingly wonderful man simply by being myself.

The world of online dating provided a different set of opportunities—and challenges. I hadn't dated meaningfully in about ten years, not since Johan and I had separated. In my earlier years, I'd—incorrectly—presented as a man who was engaging gay men. Now that I had emerged as myself and would be dating middle-aged straight men, I needed to learn a whole new set of skills and practices. I had many little gaps in my expertise, and collectively, they added up to a lot. The little things ranged from navigating chivalry and determining what to wear for a first date to figuring out how to recognize and express emotions. More significantly, I also needed to suss out how to attract and interact with the strong masculine men who lit me up—while staying true to myself and my needs for safety and comfort.

Most women learn these lessons over many years while dating as teenagers and as young adults, through trial and error, and from the other women in their lives. I was a middle-aged woman with all the dating experience of an eighth-grade girl, and I had a lot to learn. I recognized these hurdles, realized it wouldn't be a cakewalk, and was okay with that. I wasn't alone. Modern dating is hard for most people, and everyone has their own unique challenges. I was excited to finally date as myself and just get out there and explore and have fun. There's nothing like diving right in and learning by doing—so I did.

I began with the basic apps, like OkCupid, Plenty of Fish, and Match. I explored them one at a time and went on a lot of dates. True, emotional connections were elusive, but I enjoyed myself and learned more and more about dating as a straight woman. Eventually, I also signed up for some specialized apps, like Jdate, which is for Jews; an app geared toward highly educated Ivy Leaguers; as well as higher-priced apps for white-collar professionals, but disappointingly, there were very few local people on them. I also revisited the transgender apps but found little had changed; they were still largely populated by men who were just looking for sex with those who had not yet had lower surgery.

Through the course of my dating journey, I discovered another challenge: determining how and when to disclose my medical history. After I had emerged as myself but before I'd had my lower surgery, I believed strongly that it was important in this context to disclose the disconnect between my lower part and my feminine gender presentation. It's a fair assumption for a straight man to expect that he's dating a woman with a vagina, so before my surgery, I always disclosed before a date. Not only was it pragmatic, but it also ensured emotional and physical self-preservation. That was my personal decision. Another woman might see this differently, and I do believe it's her choice whether she chooses to disclose or not before a date. The tragic reality, however, is that some men react with physical violence if there's a lack of disclosure, and some will even react that way *with* disclosure. Either way, a violent reaction is horrific, even when men attempt to use panic as an excuse, as they sometimes do. Such reactions are hate crimes, manifestations of the worst kind of toxic masculinity.

After my surgery, my thinking shifted. Now that my sex and my gender were in alignment, I didn't have to worry about managing anatomical expectations, so I had more flexibility in disclosure timing. I began to experiment with my approach. Although I didn't feel like I had an obligation to, in the early years after my surgery, I disclosed up front, in my profile. This decreased some interest, and that felt okay. My medical history was an important part of me, and if a man couldn't accept it, then I wouldn't want to be with him anyhow. I also experimented with waiting until after we'd met to disclose my history. When I didn't feel a connection on that first date, it became a moot point, as we'd part ways before it could become a factor. But it did become a challenge the first time I met a man who captured my fancy.

Von and I liked each other, and the first two dates were fantastic. As our third date approached, I was wracked with nervousness. I wanted to disclose my medical history but had no idea how this alluring man would handle it—I was worried about a possible violent reaction. It was the tail end of our evening, and we were at a creperie for coffee and dessert when I decided to tell him. We were still out in public, which helped me feel safe. My fast-beating heart and trembling hands were in full nervous mode. I took a deep breath and leaned forward.

"I have something personal I want to share with you," I said, looking him in the eye. "Is that okay?"

"Of course," he said, leaning in himself.

"I was misgendered at birth due to a genital birth defect and have transgender medical history," I said, with my heart thumping faster. "I am a woman, and my heart, mind, and soul have always been female. Earlier this year, I had surgery to correct my lower part and am grateful that my body is aligned with who I am."

Von was quiet, taking it all in. I studied his body language for any sign of a reaction and was relieved to see that he was still leaning in, still holding my gaze. He seemed a little surprised, but it was clear he was open and curious.

"Wow, I had no idea," he said. "You're remarkable. It's okay—I just . . . it's a lot to take in." He smiled, still looking me in the eyes. He had a couple of questions, which I answered, and after finishing our dessert, we wrapped up our date. As we parted ways, he shared his desire to see me again and gave me an intimate goodnight kiss. And then I never heard from him again.

This could have been for any number of reasons, but I assumed it was due to my medical history. The story bumped up against my own historical phobia about those with transgender medical history and triggered a couple of painful assumptions: he didn't see me as a woman, and no man would love a woman with my medical history. I was inconsolable for days, in tears, my heart punched with pain. The experience reinforced my belief that there were extremely few men who could pique my interest and also appreciate and love me.

After that, I went back to disclosing up front, in my dating profile. I didn't want to experience feelings for a man if he didn't know that part about me. I also didn't want to go through that level of anxiety leading up to disclosure, which had taken away from my enjoyment of those initial dates. By paying attention to the reactions my profile was getting, I was able to pass on those men who weren't open-minded or who didn't see me for the woman I am, and this brought me a measure of emotional and physical safety. I knew that the right man for me would have nothing but admiration, respect, and deep, profound love for the strength I'd needed to emerge as myself.

I played around with the language and location of my disclosure. I didn't want it to be the centerpiece of my profile because it doesn't define me, and I didn't want to attract a man who was interested precisely or primarily because of my medical history. I am far more than my history, and I have no interest in chasers or their kinks.

Even with my online disclosures, my profile was still attracting a good amount of attention. However, I found that often, men didn't read, instead reaching out based on just my photos. Therefore, I needed to confirm that prospective dates had actually received the information and were accepting of it before I'd agree to a video chat or a date. Of those conversations, I sensed that about 80% of straight men were not accepting about it, and by extension, I felt that they didn't see me for the woman I am. It was frustrating and discouraging, but that left 20% who did see me for who I am. I believe in quality over quantity and was looking for only one. I worked hard to maintain my confidence, my positive attitude, and my knowledge and love of myself so that I could continue with a curious, open, and loving mindset.

Although many men had an issue with my history, I did come across a number who didn't let it deter them from seeing me as a woman or from their interest in exploring a romantic relationship. I learned that some men could evolve quickly. In many cases, they had never met someone with transgender medical history and had certainly never considered dating one, but they recognized they were, in fact, in the presence of a feminine being who was 100% woman—a woman who'd had to fight to exist. I did meet men who not only were okay with it but were also attracted to my authenticity and strength, as I deserved. I was grateful for those men, though none of them captured my full attention.

Another challenge that arose in dating were the misconceptions about transgender women. Even when these were innocent, as they often were, they tested my patience and my ability to stay positive and maintain compassion. While most men were respectful and complimentary about my profile and medical history—which I attributed in part to my well-rounded, well-written descriptions and photographs—there were some who had questions and comments that I found frustrating and sometimes offensive. Here are some of the various recurring refrains, along with my responses, which I sometimes shared and sometimes kept to myself:

- When did you decide to become a woman?

  I've always been a woman. I was born female and incorrectly assigned male at birth. It's not something I decided.

- Were you born a man?

  No, I was born a woman and incorrectly assigned male at birth.

- Are you a guy?

  No, I'm not. (I find this one particularly bothersome. It implies that they see a man in a dress. I know that's not the actual case, but it chafes against one of my own original and early limiting beliefs and fears. I'm not a man, and it feels very hurtful that I might be seen as one.)

- I don't date transgenders.

  I'm not a transgender. *I'm a woman.* Transgender *is an adjective, and using it as a noun is incorrect and offensive. And in my case, now that I've had my lower surgery, I reject the adjective for myself and refer to it as part of my historical experience. I'm a woman who has transgender medical history.*

- Do you have a penis?

  My profile makes it clear—no. It makes me feel physically ill to think about it as a penis or refer to it as a penis. I never saw it as one.

- When did you have your surgery?

  Why does it even matter when I had the surgery? (I thought that but generally didn't say it; I didn't like my own reactive tone and tried to avoid it.)

- I'm straight and only date women.

  Great! I'm a straight woman and only date straight men. (This comment conflates sexuality and gender. Also, the implication that I'm not a woman is particularly insulting.)

The primary recurring themes of these misconceptions were the incorrect beliefs that I was at one point a man and decided to become a woman or that I was something other than a woman. Both suggestions were frustrating and hurtful. No one decides to change their gender identity. It's inherently coded within each of us and is something that is out of our control. I explained this time and time again, mustering as much compassion as I could. I recognized that many men simply lacked the language to ask their questions in a way that wouldn't insult me, and I did my best to correct them gently and to give them the benefit of the doubt that they'd receive the information with open minds—at least until they demonstrated otherwise.

Since those early experiments, I've come full circle with regard to the timing of disclosure about my medical history. Sharing it in my profile began to feel like putting the cart before the horse. It didn't define me, and it shouldn't have been a required condition for those early connections. There are so many elements that make up who I am, and leading with my medical history came to feel inauthentic. I began to recognize that disclosure before a first date felt like a disclaimer, implying that I'm something less than a whole woman and feeding into misperceptions and inaccuracies about my journey. I've come to learn that I'm not obligated to include it in my profile, nor does it make sense to do so.

For the initial connection and getting to know each other, my medical history is no different from other highly personal bits of information that are only shared as intimacy deepens. A woman of child-bearing age wouldn't be expected to disclose that she's had a hysterectomy before a first date. It's the same for someone with great wealth or a lot of debt, or someone in cancer remission, or someone with a prosthetic, or someone with a history of trauma. There are countless examples and many factors that can affect the course of a developing relationship for which we have no expectations of up-front disclosures.

Unlike all of the aforementioned examples—and this is critically important—my medical history has *no* bearing on the relationship itself. It's certainly important to know to understand me better and to appreciate me, but it has no bearing on the potential for a meaningful and successful straight relationship. There are a lot of women who have boob jobs, nose jobs, facial rejuvenation, and the like, and there's no expectation that those should be disclosed up front.

Some might question my ability to have sex as a reason to disclose, but I'm able to have vaginal sex and haven't had any complaints. Like many women in their fifties, the help of a little lubricant might be needed, but it certainly doesn't rise to the level of something that needs to be disclosed before the first few dates. In the same way, a man would certainly not be expected to disclose on a dating profile that he might need Viagra to perform.

Instead of disclosing immediately, I want my history to be something I share, organically and vulnerably, as the connection unfolds. I want to confirm that he's not only comfortable but also appreciates and sees me for who I am. I do feel that it should be disclosed at some early point, like many of the aforementioned examples, to support the deepening of the relationship in the spirit of getting to know each other better.

Since that difficult experience with Von, I have found the confidence to hold for a bit before disclosing. Now, I get to know my date a bit, figure out whether I like him, and gauge if there's a connection.

This keeps those early dates fun and lighthearted and enables me to save the deeper conversations for a time when I feel safer and more comfortable. When I do feel a spark, I will disclose, always within the first three dates. I feel that it's critical information to know about me and sets a precedent for open and honest communication. Waiting beyond the first three dates feels manipulative.

The privilege of getting to know me better is my choice to make. There are those who will say that choosing not to disclose up front means I'm fooling my date or robbing him of his agency. But I'm not fooling anyone—I am a woman and present as a woman. His agency is maintained, as after I disclose, he has the right to make the decision to continue the relationship or not. For me, this is a matter of safety, security, privacy, and my own agency—which take precedence over all else.

I've refined my disclosure over the years. Today, I find that responses can be all over the board. Sometimes, he'll have no questions. Sometimes, he'll have lots of questions, and the rest of the date becomes about that. And sometimes, he needs to process, and the questions slowly drip out. The right guy will already have an intuition and not care, or he'll see me exactly for who I am and appreciate me for the qualities that my journey forged, or he will have no clue and appreciate me for the same reasons once he learns about it.

Whatever the response, it's a pivotal moment because I need to know that he'll see me for who I am as a woman and nothing different. I need to know that he won't see my medical history as having any impact on his masculinity or straightness and that he's comfortable with my agency in disclosing it as I desire. This is what works for me now; I may decide on something else as time goes on, and I grant myself the flexibility and patience to evolve and adapt.

Despite the frustrations of those early years after my emergence, I was learning. I was learning what made me comfortable and what didn't—and more about what I liked in a man and what I didn't. I was learning about middle-aged straight men and what they were looking for. I was learning how to navigate a cornucopia of typical dating experiences: endless texting that goes nowhere, ghosting, unsolicited dick pics, and so on. I continued to tend to my healing and remained receptive to new connections with an open heart and open mind.

As the fall of 2017 began, I was settling into a full, rich life with my emergence now fully behind me. I was finally walking the world as myself. People saw me for who I was. Beyond my disclosures in the context of romance and to acquaintances with whom I sensed the potential for a deep friendship, I stopped talking about my medical history. After living in purgatory for forty years and then going through a slow, lengthy emergence, I deserved to live life as myself, free of the topic of my history. The subject brought up (and still continues to bring up) the pain of my gender dysphoria. Also, there was, and still is, a subset of the population that would see me for something other than a woman if they were to learn about my medical history. Others' opinions wouldn't change my truth, but I'd worked hard to emerge and to be seen for who I am, and I had no desire to open myself up to people who couldn't handle it, especially because it had the potential to lead to discrimination and violence. Given my genetic privilege, there was little need to bring it up, so I generally didn't, which left me free to explore my womanhood and to enjoy being treated like any other woman.

Not only was I noticing differences in how the world received me; I was also discovering newness within myself. Music, for example, took on a whole new meaning for me that year. Before my emergence, it hadn't been something I noticed. As a child growing up in my parents' home, I had been well trained to keep myself busy, both to avoid Papa's assignments and to distract myself from my disconnect. I wasn't conscious of it at the time, but for me, slowing down and truly inhabiting the feelings of a given moment were dangerous acts. Subsequent to my emergence, however, I was able to settle fully into still moments and experience all my emotions. Music was a beautiful and grand discovery—I could hear and feel it for the first time in my life. In my happiness, I found a desire to dance. I'd dance to fun, happy pop music in the afternoons or evenings, and I'd rock my body to soulful jazz on Sunday mornings while preparing tea and taking care of Bosco. I'd relax into peaceful classical or easy listening while waking up and going about my dilation routine. My emergence had awakened an unforeseen part of my mind and my being.

One Sunday morning that fall, I slowly awakened, and though I was still foggy with sleep, an unexpected realization hit my consciousness: I felt a certain peace. I was happy. I remembered the modest objective I'd set out for myself with each step of my emergence, all those years earlier: to be a little less sad. I'd never imagined I could actually be happy. It hadn't occurred to me that this could be a possible outcome. I wondered why I'd set the bar so low.

I didn't need to dig deep for the answers. It had been because of my family's experience in the Holocaust, which had influenced the way I approached life. It had been because of the negative influence of phobias and related fears and the lack of positive examples within our culture. It had been because of the lack of happiness in my own life prior to my emergence.

As I lay in bed, with the first light of a clear New England autumn day falling through my window, I became overwhelmed with gratitude that my outcome had surpassed what I had even dared imagine. It was unbelievable, and I was deeply proud. I had listened to myself, honored myself, loved myself, and gone about it my way. I had leaned into fear, jumped off the high dive, and trusted that it would work out. It had been a long journey, with both an unknown duration and an unknown ending, but it had led me to my truest self. I smiled, and I felt the transformation in that small act alone. Where before my smile had been brave and superficial, it now felt brighter, transparent with weightless delight, and full of love and light. And with that, my attitude subtly shifted to embody endless and infinite possibilities and equanimity.

13

IMPORTANT LESSONS

Late that fall, I met Scott online. He knew about my medical history when he first wrote, and his response was just what I was looking for: you're a woman, you're beautiful, and I love your strength and authenticity. I was immediately attracted to his spirit, which was easygoing and chivalrous, self-assured and unflappable, with an undercurrent of kindness and deep strength. He wasn't very talkative, which lent him the air of a deep thinker. An IT leader at a local global company, he was tall, dark haired, and fit, with no kids.

We began dating. The first date became a second, and then a third. We settled into a routine in which he would pick me up at two o'clock every Sunday, like clockwork, to share an afternoon and early evening together. Our dates were low-key, in line with his personality. He planned each one, and each one was different. I loved the consistency of our dates and that he enjoyed figuring out our plans. He treated me like a queen, and I began looking forward to Sundays more and more.

We'd been dating a few months and it was a cold January afternoon when he took me to the annual auto show at the Boston convention center. I wasn't into cars, personally, but they were an interest of his, and I was excited to share the day with him and learn more about one of his passions. The convention center is massive, and the winter chill penetrated its interior; I walked close to him, enjoying holding his hand for the warmth and comfort, and following his lead as we explored the latest models and technology. The conversation came around to our relationship, and I asked him how he thought things were going between us and where he saw things going. The tone was light and casual—I wasn't trying to pin him down; I just wanted to learn a little more about how he was experiencing our Sundays, which had become a favorite part of my week. He answered that he was looking for something meaningful, which aligned with our initial online exchanges and was good to hear. But then he said, "I don't think you're ready."

I wasn't sure whether I'd heard right—and I wasn't sure what he meant. We continued walking, still holding hands. "Wait, what? Ready for what?" I asked.

"Ready for something meaningful."

I hadn't been prepared for this turn of conversation; I didn't know what to say. This was the deepest connection I'd felt in a long time, and I was caught off guard. "What do you mean?" I asked him.

"I just feel like you're not ready," he replied. "I feel like you're holding back."

"I think I'm ready," was all I could muster. I was confused—I had a strong desire for a meaningful, connecting long-term relationship and wasn't interested in dating anyone else at that point. I didn't know how to put my questions into words, so I let it drop. He didn't say anything more. We continued with our date as if nothing had happened. After dinner, he dropped me off without a kiss, which wasn't unusual. Despite what I felt was the intimacy between us, we'd not crossed the threshold into anything physical at all yet. I assumed we were just taking it slowly, but when we got together a week later, I began to wonder whether it was because he wasn't attracted to me. It was a quiet afternoon and we were in my home, relaxing on the couch after having been out. Finally, and to my surprise, he leaned over to kiss me. My heart leapt—but it was a terrible first kiss.

I didn't have the maturity or the experience to recognize that one bad kiss didn't predict all future kisses. I also didn't know that there was a way to bring it up and talk about it without completely hurting his feelings. All I knew was that I was disappointed and couldn't fathom another kiss. I didn't want to lead him on, so I had to end it.

I texted him the next morning and requested a video chat because I didn't want to do it in person or via text. He responded; we connected over video, and I broke up with him without telling him why. It was awful. He was gracious, visibly upset, and sad. I was bawling and didn't understand why.

———

Shortly thereafter, my granulation healing process took an unexpected turn. I was disappointed to learn that the silver nitrate treatments were not having their hoped-for effect. About a year after my lower surgery, my surgeons recommended a more aggressive approach, which would entail a procedure in the hospital. They would put me under anesthesia so they could look deeper inside, clean out all the granulation tissue, and cauterize the unhealed tissue, at which point I could continue with additional silver nitrate application visits. I was happy to hear there were options to help expedite the healing process, and the procedure went smoothly.

My healing progress provided some solace, but I was still struggling with my split from Scott. Over the subsequent months, I spent more nights crying than I could count. I'd wake up in the middle of the night, upset about what had transpired. It became clear to me that he had meant so much more to me than I had realized at the time. I was also feeling guilty that I hadn't given him an explanation. I still owed him that, so I reached out for another video call and shared my motivation for breaking up with him. He said that he wished I had told him at the time. He hadn't thought our kiss was great, either, and thought that we could have worked on that together.

I would have loved to give it another try, but that didn't feel like an option, so I didn't suggest it. I was embarrassed, and I didn't want to come across as wishy-washy, which he might have taken as confirmation of his declaration that I wasn't ready. We said our goodbyes and went back to our separate lives. But the pain in my heart and body didn't dissipate, and I began to feel that I would never meet another man like him—a man who floated my boat the way he did, embraced my medical history, adored me, and was in a good place for a real connection. It was anguishing that I'd let it go because of one bad kiss, and I was angry with myself.

Meanwhile, my granulation pain was decreasing noticeably from the cauterization procedure, which had permanently healed about half of the problematic tissue. My doctors recommended a second appointment, so early that spring, I had the second cauterization procedure. They told me that all had gone swimmingly; however, I went home with much more pain than I had had after the first procedure. Worse, it was a different kind of pain: I felt it on the outer surface. I undressed to investigate the source of the pain and almost passed out in horror at the sight of my vulva. My left labium bore a deep red rectangular burn, and my skin was peeling. It looked like a cattle brand. After everything I had gone through and all the care I had taken to ensure I had done my part in healing, the shock of the sight made me break down and wail, the way a grieving widow might when she throws herself upon her husband's coffin.

My dramatic breakdown dissipated within a few minutes. After pulling myself together, I called my surgeon and made an appointment. The hospital never fully fessed up to what happened, but it was clear that somehow a clamp, the cauterizing tool, or both had somehow scarred me. The surgeon told me he was pretty sure the scar would eventually heal. I was dubious and anxious but hopeful. That second cauterization surgery had successfully healed about 90% of my remaining granulation, and I had absolutely no desire to go back in for a third such procedure to heal the rest. I'd stick with the ongoing silver nitrate treatments.

That spring, Michelle's condition deteriorated to the point where she could no longer go out comfortably, and her loved ones pitched in to support her. Her other friends and I rallied around her, visiting her at her home to talk, bringing her things, and helping out when we could. Her husband, Tom, took a leave of absence from his job to be home with her full-time. When she entered hospice, we set up a rotation to visit her, keeping her surrounded by all the love she'd inspired in us. It was mid-June, and I'd just returned from California, where I'd been visiting my family to celebrate Mama's 70th birthday and my nephew's graduation, when Michelle passed away.

I'll never forget her radiant soul and spirit. She gave me perspective and gentle emotional support, and we shared lots of laughs. I'll be forever grateful for her dear friendship. She'd been effusive about how extraordinarily impressed she was with my emergence journey, and in her final days, I told her that it was her admiration and perspective that had planted the idea in my head to perhaps discuss it more publicly someday. She smiled and said that she knew I would.

With my heart full of grief, I flew right back to California. Mama would be having her bladder removed, and I wanted to be there to support her and Papa through the surgery. Although not cancerous, she had struggled her entire life with bladder issues, which had worsened with age. Bladder removal meant she would have to use a urostomy pouch for the rest of her life, a prospect she had always dreaded. It was the reason she had fought against bladder removal all those years. But now, the need could not be delayed any further without the significant deterioration of her quality of life.

The surgery seemed to unfold with no issues, and four days later, I said goodbye to everyone and flew back home to Boston. Mama was due to be released from the hospital the following day, and Amalia was going to stay another week to support her and Papa at home. Within days after having come home, however, Mama's condition worsened. She was not able to eat, had little energy, and lost control of her bowels. Amalia was there with her throughout, doing everything she could to support Mama in learning how to handle her new stoma, navigating her health care in general, playing day and night nurse, and advocating for her. Papa did his best; however, with his thick accent, inability to handle technology, and other responsibilities, like his business and their dogs, Amalia filled a critical gap.

Mama continued to worsen. A week after her release, she was in our local hospital, near death. The doctors there were unable to help her, so they put her in an ambulance for the two-hour ride back to the hospital where she'd had her surgery.

We had no explanation—we just knew that she might not survive and if she did, the recovery would be very slow.

That same night, I immediately booked a one-way ticket back to

San Francisco on the first flight the next morning. I requested family leave from work, packed two large bags and Bosco, and closed up my home, knowing I likely wouldn't be back for at least a few weeks. In the short term, we needed to figure out what was going on and get Mama through her near-death crisis. If we could manage that, we'd then need to determine her best medium-term recovery care needs.

She almost didn't survive the ambulance ride. Her abdomen had distended in the ambulance, causing the sutures from the surgery incision to rupture, spewing out feces and blood. Although the hospital team was able to stabilize her, her chances of survival were unclear. They discovered that her surgery team had accidentally left a perforation in her intestines, which caused leakage and would require a second surgery in six to eight weeks. Until then, Mama would need to survive with an abdominal opening—a wound approximately 4"×4" in size—which leaked feces and required constant care, suction, and cleaning.

Amalia and I became her twenty-four-seven health-care advocates in the hospital. During the first two weeks, we took turns sleeping on a cot in her room at night. We supported the nurses, attended to Mama's emotional and comfort needs, and became experts in cleaning her wound. All the while, we wondered whether she would make it. She suffered through excruciating pain, which wasn't brought under acceptable control for the first few weeks. While in the hospital, she also contracted a severe bacterial infection that exacerbated her condition and complicated her care. She was fully restricted from all food and not allowed to drink much water. She was constantly hot, experienced unending thirst, and eventually began to suffer from hospital delirium, also referred to as sundowning. Those symptoms included visions of dead people, attempts to eat paper napkins, and periods of severe confusion. It felt like we were watching her being tortured.

I didn't have time to contemplate her possible death while in the throes of advocacy during the day; however, in quieter moments in the night, waves of emotion fell over me. I knew I loved Mama, but the likelihood of her death illuminated just how much I loved her, appreciated her, and would miss her. Yes, I had carried resentment for how she had navigated my gender questions and for her lukewarm response to my eventual emergence. Yes, I wished she had stood up for me more and celebrated my eventual strength to emerge. But none of that mattered when it seemed I might lose her. All that mattered was that I loved her and I knew she loved me. I knew she supported me and wanted nothing but happiness for me.

I thought of what life would be like without her. I would miss her adamant requests to text when I landed. I would miss her daily calls whenever I was feeling unwell. I would miss our connections over humor and style and how we would each react to various situations. And so I grieved at night and hoped that when she did eventually die that it wouldn't be under these awful circumstances of nonstop pain.

After the first few weeks, we found—and Papa funded—private caregivers to stay with Mama throughout the night. It gave my sister and me the space to sleep at a nearby Extended Stay hotel and continue our support during the day. Papa commuted back each evening to their home to care for the dogs, which now included Bosco.

Although it was an awful time, there were some silver linings. While in the hospital, I discovered that any discomfort I'd had with using the women's restroom had completely vanished. I was able to make eye contact, smile, and engage with other women, with no fear of glares or objections.

Even better than that, my relationship with Amalia felt like it recaptured some of its warmth. In the hours we spent together in the hospital, supporting Mama and each other, I came to learn that she'd been struggling with some anger toward me. From her perspective, I'd killed the person whom she thought of as her brother. That anger manifested itself as the coolness I'd felt from her over the previous three years, since my emergence. But things shifted for her when I came back to help with Mama. Amalia told me that my jumping back on a plane without hesitation meant everything to her. She realized that although she had lost the person who she thought was her brother, she still had a sibling who would always be there. Our relationship became more easeful during that time, and after about a month, she returned home to attend to her family and her career. She was self-employed and needed to turn her attention back to that. I was fortunate to be able to take family leave from work and stayed to help care for Mama.

At that point, my relationship with Papa began to fray. The first flash point was his inability to respect my boundaries. I'd left my life—friends, gym, dating, work, and home—for an open-ended stay to care for Mama. After Amalia departed and night caregivers were in place, I found that the most effective way for me to help was to show up daily at the hospital in time for the doctors' rounds, at about five-thirty a.m., and then to stay for most of the day, with two exceptions. The first was to tend to my need for exercise, which I planned for each morning from nine to eleven thirty. That gave me ample time to leave the hospital, get to the gym, go back to the hotel to get showered and dressed, and then get back to the hospital. The second boundary on my time was around my evenings. I'm a morning person and needed evenings and nights to decompress, rest, and wash off the emotions from the day. I knew I needed to get out around six each evening to relax, have dinner somewhere besides the hospital cafeteria, and then go back to my hotel to sleep and prepare myself for another early wake-up. This allowed me to be completely present, emotionally and mentally, for what had essentially become a full-time marathon job to care for Mama—a job that I wanted to do.

It was the first time I had set hard boundaries with Papa, and he didn't like it. He didn't like my absences for the gym and wanted me to come back after my dinner. I told him that that wouldn't work for me and that she had caregivers and nurses. I knew that the only way I could maintain the existing schedule and show up as my best self was to hold on to my boundaries. He couldn't accept them and began to stew with anger. I recognized his anger was misdirected and understood that he was also emotionally and physically exhausted. In addition to seeing the pain Mama was experiencing, he was processing tremendous grief and stress. He also had a grueling two-hour commute each way, every day, and all the while, he was struggling with his own health issues. He didn't have an outlet, and I became an easy target for his frustration, which came through as negative side comments, angry energy, and efforts to engage me in fruitless conversations regarding her caregivers, which became a second flash point.

There were daily logistics for who was coming and when. There were communications, handoffs, and payment arrangements. Papa has strong opinions about how things should be run and is used to others doing things exactly as he wants them. He had issues with some of the agency policies, and I found his demands to be unreasonable, which placed me in the awkward position of having to maintain a decent working relationship with the agency while attempting to meet his demands.

To further complicate matters, he suddenly claimed that he could no longer afford to pay for the caregivers and wanted me to be at the hospital in the evenings. This was surprising—their fees were reasonable, and he had always spent money on anything he prioritized. He'd always taken pride in his refusal to let money stop him from doing the things he wanted to do. His business acumen and success had provided him with that luxury, and he had never let money be a hindrance. So I didn't believe him. I thought his claims of financial constraints were a reflection of his poor mental state, as well as both his dissatisfaction with my boundaries and an attempt to control me. About a week before Mama's surgery, his misplaced anger toward me became obvious even to her, and she asked me to cancel the caregivers altogether. Her body was close to being strong enough for the second surgery, and after confirming with her multiple times over a period of a week, I felt confident that she really did want them cancelled and no longer needed nightly support. Papa was upset, believing that I had unilaterally cancelled the caregivers.

Although it was a charged and stressful time, I didn't feel alone. Support came in from various sources across our family. Amalia and I remained in daily contact, and I found further help from the Netherlands. Mama's sister flew out to join us for a week. It was a relief to have her around, and it meant the world to Mama and me. I had also been in close, consistent phone contact with an uncle, one of Papa's brothers. He had intimate knowledge of the inner workings of his brother and of the relationship between Papa and me, so he became an invaluable sounding board to help me navigate the situation.

There was also a touch of romantic hospital intrigue, which came from an unlikely source. The guy who had inserted Mama's PICC line at the start of her hospital stay was a juicy, smart hunk of a man who seemed to have eyes for me. I was happy to reciprocate his fun and light flirtations. After a few weeks of that, he asked me to meet him for a meal in the hospital cafeteria, where I was disappointed to learn that he was a married man. It turned out that he didn't wear his wedding ring on the job. He made it clear he was open to more than just flirtation, but I'm not available for that with a married guy—unless said guy is married to me. However, I loved our flirtation for what it was. He made me feel beautiful, and it was a nice distracting ray of sunshine during a stressful and challenging time.

The day of Mama's surgery finally arrived. Tension levels were sky-high; we'd been told that this would be a make-or-break procedure. There was a chance that she would not make it. If she did, there was a strong likelihood that she would need a colostomy bag, something she wanted to avoid, as she already had the urostomy pouch.

We anxiously gathered in the waiting room—a group of her dearest friends, Papa, and I. Papa had been keeping his distance, and by that point, we were no longer communicating unless the care for Mama required it. Even though he had been stewing and had become a walking cloud of negative energy and tension, we had managed to mostly keep it civil.

It was a long, agonizing wait. At one point, I was sitting with some of Mama's friends when one of her other friends came over and shared that she had been part of a conversation in which Papa had spoken poorly of me. Learning about it and the details felt like a knife into my body and sprung a spontaneous flow of tears. She told me that he'd called me names and told the others that I had callously cancelled the caregivers, that I was selfish, and that I wasn't doing enough to care for Mama. It crushed me. It felt like such an affront given that I had been there daily, advocating intensely for her.

On the one hand, I couldn't believe that he was doing this, but on the other hand, I wasn't surprised. His actions were in line with how he'd treated me in the past, and I felt exhausted at the thought of another merry-go-round of pandering to his skewed ideas of reality. I thought about the way he'd treated me when I was young and how he'd kicked me out of the house when I was twenty-one, deserted us at my 40th birthday, and refused to talk to me for four years, with no explanation. I was done. I was done with what felt like unexplained sneak attacks. I was done with the cycle of those hostilities, which always led to me trying my best to figure out what had transpired and then take the high road to fix things for the best of the family and for Mama's sanity. I was done with the drama and negative energy. In that moment, I decided that I no longer wanted him in my life. Later, I'd discuss it with Amalia and Mama to get their blessings. That decision felt good. It felt right and freeing.

A few hours after that difficult decision, the surgeon came out with news. She came directly to me and shared that the surgery had gone really well. They were able to close the perforation and the wound, and Mama would not need a colostomy bag. She was resting comfortably. With that news, I broke down for the second time that day and gave the surgeon a big grateful hug. Mama stayed in the hospital a few more weeks and then spent some time in a nursing home, where she rehabilitated and eventually became independent enough to come home. Thankfully, Papa stepped up during those months to support her at home, and she made a near-full recovery.

I went home a few days after her surgery and took myself on a driving trip along the Maine coast to decompress and reflect before restarting work. The area is picturesque in the fall. I slowly made my way up to Bar Harbor and relished the lobster rolls, blueberry pie, nature, and sleep. I was immensely grateful that Mama had survived. We'd all had to grapple with the idea of her passing, which had seemed likely at numerous moments over the previous few months. I was also grateful that she hadn't passed in such awful circumstances, with so much pain and discomfort. We were in awe of her will to survive and her strength to push through the marathon of pain. She would pass someday, and when it was time, I hoped it would be peaceful. I also felt at peace and liberated with having made the decision, with Mama and Amalia's full support, to walk away from my relationship with Papa.

I returned to work and to my regular life, and soon, my thoughts found their way back to Scott. With distance and reflection, I'd come to realize that I had fallen in love with him, which I hadn't recognized before. I decided to tell him in hopes that we might give it another try, so I sent him a text and asked whether he'd be open to meeting me to catch up. He agreed, and we met up at a cozy gastropub in Harvard Square in Cambridge.

The moment I laid eyes on him, I felt a rush of feelings for him, and his reaction to the sight of me made me think it was mutual. I apologized about how I'd broken it off and asked whether he'd be open to another try. I didn't share the full truth of my feelings because I wanted to get a sense of where he was. He said he was open to seeing me, but he had recently met another woman with whom he'd had two dates, and he felt he should quickly decide which one of us he'd want to exclusively date. That was disappointing news, but after the pub, the two of us went back to my home to continue hanging out. He held me on the couch, and we had an intimate, connecting conversation. We both acknowledged our emotional and physical connection, and I was surprised at how many details he remembered from our time together a year earlier. We talked about why it had taken so long for that first kiss to transpire, and he told me he'd been taking it slow intentionally because he'd been concerned that my granulation issue, until more healed, would be an impediment to my enjoyment. I continued to withhold the depth of my feelings for him; that felt too quick and scary for a first reconnecting date.

In the coming days, and with the specter of this other woman haunting my thoughts, I decided to tell him more about my feelings. I reached out again a few days later, and we met to talk the next morning at his office. We sat next to each other in his near-empty company cafeteria, and I opened up about how strongly I felt about him. I stopped short of saying the words "I love you" but was otherwise forthright. I shared what I appreciated about him, how he made me feel, that I felt a deep, meaningful connection with him—and that I wanted to explore our connection further.

While I was talking, he held my hand and quietly took it all in. When I'd said my piece, he thanked me for sharing all of it and said he needed some time to process it. I wasn't sure how my words had landed. He didn't say anything further. It didn't seem to have gone horribly. He wasn't telling me that I was a crazy woman, nor was he telling me he didn't see anything between us. However, he did have limited time—which I knew—and needed to go back to work.

We sat quietly for a bit longer, after which he offered to walk me out of the building. We were alone in the elevator to the lobby, descending, when he grabbed me, pushed me up against the wall, and gave me the most passionate kiss I'd ever had. It left me feeling light-headed. We arranged ourselves just before the doors slid open, and we stepped out and crossed the lobby to the front doors.

"How was that?" he asked, pulling the door open for me.

"Well, it was a little better," I said, coyly, with a look back at him and a smile.

We made plans for a dinner date at my house on a Saturday night two weeks later, but a few days before we were to meet, he cancelled it. He told me that he'd had unexpected sex with the other woman on their third date that previous weekend, and even though she'd be out of town during our planned date, his moral compass wouldn't let him proceed with our date. He also told me he'd been shocked and disappointed about my reaction to our elevator kiss, which he'd thought was electric. He had decided to exclusively date the other woman.

I was devastated. I was devastated that he had chosen her and blamed myself for my inability to express my true feelings. I was devastated because I felt that I might never meet another man like him—someone with whom I felt such a connection and who accepted my medical history so easily. I was back to nights of loneliness and heartbreak—heartbreak that was self-inflicted, again. That made the pain even more acute.

For a long time, I wished I had told him that I'd loved the kiss, that it was the best kiss of my life. I hadn't been capable of that in the moment. I hadn't been able to articulate my feelings with authenticity or vulnerability. I'd thought it was obvious that the kiss was electrifying, and, regretfully, sarcasm had been my go-to response. Eventually, I came to understand that I hadn't been capable of anything more at the time. Scott had been right with his observation the previous year: I wasn't ready. At the time, however, that realization was still a way off.

My heartbreak lessened as the New England fall progressed. About that time, I noticed another milestone in my emergence journey: I no longer saw the masculine-featured Benni looking back at me in the mirror. My face had become entirely Ella's, truly reflecting my soft feminine self. With gratitude, I was able to dispense with the possibility of facial feminization surgery, although I consider a very small amount of breast augmentation to be an open question still. If I were to opt for it, it wouldn't be because I feel the need to be seen as female or to become "more womanly"; I would do it for myself, just because I want to.

I was still a little sad over how things had ended with Scott, but I returned to dating with confidence and an open heart and soon met another impressive man. Derek was kind, quick-witted, and athletic, and he lit me up in many ways. He was driven, a finance leader at a large health-care provider who competed in marathons and Ironman triathlons. He made me feel desired and expansive and was sweet and chivalrous. We shared a desire for experiencing great food, and I adored his positivity and penchant for fun. We met on a dating app, where I was up-front about my medical history and had playfully indicated that my vagina and I were "living happily ever after." The first volley of our exchange was his declaration that I had the best profile ever, and he loved how open and fun I was about how I presented my medical history. He hadn't dated a woman with my history before and communicated that he was open to it and would have questions along the way, but he didn't feel the need to bombard me with them from the start. I appreciated him for saving his questions as they came up. On our first date, our connection was instantaneous, and the conversation flowed easily. We found we had much in common and were on the same page about desiring a meaningful relationship.

We had numerous dates, each more fun than the last and each meticulously planned by him. I so cherished his effort. We went to a comedy show and a theater production and enjoyed delectable dishes and drinks. We loved each other's touch, and in this case, the kisses were passionate from the jump. At the end of our fourth date, he drove me home, and I invited him inside. As soon as we were inside and still in my hallway, it quickly got heated. It felt great, and I loved it. At the same time, although our clothes were still on, I felt like it was moving fast, and I wasn't feeling ready for sex. I stopped him, told him that I wasn't ready for more, and asked him to leave. He obliged.

I thought it had been a spectacular date and was excited about the potential between us. I was looking forward to seeing him for our next date, a New Year's Eve dinner at my house—which turned out to be the last time I saw him. That evening, I learned that after the previous date, he'd sat in my driveway for an hour, confused, wringing his hands, flabbergasted about what had transpired. He didn't think he'd done anything wrong, and he couldn't get his head wrapped around why I had asked him to leave. He'd decided he didn't want to date me anymore—he was only there that night because he hadn't wanted to leave me with no plans for New Year's Eve.

Much later, I recognized my role in making him feel like he had done something wrong, which he absolutely hadn't. I didn't tell him I was having a great time. He had been nothing short of a gentleman; what had transpired in my hallway had been fun and sexy, and I had loved it. But I had gotten ahead of myself about what might happen next, and that had stirred up some conflict within me. I hadn't really wanted him to go; I just hadn't known how to interpret or communicate my feelings and needs. If I had, I would have been able to tell him that I was enjoying myself but for now wanted to keep my clothes on and relax on the couch and chat. Instead, I had unintentionally emasculated him. He was unable to come back from how I'd handled the situation, and with today's perspective, I can understand.

Derek was the second casualty of my naivety in dating men. I hadn't fallen in love with him as I had with Scott, so it was less devastating, but I really liked him, and the outcome and its lessons were painful. That pain, on top of my experience with Scott, led me to the realization that I needed support to navigate the feelings of romantic loss and to learn more about dating men. I had become weary of the emotional roller-coaster ride. I wanted to either get Scott back or learn how to get over him. I wanted to approach dating more intentionally, with greater maturity and skill in navigating challenges, and I felt like I needed help shortening my learning curve. I was in my late forties now and recognized that the next time I was dating an incredible man, I wanted to show up as a more mature version of myself, more capable of expressing my feelings.

Looking back, it was not only a natural progression to arrive at that place of craving growth; it was also a special gift. I'd experienced real heartbreak, which was only possible because I had emerged. Living my truth had led me to the opportunity for a new set of experiences and lessons, which ignited a new way of being that would lead to deeper, more intimate relationships—both platonic and romantic—and even deeper inner happiness and peace.

14

COMING BACK TO LOVE

Filled with fresh pain over the premature end of my relationships with Scott and Derek, I signed up for a local workshop called Foundations of Attracting Love. There were about forty of us, with an even mix of women and men across all ages and all walks of life. The evening contained a mix of presentations, group activities, and practice. I didn't learn anything earth-shattering, but it was a good way to practice relational skills and receive some common-sense dating tips. I learned that, as with many things in life, there are elements of modern dating that are learned skills. Practice and repetition lead to confidence and ease, which lead in turn to fun, relaxed dating and ultimately increase the likelihood of a successful, meaningful connection.

There was one concept that particularly resonated: approaching dating with a head-centric approach was a recipe for likely failure. As someone who is often in her head and has found success in her career in large part because of her noggin, I hadn't considered that there could be a different way to approach dating and life in general. That evening, I learned the importance of listening to two other voices as well—my heart and body.

Because of the way my life and my transgender journey had unfolded, I had always led with my intellect. Subconsciously, I knew it had been dangerous for me to feel too deeply in my heart or my body. But now, it was suggested I do just that, and I was curious to learn more. Not only did I want to learn more about how to approach dating with my heart and body, but I was curious about what else I had missed. I liked the facilitator, and he shared that he was an intuitive and an empath who offered one-on-one coaching. Recognizing that I had nothing to lose, I took him up on his offer for a one-hour session.

That hour, which took place on a chilly Wednesday evening at a local coffee shop, changed my life. It may be that he said similar things to everyone and counted on them to fill in the gaps and details. I would have been okay with that. However, I believe he had true insight. Either way, he was quickly able to size me up and share his perspective on my blocks to love. He had three observations, and each felt big and profound.

The first was that I had unprocessed sadness related to abandonment and loneliness and that I needed to identify and heal those wounds. That felt spot-on. My loneliness and feelings of abandonment came from forty-plus years of presenting as a man while hiding my true being. During much of that time, I hadn't thought of myself as lonely, but now that I'd emerged, I could see how lonely it was to have never been seen, to have never had a deep emotional connection. In addition, I was always subconsciously braced for rejection and even anticipating possible hostility from other men. I was good at keeping interactions at the surface, and hiding my truth and feelings and thoughts, for my physical and emotional safety. The only way of being that I knew was one with my guard up. The one and only consistent man in my life—Papa—had repeatedly mistreated and rejected me, which had resulted in feelings of abandonment. In response, I had created a hard emotional shell and didn't really know how to connect and share my feelings. What I knew how to do well was sarcasm. That sarcasm had been on full display with Scott, and my concern for safety and my inability to connect with my feelings were on full display when I kicked Derek out.

The second observation was that I had uncertainty and anxiety related to myself as a woman. As part of our initial conversation, I shared with him my medical history, and he now suggested that I had some work to do to really accept myself. He recognized and acknowledged my natural confidence, and he encouraged me to rise even further and truly claim myself. He suggested I join women's groups, take more workshops, and explore other outlets where I could find community and belonging. I agreed that I still had work to do in this area as well.

The third observation was no surprise. He told me he felt all intellect in my presence, and I was not processing and engaging people from the heart—something he'd observed in the original workshop. I had heard this information before from others but hadn't known whether it was real or what could be done about it. A leader and mentor at Deloitte, the same one who had exuberantly commented about my hair, had mentioned the same thing, which he saw as a key obstacle that would hold me back from realizing my full leadership potential. He told me during a performance review, "When you enter a room, I see you calculating and looking around for the next thing. I'd like to see you better connect." I had no idea what he meant at the time and didn't know what to do about it. Hearing it again, and in this context, cemented its reality and motivated me to try to change.

Eager to grow, learn, and improve my dating game, I jumped right into tackling these three opportunities. The workshop facilitator recommended some books that could help me connect from the heart. I started with reading *The Wild Woman's Way*, by Michaela Boehm. The book resonated and led me to seek out other titles, like *The Happiness Hypothesis*, by Jonathan Haidt; *The Queen's Code* and *Making Sense of Men*, by Alison Armstrong; *The Inner Work: An Invitation to True Freedom and Lasting Happiness*, by Mathew Micheletti and Ashley Cottrell; and *The 5 Love Languages: The Secret to Love that Lasts*, by Gary Chapman.

Also as an outcome of that Wednesday-evening coaching session, I recognized my desire to connect with a community of other professional, straight, positive, growth-oriented women who shared some of my interests, like staying fit, shopping, travel, and food. I didn't have that in my life, and it was difficult to nurture new friendships in my forties and fifties. It felt even harder with remote work and with friends spread out over the country. It took time, but I tried new things and put myself out there more. I found community and joy within a few different women's groups, including a local book club and a global whiskey club, Women Who Whiskey.

I attended more workshops and was surprised to discover that there's such a thing as a love and relationship coach. I found a few coaches to follow online and soon became fascinated by the wealth of information and perspectives. I considered hiring one and sought out as many as I could on social media with the hope of finding someone well suited for me. Soon, I was following more than twenty of them. Over the subsequent years, I continued to read more books, absorbed nuggets from coaches, and strove to apply and practice everything that made sense to me.

———

Two years after my last interaction with Scott, which had triggered my inner work, I took the step of hiring a coach. I created a short list and set up interviews with each one. Bex stood out from the others—she had a thorough, holistic approach, and our chemistry felt great. My intuition told me she was the one, so I hired her, and we began working together.

I'm grateful for the work she facilitated, her guidance, and her emotional and tactical support. In addition to helping me develop a vision and inviting me to try a meditation practice, there were a number of additional practices she introduced that contributed positively to my life, each of which supported further inner growth.

One of the key practices I learned from her is identifying and recognizing my limiting beliefs. Limiting beliefs and stories impact our decision-making, our actions, and therefore the results we create in life. These beliefs are often untrue and unwittingly reinforce how we see the world, ourselves, and the possibilities for ourselves and others. I've learned to shift my relationship with these beliefs and to expand what I believe possible for my life through the practice of affirmations, which I began to incorporate into my daily routine. It's a practice that continues today. My affirmations cover many topic areas and range from recognizing that "Papa tried his best, he loves me, and I forgive him" to "I choose to live and love my moments with joy, fun, and dancing whenever it overcomes me" and "I recognize that my happiness is internal and accept that everything is perfect and complete as it is and that I'm free from attachment to desires or outcomes."

Bex also inspired me to actively practice gratitude, and I started a morning practice that began with identifying and then meditating on at least three things for which I was grateful. My meditations cover the gamut, from a good night's sleep and beautiful flowers to a win during the workday, the sound of wind through the leaves, a captivating sci-fi movie, or a creamy dessert. In these reflections, I recognize the most important things: my life, my family and friends, Bosco, my emergence, my health, and the love that is all around me.

As I got deeper into my inner work, the concept and impact of *vibrations* or *vibrational energy* started to come up regularly. I heard that I had good vibrational energy or that I was *high vibration*. I learned that one's vibration is aligned with one's thought patterns and emotions, which impact how we are perceived by others. Those who are high vibration are thought to practice acceptance, experience joy, and have peace while thought patterns and emotions like anger, despair, and fear are labeled as *low vibration*. Those low-vibration emotions are an important part of the human experience and should be embraced; however, a lower vibration might emerge when one is ruminating on them rather than accepting and then releasing them. There's not much scientific research to support a correlation between emotions, thought patterns, and how we appear to others, but it makes sense that a generally content and happy person would be more attractive to be around.

My ongoing inner work led to a more fun and easeful dating experience and taught me to approach love as a practice and way of being. That mindset further supported finding happiness in the moment, experiencing life with more joy, strengthening my vibration, and improving all my relationships. I feel more and more gratitude for my emergence; without it, I would not have had the opportunity for heartbreak, which gave me the motivation to do this work.

All the while, my body continued to heal, first from the procedure that had left me branded and then from the granulation itself. The brand did fully resolve and clear up. The granulation healed unusually slowly, and only after I'd completed three years of silver-nitrate applications was I able to stop those appointments. It wouldn't be until the four-year anniversary of my surgery that I'd be 100% healed. The pain associated with nerve connections and healing had also slowly tapered, eventually ceasing to be an issue. I no longer found myself needing to rub my crotch in awkward settings. Finally fully healed, I felt immense gratitude that the results were finally what was intended.

I continued to attend therapy sessions, but now it was sporadic—after four years of full-time therapy, I'd dropped down to part-time for two years, and I was only seeing my therapist once in a while, as needed. My work with Bex was generating a powerful impact, and I was eager to keep the momentum going, so I registered for a three-day silent meditation retreat at the Art of Living Retreat Center in Boone, North Carolina. I set an intention to see whether the experience could help me answer three questions:

1. Who was I? What was my light, my core, my inner being?

2. How could I find ease in my body during the work day? I continued to operate almost entirely from my head, which was pressuring my body into a tight, painful, stressed-out mass. It wasn't sustainable for my health, and it was also counterproductive to my preferred feminine way of being.

3. Why did I want to write a memoir? For years, I'd felt a nudging to do so but didn't understand my motivation.

I flew into Charlotte, picked up a rental car, and drove two hours into the Blue Ridge Mountains to the retreat center, which is nestled in the hills not far from the Tennessee border. That night, I'd make the transition into silence, but the first day was for getting settled and meeting the rest of the cohort, which consisted of thirty or so others, most of them women. We had some time to connect and learn a little about one another, and then we gathered for yoga and meditation sessions before dinner. After an evening walk, we made the shift to silence, which also meant no reading and staying off our phones.

The next day dawned clear and cold. After morning sessions of yoga and meditation, followed by breakfast, we had some free time. The dining hall was nearly empty by then, so I relaxed into a rocking chair at the picture windows, which looked out over the serene mountain range. As I sat before that magnificent open view, a memory suddenly returned to me: that bright Tuesday morning when I was four years old, walking into the living room to see Mama. The memory and its power had been set aside somewhere along the way, but now the details all came flooding back: the light and the warmth, the dust in the sun rays, the orange and green colors, and most of all, the feeling of receiving love and that I *was* love. Tears of gratitude flowed, there in the center's dining room, before that expansive panorama. Over the course of my life, I had moved away from love. I had become incapable of it because of the pain and confusion that stemmed from the deep disconnect inside of me. With that burden gone and with the subsequent work I'd done, I was able to remember who I was. I rediscovered myself.

I am a light of love, exactly the same now as I was when I was four years old. My inner light never changed. It had been dampened and then forgotten, but it was always there, beneath a hard shell that had covered my pain and confusion. On that morning at the retreat center, I felt that pure love again. My life had come back full circle to who I was at my core, and now the love was able to shine back through. Not only did I reclaim it, but I made the conscious decision to prioritize and strengthen it. I had the answer to my first question.

For the rest of the time at the retreat, I practiced getting out of my head by actively recognizing present moments, engaging in embodiment exercises, committing to my meditation practice, and recognizing and celebrating my breath. I had already begun these practices, but my time at the retreat emphasized their importance and further motivated me to prioritize them.

I came to see that my spark for this memoir was rooted in wanting to make a difference where I have access and influence. I was immensely privileged to be connected to business leaders through my profession, through grad school, and through the Massachusetts LGBT Chamber of Commerce. These were leaders who could influence policies, processes, and culture within their enterprises and, as a result, reduce inequities and increase belonging for gender-diverse and transgender employees. Most of these business leaders had never had to struggle with their own gender identities, and I sympathized with how difficult it was to comprehend something that had been nearly incomprehensible even to me. I realized my story could make a real difference. I could go public about my medical history through a medium that could tell the whole story, provide the full context, and focus on the internal rather than the external. Told through that lens, my story could help deepen understanding of gender identity, build compassion, and inspire leaders to demonstrate meaningful enterprise allyship.

Additionally, the retreat also illuminated my resistance to the openness I'd need in order to write about my medical history in a memoir. This resistance had been evident over the preceding years each time I'd declined speaking opportunities about my journey. I'm naturally private, and my genetic privilege enabled me to fully present as who I was as a woman without questions about my medical history. My resistance was rooted in the fear that there would be some—or many—who wouldn't see me for who I am. Over time, there were fewer and fewer people who knew my medical history. And I had no reason to share it with anyone, with the exception of deepening friendships and within the dating realm.

I felt that after everything I had gone through, I deserved to relish being seen for who I was by those who otherwise might not have seen me that way. I was enjoying settling into myself, growing, and living free without fear of harm. I could have continued this way, which would have been a fine choice—and one that I would have had every right to make. However, my experiences had also taught me that confronting fears and resistance is where life is juiciest. I recognized the negative impact of forty years of resistance to my disconnect and the harm I'd caused by not following my intuition.

Somewhere along my growth path, I had discovered a framework to help make decisions about whether to take action on something that could be impactful. It starts with the invitation to determine whether the desire for action is coming from a place of impulse, ego, or intuition. The proposition to write a memoir had lingered for years, so I knew it wasn't an impulse. The decision certainly hadn't come from a place of urgency. It wasn't ego, either—in fact, my ego had kept me from doing it, out of fear. During the retreat, I came to understand that my desire to write came from my intuition and had been a steady, patient, loving desire.

So I grew determined not to allow fear-driven resistance to defeat my intuition. I'm scared as all hell to go more public, and at the same time, I am letting go and trusting. I'm ready to dive from the high dive again. I know I'm doing it for the right reasons and know I'll be okay.

EPILOGUE

UNFOLDING AS IT SHOULD

Today, the feelings of gratitude, joy, and happiness can be so powerful that I feel them bubbling all through my body. Sometimes, they cause me to stand up, turn on my favorite playlist, and dance, dance, dance. I dance because there's peace and stillness in authenticity and because I've learned to experience happiness in the moment and to connect to life through the prism of love. I experience happiness that I'm seen for who I am—as I should be and as we all deserve to be—and happiness for hope, possibilities, and the knowledge that life is lived by focusing on the present moment with love and appreciation. The joy, gratitude, happiness, and inner peace that inspire my impromptu dance parties are a reflection of the changes both to my exterior and my interior. The external changes were life-affirmingly critical and set the stage for the subsequent inner work, which provided peace and the ability to fully experience my life. Both were only possible because I stopped allowing fear and others' opinions to dictate my inaction and instead followed my intuition and truth.

Emerging led me to spirituality, and it led me back to love. It taught me to love myself and reminded me that I am love and to connect with love. The experience and arc of my story have gifted me with the understanding of how it feels to go from living inauthentically, without peace or the love of self, to living with supreme ease, with love of self, and with love for others. It taught me gratitude for everything from my breath to a chocolate chip cookie.

Through my authenticity and with my newfound peace and focus, it has become possible for me to show my interest and to invest my time into the well-being and lives of others. I'm able to hold more substantive conversations with friends and colleagues, and I'm able to be more present and be a better a friend. As a result, my relationships have deepened. One in particular has been meaningful and has shown me the potential for the depth of interconnectivity. I met Erik through a mutual friend a few years before I emerged. He had done a lot of deep internal work, and once I began progressing with my own self-growth, we discovered a resonance in one another that moved us beyond our casual acquaintance to a deep friendship, and he has since become my best friend. He provides the space for introspection and for me to share and feel understood, and he shares his own meaningful perspectives, free of judgment. Our relationship has evolved into the type of a deep platonic friendship that I had never had the joy of experiencing because I was not being authentic within myself. I was honored to be the best woman when he married his husband, and standing next to him at his wedding was one of the best days of my life. The mood of the day reflected perfectly how I had shifted my life to one that celebrates love, joy, and fun. The day delivered an abundance of moments when I felt vibrantly alive with love and gratitude.

Somewhere along the way, Mama stopped asking me what was wrong, as she had been doing in so many of our conversations dating back to my childhood. My short fuse was gone; my sadness had dissipated. My relationship with her, as well as with Ryan, has continued to feel lighter and more connecting as I've gone down the path of the inner work. Mama shares more about what's going on in her life because I'm less curt, I'm less self-involved, and I have much greater access to love, compassion, and curiosity. I notice that others, too, react to me with more smiles, joy, and connecting energy. I can't say with certainty why that may be, but I am more open, smile more, and seek eye contact with those who cross my path, and I believe that one's energy can uplift another and vice versa.

My 50th birthday arrived in 2021, and I hosted a celebration in Santa Fe. COVID restrictions and concerns prevented some people from attending, but many who had been at my fortieth in Palm Springs were able to make it, along with several new friends. Like Erik's wedding, the weekend filled my cup with joy and love. I felt immense gratitude to be able to celebrate the big 5-0, having made it through to the other end of a journey that had only been a suggestion in my mind at my fortieth. Papa was not invited to this one, and Mama's health kept her home, but Amalia was in attendance. Although I still feel an emotional distance from her, our relationship has improved a bit, and for that, I'm also grateful.

I love my family for having stood by my side and loving me through my journey. At the same time, I carry some sadness for not having been recognized or celebrated for the strength and power it took to be true to myself. Even though Mama has pictures of Amalia and her kids and other friends up in her house, there are no pictures of me. However, I feel their support and love in other ways. I see it in their acts of service, usage of the correct pronouns, and, most importantly, the way they fully accept me for who I am in all areas that matter. Our relationships feel enduring. We are present in one another's lives, and we love one another. Occasionally, I hear that Amalia and Papa are still struggling with my emergence, but when I inquire to learn more—the how, the why, and the feelings involved—I don't get much in the way of answers. I'm told only that my emergence was hard on them and continues to be in some ways. My family doesn't really practice talking about feelings, and beyond what I've shared, I've refrained from speculating. I love them for exactly who they are, and I practice understanding that their perspective is perfect and exactly how it's supposed to be. Upon reflection, I've come to appreciate that it's Papa, ironically, who has provided me with positive affirmation for my emergence even though he still struggles with it. I never expected flag-waving, car-stickering, parade-joining support from him or from anyone in my family, but he has told me that he's proud of me, and that matters. He has also offered to buy me dresses and has surprised me with jewelry. These acts have meant the world to me, both at the time and even more so as time has passed. They're countered, however, by his inability—or unwillingness—to consistently refer to me with the correct pronouns. I also recognize that he's a very complicated man who struggles with unresolved traumas.

I've come to understand that beneath his internal conflict about me, he always had some level of acceptance. I know I was accepted into his heart as his child and he embraced my eventual emergence with words of pride. I also know that, in his own way, he loves me. And the only way he knew how to show his love was to provide. I love him and have forgiven him. He did his best with his hand of cards, which was the result of how he was raised, his circumstances, and his unique experiences.

Four years after Mama's dramatic medical adventure, after which I went no contact with him, he made an unprompted effort to reach out to me. In the interest of love and compassion and for Mama's benefit, I accepted his invitation to join them for Thanksgiving dinner at their house. I hoped that perhaps we could have an arm's-length relationship in which we see each other once or twice per year.

Going into it, I'd decided I would immediately flee, graciously and with love, if I sensed any rumblings of anger or misplaced drama. It wasn't necessary. The conversation was neutral, but I felt the love a dad has for his child. I felt Papa's respect for who I am. He tried to get my pronouns correct, and he was mostly successful during the evening. The meal unfolded with no discussion of the four-year silence, which was strange but likely for the best. The week prior, he had made a batch of his famous dried sausage and made sure that I had plenty to take back to Boston with me. That gesture took me back to my child-hood and made me tear up. Receiving the sausages that Thanksgiving trip reminded me of my earlier self, before the disconnect took over. The evening ended with him giving me a long hug. The entire experience was an affirmation that, at his core, he loves me deeply and his harmful actions have had everything to do with his own demons and issues; they've never really been about me. And it was also a reminder of the love I have for him.

I will always have great respect and admiration for my parents' decision to move us to the US, which took chutzpah and courage. It was a big risk, with no home, no jobs, and limited English. They had a dream and dove headlong into it, and the challenge strengthened their partnership. Their boldness, dedication, and resolve became imprinted into my psyche. I didn't realize it for decades, but the example they set—recognizing a dream, initiating steps to bring it into motion, and seeing it through to fruition—gave me the courage to follow my truth. They showed me how important it is to follow intuition and not to hide or shrink into mediocrity.

In the professional realm, the positive impact I made at Deloitte increased after my emergence and even more so after my subsequent growth. The benefits of my more easeful, confident, and connected approach are hard to quantify, but they were evident in the results, the feedback I received, the effectiveness and support of my teams, and the promotions I earned. None of that would have been possible without Deloitte's supportive role, including its policies and people, which helped to ensure my successful emergence in the workplace. Within three months after the meditation retreat, I requested and Deloitte granted a sabbatical to allow me the time to write this memoir. Upon returning to work, with a draft memoir completed, I was offered an opportunity to serve in a newly created global leadership role. The role was aligned with my skill set and would allow me to make a meaningful impact within Deloitte. However, upon reflection, I understood I needed to follow my heart to focus on getting this memoir completed and launching a new venture—Emerge Collaborations—aimed at guiding enterprise leaders to overcome the structural challenges that inhibit gender equity within their organizations.

Emergence reflections and a shift in values

Prior to my emergence, I was flat and compressed. My life was black and white, and even though I was doing pretty well from an outsider's perspective, I was trudging along as best I could, and life felt meaningless. There was no music, no color, no vibrancy, no hope, and no authenticity. I lived with an undercurrent of sadness. I didn't love myself and was incapable of truly connecting with others. I couldn't live in the moment, so I kept busy multitasking and was mostly in my head, thinking about the past and future. I had no hope for ever having romantic connecting love, something for which I had a deep desire. I lacked peaceful inner calm and was inwardly focused with selfish tendencies.

My emergence was a vital and transformative act of self-love. That act allowed me to live as my authentic self and, in doing so, gave me the gift of hope and allowed me to eventually become a better person and give more of myself to those around me and the world. Living authentically was a prerequisite both to my happiness and to learning that I had more growth to accomplish. My emergence into the full expression of my female self gave me peace and opened my world to truly living with music and love. That quickly and inevitably led to a first real romantic heart connection, with Scott, which then led to another first: true heartbreak. I am grateful to have had that heartbreak. It triggered hard lessons and pain, which prompted an inner growth journey—growth that would never have been possible without my emergence.

That growth journey led to a realignment of many of my values. Love became a central part of my life—love, the secret ingredient that makes life shine and provides meaning. I'm referring to all types of love: the love between friends, the love felt by couples walking together in the park, the love of the beauty around us. And it starts with the most critical love of all: love of self, including compassion for myself, trusting myself, and learning to recognize negative self-talk. My approach to happiness also shifted. I learned that happiness is not an end to itself but a treasure to be found within individual moments—something that's sourced from within and from living one's truth. This discovery led me to a much greater appreciation of the immediate and the hard practice of remembering to live life where and when it happens. The best moment of my life is right now, as I'm typing these words. This moment. Now this moment. It doesn't always come easy, but my newfound meditation practice helps. I've come to appreciate that I can live in the moment while also cultivating and honoring desires.

In romance and in my other relationships, I strive to prioritize presence, which allows for the magical sparks of real connection. As a result, I'm no longer carefully monitoring what's coming out of my mouth and thus more easily connect with people. One day, I was doing a walk-through of my rental property with my realtor, and we noticed that the previous owners had left the crawl space full of junk. I was wearing a dress, but that didn't stop me from diving in to remove the contents. In doing so, I broke a nicely manicured nail and exclaimed, "Oh wow, I broke a nail!" I quickly followed it with a laugh and added, "I've always wanted to say that!" My realtor might still be laughing to this day, and I think it's because we shared an authentic moment. Whether with friends, family, work colleagues, or a date, I've come to appreciate the value of connection and that meaningful conversations require open-mindedness, curiosity for both listening and expression, and authenticity through expressing feelings and needs.

My relationship with my body also shifted. Connecting with my physical presence brightened the colors and injected juiciness into life. I'm not just my brain; my emergence gave me greater access to my heart and therefore my authenticity. I've learned how to pay attention to the wisdom of my body in the way it expands or constricts, which has deepened my powers of intuition. This new connection to my body also led to a greater priority for pleasure and self-care. Discovering and pursuing fun things balance the hard moments, raise my vibration, and serve as a light for others.

One of the most eye-opening concepts I uncovered as part of all the reading, coaching, and workshops is the idea that everyone has feminine and masculine energies. Most people tend to lean one way or another, which has implications in the workplace, with family and friend dynamics, and in romantic partnerships. Some women have a lot of feminine energy while others have a more masculine energy. It's the same with men. It's healthy for people with more masculine energy to be able to tap into and express their feminine side, and vice versa. Like many women in the workplace, I have found success in my career in part by tapping into my masculine energy. I know how to be a doer and push. However, this doesn't feel aligned with my true self. It's draining. I prefer the dynamic to be different in my personal and love life. Romantically, I'd much rather connect through my femininity: sharing my feelings, desires, and needs; showering my man with appreciation and adoration; and nurturing my relationship.

Through my growth journey, I've also refined my faith system. I've always felt firmly rooted in my Jewish heritage and have never thought there's an Almighty. That remains the same, but now I believe there's some magic to the universe. I use the word *magic* loosely, as a way to refer to things I don't understand. I believe the universe works in mysterious ways and use the word *universe* to describe the unexplained. I have come to accept things as they are and to refrain from having expectations about outcomes. I trust that everything is unfolding perfectly as intended. This helps me to appreciate what is and let go of control. It makes it easier to live in the moment.

Finally, I've had a shift in my mindset from one of scarcity to one of abundance, which has made it easier for me to step into the natural flow of life and all it has to offer. I have found abundance to be self-fulfilling: the mindset opens my eyes to it, and through improved inner ease, authenticity, and confidence, more abundance might even come my way. This has significantly shifted how I approach and experience dating. Although I once believed that there were very few men with whom I could connect and who would be accepting of my medical history, I now believe there are many, and the best of them will cherish my medical history as a testament to my strength, authenticity, and beauty. Recognizing abundance allows me to approach dating with a more lighthearted attitude and have more fun, and it makes it easier to get out of my head and into my body.

These shifts in my thinking and feeling have been profound, and I strive to adhere to them. I'm human, however, and it's easy to fall into old habits. And that's okay. When I notice this, I'm compassionate with myself, and I gently guide myself back.

Some of these shifts are much more challenging than others. For example, I find that I'm more often *not* in the moment than I am, but I'm grateful to be more present now than I was a year ago and more in the moment a year ago than I was two years ago. Remembering to be in the moment is a practice.

With the refinement of my values and with my daily gratitude, meditation, and affirmation practices, my relationship with loneliness has also shifted. I'm a single woman without children who works remotely, with family and dear friends spread out across the US and Europe, so loneliness can be difficult to escape. My journey has made me realize the importance of meaningful belonging, which I define as a community in which someone can be their authentic self and feel connected to those around them. Even though I am authentically myself, my introversion and historical inclination in moments of opportunity to abstain from talking about my journey constrain meaningful belonging. Now, I'm challenging myself to be more open about it; not only can it make a meaningful, supportive difference, but it's also an antidote to loneliness. Authentic sharing leads to connections. Belonging is self-fulfilling.

The tea on my journey to love

I continue on my journey to romantic love and very much look forward to meeting my guy! My relationship with the journey has shifted. Whereas I used to feel constricted, sad, and perhaps even a little jealous when I saw romantic scenes on the television or in public, my body now expands when I see those scenes, and I celebrate the love around me. I feel it and am happy for other couples in the same way I was for Erik. I now have hope. I know my guy is out there and feel we are dancing the perfect dance. I practice staying open and in the moment with connecting love while continuing to enjoy the dating journey, growing, and trusting in the universe.

My dating experience has shifted a great deal since the days of Scott and Derek. It no longer feels stressful or angst ridden. The Ella who shrank from men and stumbled through dating with awkward naivety is gone, and in her place is a more mature Ella, who is playful, curious, confident, vulnerable, loving, and authentic. My practices of sharing needs and desires, allowing myself to receive, letting go of control, showing appreciation, and internalizing abundance have entirely changed dating. It now feels easeful, natural, sexy, and exciting. Also, I've noticed that the negative experiences in dating, like ghosting and dick pics, have become almost nonexistent. In fact, I'm attracting and meeting captivating men who light me up, online and in my day-to-day life. It took some time to believe that phenomenal single men exist in abundance, but now my experience has taught me that is true.

The approach and timing of disclosing my personal history remains tricky, and I grant myself the compassion and flexibility to adjust as needed, based on what feels right. There are many men who turn out not to be comfortable with my medical history, but my feelings of disappointment and hurt are less deep and move through me faster than they used to. If he's not accepting about it, then his reaction doesn't bother me as much as it used to. I strive to recognize gratitude for elements of the connection, search for lessons to better myself and crispen my vision, and remind myself that I'm one step closer to my guy. I release these men with love and appreciation for what they have provided and for what I learned and move on.

I've discovered there are wonderful men who fully accept my medical history. I approach dating with discernment, however, and just because a guy is okay with my journey doesn't mean that I would settle if he's not the man for me. I owe that to myself and to the right guy. As much as I'd love to be in a relationship, I am doing fine as a single woman. My single status does not stop me from doing the things I love, such as exploring the world, solo or with friends. I'd rather be alone than fall into something fleeting that doesn't feel right or be in a relationship in which I lose myself or settle for something less than I deserve. This time alone has taught me what I need to make myself happy, and I am steadfast in seeking longevity, not convenience. Now that I have finally emerged and found love for myself, my desire has slowly merged with the secure knowledge that our paths will lead to each other exactly when intended.

Many years after my emergence, I was catching up with a close single friend over a delicious dinner at a Greek taverna. We were commiserating and sharing about our respective recent dating experiences. He asked me why I hadn't just picked up and started a new life elsewhere. Given how I present, he felt it would have been easy for me to have a fresh start, where I'd never have to disclose my medical history, and where I might be able to fully experience life, romance, and partnership without ever talking about any of it. I smiled, aware of two strong emotions rising in me: gratitude and satisfaction. I was grateful for my friends and family and the course that my journey to emergence had taken. I explained that at the beginning of my journey, the thought of relocating and leaving everything behind was not an option. It had always been important for me to bring as much of my life and friends and family along with me through the emergence. And I felt satisfaction knowing I had made the right decision. Even with the additional challenges it provides in dating, the decision still feels absolutely aligned with my core values, and that feels immensely satisfying.

An unexpected challenge

Around the time I started writing this memoir, I began to notice some unexpected hair loss. Along with the hair loss came stinging and itching along my hairline. It felt distressing and triggered a lot of questions ranging from why it was happening to how much would be lost, and I harbored fear that it might eventually make me appear more masculine. I lost a lot of sleep, both from the related anguish and because the sensations themselves often woke me during the night.

I sought out a dermatologist specializing in hair loss and began a multiyear journey to diagnose and treat my condition. Two and a half years into this journey, she diagnosed me with frontal fibrosing alopecia, a condition without a cure that tends to follow a prolonged course. It primarily affects women in their fifties, and it provided me with some solace to know that it was mainly women who experienced this condition. By then, I'd lost more than half of my hair, and the loss continues. It's been difficult to accept this change partly because I feel that my hair has helped me be seen for who I am. It's also tied into my sense of beauty and femininity. I'm grateful that my hair is naturally thick and curly and that I had a lot of it, so people don't yet notice the dramatic change. At the same time, this experience has tested my ability to practice acceptance, given the constant reminder of the stinging sensations. I remind myself that it doesn't define me, that it doesn't impact my ability to enjoy the moment, and that things unfold as they should.

And then came Executive Order 14168

When Executive Order 14168 came out on the day of President Trump's second inauguration, this memoir was in the last stages of copyediting and a month away from completion. On January 21, I woke up at two a.m. and looked at my phone to see whether the executive order had been published. And it had. I blearily read it. The first thing I noticed was the title, which had been written to manipulate, provoke fear, and scapegoat an already vulnerable group. It was officially called "Defending Women from Gender Ideology Extremism and Restoring Biological Truth to the Federal Government." I couldn't absorb it all in those moments, but it was clear that it would be harmful to gender-diverse and transgender people and their families.

The next morning, I set aside dedicated time to read it. I printed it out, sat down, and took in each word slowly. As I read, a mix of emotions hit all at once: horror, fear, anger. My body constricted, and I began to feel what I would later recognize was a loss of psychological and emotional safety. The order stood against the freedom that this country that I love stands for. I absorbed its basic facts, starting with the federal policy framework that redefines *sex* strictly as an immutable biological classification assigned at birth and excludes gender identity from legal recognition. Under this definition, all federal agencies were required to eliminate terminology and policies referring to gender identity and to revert official documentation—including passports, personnel records, and other legal documents—to reflect sex assigned at birth. The order also directed agencies to withdraw funding from programs and research involving transgender health care, gender-affirming treatments for minors, and diversity, equity, and inclusion (DEI) initiatives that address gender diversity. Additionally, it mandated that access to single-sex spaces such as restrooms, prisons, and sports programs be governed exclusively by biological sex, thereby rescinding previous protections extended under laws such as Title IX. Finally, the order nullified prior executive actions that had expanded federal protections for transgender people and instructed departments such as the Departments of Health and Human Services, Justice, and Homeland Security to implement new guidance and reporting structures consistent with the order's binary framework.

The order came as little surprise. Trump's attack on transgender people and transgender rights had been a centerpiece of his campaign:

- Throughout Trump's 2024 presidential campaign, GOP-aligned groups spent more than $200 million on ads attacking transgender rights, including "some $37 million" by the Trump campaign alone (Witt, 2025). These ads aired "during the World Series and other major sporting events," essentially "mocking trans people" for mass audiences, and reflected how Republicans had explicitly "made an anti-trans stance central to [their] political platform."[1]

- In a two-week span in October, Trump-aligned groups ran a TV "blitz" portraying transgender people as "menacing, disgusting, and a threat to middle America," framing trans identity as a social and moral threat tied to families, public safety, and national values.[2]

- In the final days of the campaign, Trump made opposition to transgender rights "central to his closing argument," airing ads that featured "a spoof video mocking transgender people and their place in the US military," along with "false claims" about transgender athletes and surgeries for minors, depicting transgender Americans as a threat to national identity.[3]

- Nearly one-third of all Trump campaign broadcast TV ad spending in October 2024 targeted transgender people, totaling "more than $21 million out of a total of about $66 million."[4]

I had tried to avoid exposure to these attacks, but that was nearly impossible because I like to stay informed, and the attacks permeated through every news source, including social media. Generally, I strive to see all sides of an issue, but in this case, this was impossible; the attacks struck me as malicious because they weren't based in truth or science and were grossly misleading. Assuming the disregard for science wasn't accidental, I could only conclude that the campaign deliberately used false messaging and fearmongering to win votes. Leading up to Inauguration Day, I had opted to take a wait-and-see attitude to determine whether the attacks on transgender people would translate to policy. I didn't want to worry about something that might not materialize. With the passing of Executive Order 14168, however, the transphobia and fearmongering became federal policy.

The scientific and medical communities—including major associations in pediatrics, psychiatry, psychology, endocrinology, and public health—consistently affirm that gender identity is a real and distinct aspect of human development and that gender-affirming care can be medically necessary. The administration's reversal of prior guidance effectively removes federal protections against discrimination for millions of Americans and it ignores and erases the reality of intersex people. Further, by cutting funding to medical, academic, and public programs involving gender diversity, the order will restrict access to health services and reduce accurate public information. Although it claims to promote fairness and safety, the realistic impact of Executive Order 14168 heightens exclusion, disrupts service access, and creates legal conflicts with states and institutions that recognize gender identity within civil-rights frameworks.

It was difficult that morning to get my head wrapped around the full possible impact and reach of the executive order, but a few things were immediately clear. First, much of the content of the order was based on falsehoods and flew against everything that the entire scientific community (as well as my personal experience) has proven. This order erases people's lived realities, including my own. I have a transgender medical history, and this policy attempts to invalidate and politicize that history. That and the fact that this minority population—when not supported with appropriate medical care and general support—is already at increased risk make this order mean-spirited, cruel, and hateful. It also strikes me as a calculated political wedge, aimed at mocking and rejecting something poorly understood. And in doing so, it ends up harming those who are already most at risk. The impact of amplifying and institutionalizing falsehoods through the US federal government significantly endangers an already-marginalized community and amplifies hatred, emboldening others to do the same. The order effectively weaponizes identity in a way that renders people like me invisible and unsafe.

Second, the order felt ironic. It claims to protect women by enforcing single-sex definitions in public spaces. However, not only will it harm transgender people; it will have the opposite effect and harm all women. It compels transgender men, many of whom present fully as male and whose hormones are aligned with the level of cisgender men, to use women's facilities, raising privacy and safety concerns. At the same time, cisgender women who do not conform to traditional gender expectations may face increased harassment or wrongful exclusion, as the policy encourages subjective judgments about who "belongs" in a given space. And finally, what about me? I'm a woman and present as one and have had my lower surgery. If I'm to follow the order, the risk of harassment or even harm to me is much higher if I were to try to use the men's room.

I was hyperaware that, physically, I was likely very safe and very privileged to be able to feel this way compared with others who share my experience. All my paperwork was fully updated, and I had genetics on my side. At the same time, the loss of emotional and psychological safety felt like a surprising mindfuck—the kind where your body is technically safe but the state is still coming for your truth.

Setting that dissonance aside, I tried to understand the realistic and more likely impact on me. My US passport had just been renewed, so that would still be good for another ten years. Although passport renewals were already upending lives and putting travelers at risk at border crossings, that was a not-now worry for me. There were already reports of women being placed in men's prisons. I wasn't planning on breaking any laws and landing myself in jail, but it crossed my mind that if I were to somehow get myself in trouble, the risk of landing in a men's jail was real. It didn't feel like a big worry since all my paperwork was correct, but I've lived enough to know that things don't always go as expected. My biggest concern was that health insurers would use the order as justification to deny coverage for hormone therapy. I also feared the loss of dignified patient-centered health care that would recognize who I am.

Some effects of the order I wouldn't have to worry about for some time, but others had immediate impact. Although a handful of Emerge Collaborations clients had stated their intent in late January to move forward with consulting services, by the end of February, each one communicated that they were unable to move forward because of the risk of federal government retribution. Emerge Collaborations lost its entire sales pipeline in four weeks. I had invested my house in the business, and the loss was devastating—emotionally, mentally, and financially. The election itself and the prospect of publishing a highly personal memoir had already impacted my ability to sleep through the night for the previous three months. The order further affected my feelings of safety and wiped out my business, thereby impacting my financial security and threatening my home. It pushed me into full survival mode.

I knew that the order and its impact would last for only a moment of time and things would shift back. But when? It wouldn't be in time to reverse my financial predicament. By the end of March, I decided to pause the publishing process until I could stabilize my life. And because of the dramatic shift in the landscape for gender-equity consulting services, I also decided to pause the consulting side of Emerge Collaborations and start a full-time job search. I identified my target roles, refined my resume, developed a list of target companies, and began networking.

Those decisions helped me find some psychological footing and provided space for me to reflect on what else I could do to keep my house, improve my finances, and increase my sense of safety. I knew I could find a great opportunity, but I was worried about the timing, especially given the tough job market as well as the biases against women, against people in their fifties, and against people with my medical history.

The objectives of reducing my spending and living in a society where my existence isn't invalidated led me to consider moving back to Europe. I am an American citizen, but I am also a Dutch citizen with a Dutch passport. When I dug deeper into that idea, it made so much sense. I would be able to live a bit more economically there, and I speak the language and have family there whom I love. Additionally, the Netherlands has a thriving business economy, and it's a progressive and open culture where the state hasn't invalidated gender identity. I had nothing holding me back—no boyfriend or husband, no kids, and no predictable income. So why not? I could move, and it would be an exciting adventure. It began to feel like an opportunity that was begging to be claimed. By mid-April, I made the decision.

In order to make it work, I needed to rent or sell my house. I was determined not to sell it, so I paused my job search to focus fully on getting the house rented and to prepare for the move. The intensity and speed didn't help my exhaustion, but over the next two months,

I found a tenant, secured a furnished apartment in the Netherlands, rented a local storage unit to store my furniture and belongings, booked ocean passage for my clothes and personal items, and began to plan all the steps for a one-way flight for Bosco and me. I sold my car to fund all of it. I felt so fortunate and grateful that I was able to make it happen.

Once I'd made the decision, the weight lifted. Reducing my financial burden, ensuring continuity for my hormone therapy, and moving to a country where the government isn't actively erasing a community was a step toward stability, a return to safety, and the chance to finally breathe again. At the same time, the weight was replaced with a cornucopia of emotions—so many that it was difficult to discern them all. Most prevalent was a bittersweet feeling with deep sadness and nervousness: deep sadness for the facts that led to the move and being so far away from Mama as well as my community, and nervousness for the change and the question of whether I'd be shooting myself in the foot, socially or financially. Time would tell. However, I also felt occasional sparks of excitement about the move. I was moving toward something that was pulling me. Outside of the US, the Netherlands had always felt like home. I was excited to be closer to my Dutch family, to speak the language, and to experience the culture—in particular the food and its people. I was excited about the adventure and about experiencing something new and different. Layered beneath all of that was a recognition of the irony of moving to Europe, from the US, no less, given what had happened there less than eighty years ago and the lasting impact it had had on my family.

That same spring, just as I was moving toward the decision to relocate to the Netherlands, I had the opportunity to partner with two large enterprises for separate in-depth conversations about gender identity. Both companies received an advance copy of the memoir, and we collaborated to have intimate fireside chats about gender identity through the lens of my experiences. The first was a large technology company, which invited me as part of their Women's History Month celebration. The second was an Am Law 100 firm—I had the privilege to join them in person at their annual on-site Pride retreat. Each event made a positive impact and a real difference in improving understanding and telegraphing belonging and hope. It felt special to be able to make an impact on a topic for which I feel passion.

Once I'd completed most of my key move-related activities, I had the opportunity to revisit whether I wanted to return to my job search or to publish the memoir as soon as possible and focus my time on more opportunities to have conversations about gender identity with enterprise leaders and their organizations. After much reflection and feeling into my heart, and despite an ungodly amount of angst and fear, I resolved that I should publish the memoir and continue what I had set out to do when I left Deloitte. It felt highly risky, and it might look a bit different in this changed environment, but there is still much important work to do to foster professional belonging and inclusivity among the gender-diverse and transgender population. The first half of 2025 was challenging and gut-wrenching, but I believe it needed to happen to get me exactly where I needed to be. I'm choosing this work. I don't know everything ahead, but I know it's mine to do.

Taking a look at the word *transgender*

When I began my journey with gender identity, I had very little understanding of it. I had been conditioned to believe that sex and gender were one and the same. Over many years and with much pain, reflection, and my analysis during therapy, I came to realize that the two were different. Once I understood this, I dove into investigating the meaning of the word *transgender*.

The origin of the word *trans* comes from Latin and means "across," "beyond," "through," or "the other side of." *Gender* also comes from Latin and means to divide by kind or sort, which has evolved to mean separation into the masculine, feminine, or related other.

A literal interpretation of *transgender* implies that someone went "beyond their gender" or "crossed their gender." Said differently and as interpreted by most, this means they changed their gender. This is false, misleading, and does more harm than good.

Merriam-Webster defines *transgender* as "of, relating to, or being a person whose gender identity differs from the sex the person had or was identified as having at birth." This definition of transgender is widely accepted by most sources, but this definition does not fully capture my experience. It's rooted in making a connection between sex and gender identity and does not reflect who I am today. The existing definition hinges on gender assignment at birth as a result of sex organs and doesn't leave room for an inaccuracy in those sex organs that later might be fixed. Assignment of a gender at birth is fine, but it is based on incomplete information and should be considered placeholder information until confirmed by the person being assigned. The current definition—which stems from a doctor's assignment—encourages us to see people who are labeled as transgender as something different from their gender, which is misguided. Gender is gender identity. Gender is not sex. A transgender woman is no less a woman than a cisgender woman. Both their gender identities are woman, and both were born with the same gender identity. A transgender man is no less a man than a cisgender man.

It's time for this definition to evolve into something less subjective, with the power to have a positive impact. I propose the following: "of, relating to, or being a person whose gender identity differs from the sex the person has."

There are two key changes: "has" replaces "had," and the trailing verb phrase "or was identified as having at birth" is gone. This definition posits that once a transgender person has remedied their congenital malformation (for those who need or want to) and aligned their sex with their gender identity, they are no longer transgender. The updated definition makes the *transgender* adjective irrelevant for women and men whose sex has been fixed and whose gender identity matches their sex and is aligned with their presentation.

Transgender at its core means that there's a variance between sex and gender. The updated definition retains, acknowledges, and validates the existence of people who do not need or want to change their sex, who choose to not have lower surgeries, and whose gender identity differs from their sex.

While I bear no animosity toward the doctor who assigned me, I believe that assignment at birth is ultimately irrelevant. That historical state doesn't matter. To trust that my updated definition is an improvement is to acknowledge that gender identity is separate from sex and isn't something that changes after birth. I'm not a medical professional or a scientist, but I believe that my disconnect—a variance that I've had since birth—was ultimately the result of a defect during gestation and feels to me a congenital anomaly. The genetic causes of congenital anomalies are most often single-gene defects and chromosomal abnormalities. A congenital anomaly can be fixed, but gender cannot.

My gender never changed. I was born female and have always been female. I was incorrectly assigned male at birth because my lower part—my sex—was wrong. I was transgender when I was born and for the first forty-plus years of my life. My congenital anomaly has been fixed, and my gender identity, sex, and presentation are aligned. There is nothing transgender about my current state. The label doesn't apply. I'm not transgender at this point in my journey. It doesn't make sense that my doctor's understandable but incorrect assignment would lead to an erroneous adjective—*transgender*—stickered before the noun—*woman*—that is and has always been my truth.

At the same time, my transgender experience is an important slice of my medical history. The transgender information is important as a historical record for medical purposes for the few instances when it's relevant. But more importantly, my transgender journey has shaped who I am and contributed greatly to how I relate to others. It has provided me with more compassion and strength than I would have otherwise had.

I would add that it's never appropriate to ask a transgender person what they have between their legs. One's sex is private information and doesn't take away from gender. Given the arc of my journey, I gladly, giddily, and joyously shout my sex from the mountain tops; however, that is my decision to make and not one that others might choose.

Musings on courage

Through my growth, I have developed additional confidence and an increased love for self so that I'm better equipped to handle the idea that strangers and new connections might incorrectly see me as a "man in a dress" or something other than a woman. It's rare, but the constriction in my body over the thought and the fear surrounding it persist. Although I have shed the word *transgender* as an adjective preceding *woman*, I am proud of my transgender experience and am getting more comfortable sharing it when I want to deepen a relationship. I don't mind when strangers and new connections see me for who

I am as a woman *and* also see me as a woman who has had an extraordinary journey. At the same time, I continue to practice not caring what other people think. There will always be some people who don't believe gender identity is real or believe themselves to be in opposition against the very concept. I think such stances are fear driven, as fear is a common reaction to things people don't understand. At the end of the day, my emergence doesn't impact anyone negatively. In fact, it's the opposite. I'm a better person who is kinder, nicer, and quicker to help those in need, and I have returned to putting love into the world. My emergence is a net positive for everyone.

When the topic of my emergence comes up, I'm at times told that I'm courageous. On the one hand, it feels good to have words like *courage* and *bravery* directed at me, and I recognize the good intentions behind it, but on the other hand, it is sometimes dismaying. It has the potential to communicate, perhaps unintentionally, that they see me as something other than a woman. I also feel that the congratulations and labels of courage refer to my perceived alignment with a marginalized and misunderstood group, as if that's something to feel bad about.

Neither the acts of emerging nor the day-to-day of living my truth are courageous. I had to do both. There was no choice. My emergence itself—in the moment when I emerged at work—was scary for a split second, only because there was no putting the genie back in the bottle. But jumping from the high dive was the easy part. I didn't have a choice. When you don't have a choice, you don't need bravery or courage. The act is easy. Perhaps a better analogy is standing on the edge of a cliff with a parachute when a herd of buffalo is coming at you. I was prepared. I knew the herd was coming. I had everything I needed.

The actual brave part was looking in the mirror five years earlier: truly looking, seeing, and then doing something about what I saw. I had to summon my courage years prior, when I was desperate and made the call from O'Hare to Papa, and through all the subsequent actions to get myself off the road and into a world of unknowns, beginning with therapy, to follow my truth. When I'm told I'm brave, I hope that it is intended for all those past moments that led to me being true to myself rather than for what I am now: a woman simply living her life.

Often, when I'm told I'm brave or courageous, I pick up on non-verbal cues—facial expressions, tones, body language—that carry the possible implications that the speaker feels bad for me, doesn't see me for who I am, or both. Those cues suggest that I'm something different from another woman who didn't have to fight to express her gender differently from assigned. That implication, which I understand comes from a place of ignorance rather than malice, bothers me. Yes, I had to fight for it, and I'm different because of it, but we are all different in all our varied experiences. My journey is no different, and now that the journey is in the rearview mirror, there is nothing courageous or different about this woman, who just gets up in the morning and goes about her day like any other woman.

I've had a great adventure while fighting for my birthright to walk the world for who I am, and I love to be congratulated for that. Tell me you see me for the full woman I am, and congratulate me for having been courageous enough to look in the mirror, recognize the truth, accept the truth, and fight for it.

In closing

In the years following my emergence, I've undergone a profound shift to general happiness. I'm prioritizing living with love and self-compassion. I strive to trust that everything is perfect as it is and will unfold exactly as intended. My growth and all the related shifts have not only improved how I experience my inner being; they have also profoundly impacted all areas of my life, including family, friends, and the workplace.

So much goodness has come from my emergence, and I am forever grateful for it. It has brought forth the truth of who I am. It has irreversibly and positively changed how I treat myself and how I approach and connect with the world and those around me. It has delivered gratitude and appreciation for life and the divine breath. It has shifted my priorities and the decisions I make and led me to see hope, abundance, and love where I once saw hopelessness, scarcity, and suspicion. It has confirmed the importance of following my intuition, especially when there is fear and resistance, and it has also proven the power of just taking one step at a time. It has brought me peace and relaxation, allowing me to finally live in the all-important moment, when one finds happiness. Most importantly, my emergence has brought me back to love. I do believe that the purpose of life is to love—to love oneself, to live with love, and to put love into the world, into each moment when life happens. I consider myself to be immensely fortunate. I had the support, resources, and genetics to help me through my journey with relative smoothness and success. I am grateful and at peace, and I feel that anything is possible.

If you made it this far, thank you. I hope you've gained the slightest bit more understanding and compassion for what's happening on the inside for those who struggle with gender identities that are misaligned with what others see. It's my hope that after having read this memoir, you consider yourself to be an ally—or a stronger one if you already were.

With love,

Ella

AFTERWORD

AN INVITATION TO SENIOR LEADERSHIP

Dear enterprise leader,

Having shared my story, I trust it provides some insight into gender identity and a deeper appreciation for the challenges faced by those who are transgender, have undergone transgender journeys, or identify as nonbinary (including gender-fluid and gender-nonconforming individuals). If so, I invite you to reflect on your role as an ally. Consider the following sobering statistics regarding the gender-diverse and transgender workforce:

- 67% of gender-diverse people felt extremely uncomfortable in their job settings, and as such "reported negative outcomes such as being fired or forced to resign, not being hired, or being denied a promotion."[1]

- 59% of transgender people do not "pursue certain industries" because of fear of safety.[2]

- "30% of transgender employees have been fired, denied a promotion, or experienced another form of workplace mistreatment due to their gender identity or expression (Human Rights Campaign, 2018)."[3]

- 50% of transgender and nonbinary employees reported experiencing verbal harassment at work compared to 28% of cisgender LGBQ employees.[4]

- 66% of gender-diverse employees won't even apply for a job in a company "where they perceive the culture to be noninclusive."[5]

- 1.6% of US adults reported being transgender or nonbinary, according to the Pew Research Center's 2022 study results.[*][6]

- 28% of Gen Z adults identify as LGBTQ, according to a 2023 PRRI study, and according to a 2023 Trevor Project study, 59% of LGBTQ+ Gen Z members identify as transgender, nonbinary, or questioning.[7]

As of 2024, it was reasonable to conclude that at least 2% of the US workforce was gender diverse or transgender, representing more than three million employees. By 2030, it's estimated that Gen Z will make up at least 30% of the workforce, potentially increasing the number of transgender, nonbinary, and questioning employees to more than five million. Furthermore, research suggests that upward of two-thirds of this segment of the workforce feels a lack of belonging. While many enterprises have made commendable efforts to address the issues that inform belonging, most have only scratched the surface, focusing primarily on training and human resource policies. Although these measures are important, they are not comprehensive and fail to create lasting change.

---

* These numbers are underreported because of fear of identification.

The daily experiences of a gender-diverse employee can often feel like a death by a thousand cuts. True equity and inclusivity require a deeper commitment. Hundreds of small but important changes to policies, processes, and culture should be made across the entire enterprise—including IT, finance, marketing, and the C-suite—to create genuine feelings of belonging for gender-diverse and transgender employees. This is not only the right thing to do morally, but research also shows that fostering belonging directly impacts the bottom line, driving increased revenue, organizational efficiency, and sustainable growth.

With my emergence journey behind me, I've shifted my focus to making a difference by improving feelings of belonging for the gender-diverse workforce and would love to work with you to do that. You are in a powerful position to make a significant impact, and you are uniquely positioned to do so. As a starting point, I now offer memoir-based gender identity fireside chats. These sessions open space for authentic dialogue, empathy, and insight, which are precursors for sustainable organizational change. Additionally, a cross-enterprise review can uncover opportunities to strengthen processes, policies, and cultural practices to foster belonging that truly sticks. At my company, Emerge Collaborations, we are ready to partner with you in this essential work. We offer tailored recommendations designed to meet an organization's specific needs, ensuring that they are relevant and impactful. Our approach drives transformative change in workplaces, fostering environments where the gender-diverse and transgender workforce can thrive. Thanks again for taking the time to read my story. I hope it has made a positive impact, and I hope to hear from you to begin this much-needed work together.

With gratitude,

Ella Samson

EMERGECOLLABS.COM

ACKNOWLEDGMENTS

This memoir—and my journey—would not have been possible without the unwavering support of so many. I am endlessly grateful to each of you.

To my family—Mama, Papa, and Amalia—for standing by my side and loving me as I am, despite your struggles with my emergence.

To those who truly saw me—Bex, Bosco, Carl, Erik, Lynn, Michelle, and Ryan—for showing up in ways big and small, offering love, understanding, and light in the hardest moments.

To my therapists—for your presence, for your wisdom, and for helping me recognize the truth.

To Dr. Bowers—for your expertise, for your care, and for gifting me something beyond measure: a miracle.

To my dear friends and early readers—Andrew, Assaf, Bex, Bob, Brenda, Cheryl, David, Doug, Erik, JP, Kari, Kathryn, Lynn, Rachel, Robert, Ryan, and Stuart—for your encouragement and thoughtful feedback that kept me going.

To Deloitte, with your remarkable culture of belonging, and to my colleagues, leaders, and friends—for your extraordinary support, without which my journey would have taken a very different path.

To my editors—Ben, Christopher, and Jason—for your passion, for your skill, and for pushing back when it mattered.

To Dr. Sullivan and Dr. Toth—for your invaluable input in sharpening the medical and biological details of this memoir.

To Sam, Sarah, and the entire team at Greenleaf—for believing in this mission and for the research, creativity, and expertise that helped bring the memoir and its message to life.

And finally, to everyone—past and present—for being part of my story in ways large and small. Thank you. This memoir exists because of and for all of you.

RESOURCES

To explore gender identity further and engage more deeply with the memoir, scan the QR code to access additional materials, including

- a glossary with key definitions related to gender identity;

- a visual framework illustrating the relationship between gender identity, birth-assigned sex, sexual orientation, and gender expression;

- a reader's guide for reflection and discussion.

EMERGECOLLABS.COM/BOOK

NOTES

Introduction

1. Andrew R. Flores et al., "Gender Identity Disparities in Criminal Victimization: National Crime Victimization Survey, 2017–2018," *American Journal of Public Health* 111, no. 4 (2021): 728, https://doi.org/10.2105/AJPH.2020.306099.

2. "What Is Diversity, Equity, and Inclusion?" McKinsey & Company, August 17, 2022, https://www.mckinsey.com/featured-insights/mckinsey-explainers/what-is-diversity-equity-and-inclusion.

3. Brad Sears et al., *LGBTQ People's Experiences of Workplace Discrimination and Harassment* (UCLA School of Law Williams Institute, 2024), 10, https://williamsinstitute.law.ucla.edu/wp-content/uploads/Workplace-Discrimination-Aug-2024.pdf.

4. Ann Hergatt Huffman et al., "Workplace Support and Affirming Behaviors: Moving Toward a Transgender, Gender Diverse, and Non-Binary Friendly Workplace," *International Journal of Transgender Health* 22, no. 3 (2021): 226, https://doi.org/10.1080/26895269.2020.1861575.

5. Kim Parker et al., *Americans' Complex Views on Gender Identity and Transgender Issues* (Pew Research Center, 2022), 4, https://www.pewresearch.org/wp-content/uploads/sites/20/2022/06/PSDT_06.28.22_GenderID_fullreport.pdf.

6. "Mapping Attacks on LGBTQ Rights in U.S. State Legislatures in 2023," American Civil Liberties Union, last modified December 21, 2023, https://www.aclu.org/legislative-attacks-on-lgbtq-rights-2023; Movement Advancement Project, *Under Fire: Erecting Systemic and Structural Barriers to Make Change Harder* (Movement Advancement Project, 2023), 2, https://www.mapresearch.org/file/MAP-2023-Under-Fire-Report-3.pdf.

7. Pierre Dupreelle et al., "Companies Are Failing Trans Employees," *Harvard Business Review*, March 31, 2023, https://hbr.org/2023/03/companies-are-failing-trans-employees.

8. Human Rights Campaign Foundation, *The Epidemic of Violence Against the Transgender and Gender Non-Conforming Community in the United States* (Human Rights Campaign Foundation, 2023), 40, https://reports.hrc.org/an-epidemic-of-violence-2023#epidemic-numbers.

9. Caroline Medina et al., *Protecting and Advancing Health Care for Transgender Adult Communities* (Center for American Progress, 2021), 6, https://www.americanprogress.org/wp-content/uploads/sites/2/2021/08/Advancing-Health-Care-For-Transgender-Adults.pdf.

10. Medina, *Protecting and Advancing Health Care*, 5.

11. UNAIDS, *UNAIDS Data 2023* (Joint United Nations Programme on HIV/AIDS, 2023), https://www.unaids.org/en/resources/documents/2023/2023_unaids_data.

12. Public Religion Research Institute, *A Political and Cultural Glimpse into America's Future: Generation Z's Views on Generational Change and the Challenges and Opportunities Ahead* (PRRI, 2024), 10, https://www.prri.org/wp-content/uploads/2024/01/PRRI_Jan-2024-Gen-Z-final.pdf; R. Nath et al., *2024 U.S. National Survey on the Mental Health of LGBTQ+ Young People* (The Trevor Project, 2024), 33, https://www.thetrevorproject.org/survey-2024/assets/static/TTP_2024_National_Survey.pdf.

Epilogue

1. Emily Witt, "Where Do Trans Kids Go from Here?" *The New Yorker*, February 19, 2025, https://www.newyorker.com/news/the-lede/where-do-trans-kids-go-from-here.

2. Diana Goetsch, "2024 Was the Year Trans People like Me Became Untouchables," *San Francisco Chronicle*, December 31, 2024, https://www.sfchronicle.com/opinion/openforum/article/2024-transgender-people-untouchable-19998762.php.

3. Bill Barrow, "Trump and Vance Make Anti-Transgender Attacks Central to Their Campaign's Closing Argument," AP News, November 1, 2024, https://apnews.com/article/trump-harris-transgender-politics-61cff97a64fac581ffc5f762be4c57d3.

4. David Wright and Alex Leeds Matthews, "Here's How Trump, Harris and Their Allies Have Altered Their Ad Spending Strategies in October," CNN Politics, October 19, 2024, https://edition.cnn.com/2024/10/19/politics/campaign-advertising-tv-trump-harris/index.html.

Afterword

1. Christian N. Thoroughgood et al., "Creating a Trans-Inclusive Workplace," *Harvard Business Review*, March–April 2020, 4–5, https://hbr.org/2020/03/creating-a-trans-inclusive-workplace.

2. David Baboolall et al., "Being Transgender at Work," *McKinsey Quarterly*, November 10, 2021, 9, https://www.mckinsey.com/featured-insights/diversity-and-inclusion/being-transgender-at-work.

3. Ann Hergatt Huffman et al., "Workplace Support and Affirming Behaviors: Moving Toward a Transgender, Gender Diverse, and Non-Binary Friendly Workplace," *International Journal of Transgender Health* 22, no. 3 (2021): 226, https://doi.org/10.1080/26895269.2020.1861575.

4. Brad Sears et al., *LGBTQ People's Experiences of Workplace Discrimination and Harassment* (UCLA School of Law Williams Institute, 2024), 10, https://williamsinstitute.law.ucla.edu/wp-content/uploads/Workplace-Discrimination-Aug-2024.pdf.

5. Pierre Dupreelle et al., "Companies Are Failing Trans Employees," *Harvard Business Review*, March 31, 2023, https://hbr.org/2023/03/companies-are-failing-trans-employees.

6. Anna Brown, "About 5% of Young Adults in the U.S. Say Their Gender Is Different from Their Sex Assigned at Birth," Pew Research Center, June 7, 2022, https://www.pewresearch.org/short-reads/2022/06/07/about-5-of-young-adults-in-the-u-s-say-their-gender-is-different-from-their-sex-assigned-at-birth/.

7. Public Religion Research Institute, *A Political and Cultural Glimpse into America's Future: Generation Z's Views on Generational Change and the Challenges and Opportunities Ahead* (PRRI, 2024), 10, https://www.prri.org/wp-content/uploads/2024/01/PRRI_Jan-2024-Gen-Z-final.pdf; R. Nath et al., *2024 U.S. National Survey on the Mental Health of LGBTQ+ Young People* (The Trevor Project, 2024), 33, https://www.thetrevorproject.org/survey-2024/assets/static/TTP_2024_National_Survey.pdf.

ABOUT THE AUTHOR

 **Ella Samson** (she/her), founder and strategic operations leader of Emerge Collaborations, author, and speaker, is transforming how organizations approach gender equity in the workplace. She creates safe spaces for authentic dialogue about gender identity, helping enterprise leaders deepen their understanding, foster meaningful allyship, and improve belonging.

With an MBA from the Wharton School and more than thirty years of cross-functional leadership experience at organizations including Deloitte Consulting and Peet's Coffee & Tea, Ella has guided companies through complex transformations, operational improvements, and culture shifts. Today, she applies this expertise to enable organizations to address structural inequities related to gender identity through actionable enterprise-wide recommendations in policies, processes, and culture.

Ella's memoir, *The Power of Emergence*, helps readers understand gender identity and inspires meaningful allyship through authentic storytelling. Drawing on decades of operational leadership and lived experience, Ella collaborates with clients across the US and Europe to build understanding and enable enterprise-wide impact.

9 798900 520278